D1689898

Published by Central Park South Publishing 2022
www.centralparksouthpublishing.com

Copyright © John E. Mayer and Koji Steven Sakai, 2022

All rights reserved. No part of this publication may be reproduced, stored in a retrieval system, or transmitted in any form or by any means, electronic, mechanical, photocopying, recording or otherwise, without the prior written permission from the publisher.

Typesetting and e-book formatting services by Victor Marcos

ISBN:
978-1-956452-26-6 (pbk)
978-1-956452-27-3 (hbk)
978-1-956452-28-0 (ebk)

SECESSION

John E. Mayer and
Koji Steven Sakai

Contents

Chapter 1:   *When in the Course of Human Events*   1
Chapter 2:   *It Becomes Necessary to Dissolve the Political Bands*   14
Chapter 3:   *The Preamble*   24
Chapter 4:   *A Decent Respect to The Opinions of Mankind*   35
Chapter 5:   *These Truths are Self-evident*   48
Chapter 6:   *All Men Are Created Equal*   60
Chapter 7:   *The Form of Government Becomes Destructive*   72
Chapter 8:   *Organizing its Power in Such Form*   89
Chapter 9:   *The Right of the People to Alter or Abolish It*   100
Chapter 10:   *Life, Liberty and the Pursuit of Happiness*   114
Chapter 11:   *It is Their Duty to Throw Off Such Government*   125
Chapter 12:   *He Has Excited Domestic Insurrections Amongst Us*   140
Chapter 13:   *A Long Train of Abuses and Usurpations*   149
Chapter 14:   *Right Ought to be Free and Independent States*   165
Chapter 15:   *He Has…sent Hither Swarms of Officers to Harass Our People*   176
Chapter 16:   *For Quartering Large Bodies of Armed Troops Among Us*   188
Chapter 17:   *To Bear Arms Against Their Country*   199
Chapter 18:   *He Has Kept Among Us Standing Armies*   217
Chapter 19:   *He Called Together Legislative Bodies*   228
Chapter 20:   *In Every Stage of These Oppressions*   247

Chapter 21: *We Mutually Pledge to Each Other Our Lives,*
  Our Fortunes and Our Sacred Honor 254
Chapter 22: *He has Made Judges Dependent on His Will* 271
Chapter 23: *The Civil War* 280
Chapter 24: *The Enemy at our Gates* 291

CHAPTER 1

When in the Course of Human Events

It was one of those late summer mornings when the air was crisp and fresh. Amid the glut of bureaucrats rushing to offices in the morning traffic in northwest Washington D.C., a mid-length shiny clean Mack truck stood out like a sore thumb amongst the other few dirty and banged up urban oxcarts burling their way through traffic. The Mack's engine labored as it drove through crowded streets looking for a place to settle.

You can tell a lot by a person's choice of vehicles and the 26-foot Mack truck reflected the identity of its owner, Daniel Rivera. The cab was immaculate inside and out, even after the 2,800-mile trip from Santa Maria, California. The cab of the truck sat two comfortably, and the sleeper was adequate for two buddies on a mission. More precisely, one buddy on a mission and the other along for the ride.

The GPS on Daniel's phone was nagging him about every upcoming turn, still haranguing him well after the last turn.

"We know, we know! Now shut up, you cracker bitch!" his passenger Ricardo Lopez said, laughing at the device's repetition. He then took a greedy swig from the Jack Daniel's bottle and passed it to Daniel. The two had been best friends since childhood with a Lennie (Ricardo) and George (Daniel) relationship ever since a farm accident left Ricardo feeble-minded when he was six-years-old. After Ricardo's parents died, Daniel's loyalty expanded into taking Ricardo into his home and they have been inseparable ever since.

Daniel tilted his head slightly toward his traveling buddy, let out a polite laugh and shook his head in refusal. The truck continued to amble down 1st Street NW and then made an illegal right turn on 15th Street NW and parked at the corner.

"Ya can't do a right on that street amigo. It's one way," Riccardo said, sitting upright in the passenger seat and hiding the bottle underneath it.

"Shhhh! It's OK. This is the best spot and the best angle for them to get my message. Right here. This is it." Daniel calmly assured him, softening his voice toward his friend, then the rage inside him resumed as soon as he turned back to the steering wheel.

"Ok, man. But, if a cop comes, this is going to be one short protest. He'll shag you right outta here." Ricardo said.

"I got it covered, man. See that restaurant a couple doors down," he said pointing with his outstretched hand. "What's that called, Georgia Brown's? We'll just say we're delivering to that place. Nice load of broccoli right from our hometown." Daniel slid down in the driver's seat. "What, the cop's going to shag us after…" He looked at the odometer. "2,878 miles? Besides, I got my blinkers on." They both chuckled.

Ricardo resurrected the bottle of Jack from under the seat and took a large swig and passed it to Daniel. Ricardo slumped in his seat and relaxed to enjoy the buzz.

"You're always so cool, man." Ricardo closed his eyes and licked his lips to savor any of the liquor that may have lingered on his lips. "I wish I could be as cool as you."

Daniel smiled at his companion, then turned his head back to look out the windshield.

"I only saw you lose your cool once and that was a couple of weeks ago when you got that letter about your benefits. You went wild!" Ricardo stopped himself, then reflected, "You've been so angry ever since, like you want to hurt somebody all the time." He paused again. "You're angry all day, you've changed."

Daniel looked over again, and without a word put his hand on his friend's shoulder.

The blue tarp draped snuggly on the frame that sat on the full length of the Utility brand flatbed trailer. The tarp and the frame were new, bought for Daniel's special trip to D.C. He had the cab and the trailer for years, using it to pick up loads in the fields around Santa Maria. He picked organic vegetables from small boutique farms driving right into the fields. The versatile flatbed allowed the farm workers to stack the crates in all directions quickly. He delivered to some of the best restaurants in California, which was why it was good for business to keep his cab and the trailer extra clean. The white cab always had the sparkle from a coat of wax. The five-star restaurants didn't want to pay a premium for products hauled in a filthy truck that looked like it would break down any minute. He was delivering the best produce in the best truck. Daniel was proud of his business. He did well financially, driving long hours often seven days every week. But, when it came down to it, Daniel was a truck driver living halfway between Los Angeles and Santa Maria. The property values and the cost of living were not cheap, so his veteran's benefits were vital to keep him and his family afloat. After all, he reckoned four hairy tours of duty in Afghanistan, which resulted in two purple hearts, gave him entitlement to the checks and the health benefits that made self-employment work after he retired from the army.

Daniel unwrapped a long churro from a wax paper wrapper to wash down with his next swig of Jack. "This is the best man. A bite of sweet, get that cinnamon and sugar in your mouth and then choke it down with a mouthful of Jack. Mmmmm, mmmm! Noth'in better." He had an unusual gusto for this familiar treat.

He did it just as he described, taking a big bite of the churro, chewed it up some and then sipped from the bottle, letting the sugary dough absorb the whiskey. He savored the delight with half-closed eyes until he swallowed the whole mixture down. He offered Ricardo the rest of the churro and the bottle. Ricardo didn't hesitate, mimicking Daniel's way of washing it down.

The men sat comfortably and watched the traffic stream toward them down the one-way 15th street. They people watched the Washingtonians in their cars and the light foot traffic. Oddly, not a single driver that passed them looked at the backward facing truck. This assured Daniel and relaxed Ricardo as much as the whiskey buzz that was growing inside his head.

They stared for a good long time before Daniel broke the silence. "See those windows up and down on that flat corner of the building?" Daniel said, craning his neck out his window to glance towards the rear of the truck.

Ricardo opened his window and viewed the building just as his friend described. "Yeah, I see them," he answered.

"That's where all the big wig executives have their offices. Figures, corner office, best view." He paused and took in the sight. "That's who I want to get my message. Every single one of those bureaucrats that decided to take my benefits away from my family and put me out of business," Daniel said slowly and measured while he studied the building. His breathing was now rapid and deep.

"You'll show 'em. Whatever kind of light show or sign you got back there, you'll wake them all up. You'll show 'em. How they are take'n away from the simple man," Ricardo smirked. "I can't wait to see what we dragged all this way. I hope it's okay from the drive. Ya never even checked on it the whole time we were drive'n. I hope it's alright?"

Daniel pulled his head back into the cab. "Oh, it's fine. It's a rugged piece of work. That's the least of my worries."

"How long do you think you'll be able to show it before the cops come and shag us outta here?" Ricardo asked.

"Enough to get my message across. I don't need a lot of time."

"Can't wait, it's going to be some protest, *ameeego*!" Ricardo played up an exaggerated accent and laughed. With a limp arm, he threw a defiant fist in the air. The good times continued to roll inside the cab.

Daniel looked at his friend, smiled and reminded Ricardo of the time when the boss at the avocado field grilled them about stealing. Ricardo never questioned why Daniel was taking produce home every day and he didn't give up his friend to the boss as the one who was stealing. Years later, Daniel revealed to Ricardo that those avocados were all his family had to eat during that time. As itinerant help, Daniel's family brought home wages so low that they couldn't eat after paying the rent on the rundown camper his family lived in on the farm.

Daniel took a long pull from the bottle, closed his eyes, took a deep breath and sighed, "Well, it's that time."

"Need my help?" Ricardo asked.

"Naw, just sit back and enjoy the show. You've been a good *amigo*, coming all this way... never nagging me to see my piece of work back there. I really want to thank you. *Gracias amigo.* You've trusted me all this way and been a loyal friend as always. Thanks." Daniel's eyes slightly welled with tears.

"You've been through a lot in the last few months, my friend. Your benefits cut by that ass of a president. I know it was hard deciding whether to close your business. Been a lot on your mind, I know ya had to do this, whatever we're doing here. I hope this all makes a difference," Ricardo said. He then locked eyes with his life-long friend and employer.

Daniel jumped out of the cab and unhooked an opening of the trailer tarp and climbed onto the trailer bed. The clang of metal parts echoed inside the tarp. Ricardo eased back into his seat in and stared at the large side mirror.

In unison, the top and all four sides of the black tarp covering the trailer bed fell from the frame—and Daniel's message was fully exposed. There in the middle of the trailer bed sitting on a tripod was a Browning M2A1 .50 caliber machine gun. On each side of the fierce weapon was a wooden vegetable crate overflowing with jacketed ammo feeding into the weapon.

Daniel put on military googles and large earphones. With a jerk, he pulled the load lever, and without hesitation, he fired at the office windows up and down that flat corner of the United States Department of Veterans Affairs. The power of the shells hitting the side of the building exploded glass and concrete off the structure. Glass, metal, and brick splashed everywhere. Out of context from a war zone, in the lazy quiet of a Washington morning, the weapon made a sound like cannon fire with each discharge. He had a determined expression on his face, eyes focused, jaw clenched and brow furrowed. His body was rigid and his arms tense controlling the massive weapon.

In the cab, Ricardo immediately froze with shock. His eyes popped wide open and his adrenaline propped him erect in his seat. His Jack Daniel's buzz evaporated quicker than a drop of water in the Sahara. He dropped down onto the floor and covered his ears from the booming of the machine gun. The entire truck shook with the explosion and speed of each shot so much that Ricardo feared it might implode. He lifted up his arm to open the passenger door and rolled out onto the street and crawled away on all fours as fast as he could scamper. After a half block of crab crawling, he got up and ran as fast as he could and began to yell, "I ain't part of this shit!" repeatedly until he disappeared.

Each round destroyed huge chunks of the tired concrete of the 100-year-old building that was made to withstand World War I vintage weapons not high caliber shelling from a modern implement of war. Instantly, the windows, the window frames and the rectangular shape of that corner were practically non-existent and in their place was a giant gaping hole, which Daniel was now aiming directly at with the rounds striking the interiors of different floors with random aim. The attack destroyed the side of the building, along with whatever was behind the picture windows on each level of that corner. There was no telling how many lives were lost inside.

The Browning fired 500 rounds a minute and in both of Daniel's crates held 1,500 cartridges. 3,000 rounds fired in approximately six minutes. Daniel calculated that if he was to fire another 1,000 rounds at this intensity, the barrel would overheat, and the Browning would malfunction.

It was time to end six-minute protest. Daniel began kicking the spent shells off the trailer bed nonchalantly, as if he as tidying up after a delivery. He fussed with the tarp and inspected the tarp frame. As he went about his clean-up, two dozen police vehicles raced into the scene and cornered the Mack and Daniel. Daniel put his hands high in the air and stood motionless. The police, FBI, and Homeland Security officers approached him cautiously.

"I surrender. No weapons. I surrender," Daniel yelled to the crowd of law enforcement. They still approached him slowly. One officer, then another climbed up onto the trailer, all keeping their firearms trained on Daniel. Cautiously, they were on Daniel in seconds, and an officer grabbed Daniel and forcibly lowered his arms one by one and handcuffed them tightly behind his back and then pulled him down off the truck. The police executed all these actions without uttering a single word to Daniel, who soon found himself placed in the back seat of a patrol car where he sat quietly.

With the focus of the attack on the far corner of the building, the main entrance to the Veterans' Building on

CHAPTER 1

15th street appeared safe for the firetrucks and ambulances to park in front. Emergency personnel rushed into the building with all sorts of life-saving equipment. Dozens of responders entered the building including doctors and nurses flanked by firefighters in their turnout gear.

As the first of the responders entered the building, the grand foyer was completely still. The firefighters leading the rush into the building yelled for any of the occupants. "Where are you? Is anyone hurt? Where are you located? We need to evacuate the building. The attack is over."

After a few moments, sounds and voices echoed from the left of the large foyer, and then a stairway door burst open and a flood of office workers came rushing out of the staircase.

The responders met the workers immediately and repeated their messages, "The attack is over. Do not run. Try to stay calm. Everything is under control. Where are the wounded? Where are the hurt? Tell us where the injured are?" None of the workers spoke up. Many shook their heads, shrugged their shoulders and stated they didn't know of any wounded. The first responders ushered the workers in an orderly fashion out the main entrance and into the street.

A fire captain, Tim Bellamy, stood in the middle of the foyer standing on the veterans' administration seal with a two-way radio. He had stationed himself there after being the first of the emergency responders to enter the building.

As the flood of workers tapered down, two men and a woman all in business suits approached Captain Bellamy. "Are you in charge here, sir?" the woman named Selma Jackson asked.

"Yes, Captain Tim Bellamy." He said, offering her his hand.

"Well, Captain, by the grace of God and Google Calendar, we don't seem to have many or possibly any casualties here," she reported. "Oh, I'm Selma Jackson, the director of the Veterans' Administration and these are my assistants, Dwight Washington and Jim Steele."

The men shook the captain's hand and exchanged hellos.

"What do you mean you have no casualties? You haven't seen anyone hurt?" Bellamy asked with the urgency to act in his voice.

Selma responded in that shaken, talk too much/talk too fast vibe, giving way too much information in a post-trauma chatter: "Every Monday is our full administration briefing. The staff is in the auditorium at the far end of the building. I started this long ago based on the Steve Jobs model with a little Costco mixed in. Everyone gathers in the auditorium, and I facilitate an info meeting. At the end, we do a short group exercise. It's our largest conference room, and since the majority of people in this building are administrators of some or another program, ninety-nine percent of every human being in this building was in that meeting at 9:30 when we heard the noise start up. Only a couple of maintenance people or such were not in the auditorium. What the hell happened out there?" She asked, but continued without waiting for the answer: "I paused my opening presentation and cursed the construction taking place outside right during our weekly briefing."

"Well, your meet-up idea just saved a bunch of lives because the corner of your building was just completely shot out by some crazy person," Captain Bellamy said.

Selma almost fell down from the shock, and was forced to grab onto Jim to steady herself. As her eyes widened, she took a long deep breath and then shook her head as if to prevent herself from passing out.

A visibly shaken Dwight spoke up, "All our executive offices are up and down that corner! My desk faces out the window!"

Steele and Jackson looked even more stunned, bracing themselves on each other with their heads lowered toward the floor.

Bellamy's voice slapped them to attention: "Listen, I know you're in shock here, but we have to get a head count, your complete personnel immediately." He looked toward all the responders rushing into the building and barked, "Sweep every floor. It's OK to take the elevators. Get there now! Three blasts on the air horn is all clear, NOW!"

The responders raced past them.

"Is there a way to make an announcement throughout the building right now? You have a building intercom or something?" Bellamy asked, before speaking into his two-way, "Keep all the building people together outside until we get a head count."

Bellamy's call to action snapped Selma into work mode again. "Yes, come on into the reception office," Selma said, leading him and her assistants to the central reception office just off the grand foyer.

Walking through the large all-glass double doors, they immediately heard multiple landlines ringing constantly. Selma picked up an old fashion microphone, pressed a button on its base, tapped it twice to make sure the ancient thing worked, and she announced, "Attention, attention! All personnel must evacuate the building immediately. No exceptions! Repeat, all personnel evacuate the building immediately. No exceptions!"

"Good. Now let's all get outside and see if you can account for all your people. I'm getting reports from the floor searches right now as well. The top two floors are clear. No one found yet," Bellamy said.

The group exited the building through the undamaged main entrance and stood outside beside the emergency barricades in front of a large crowd of curious spectators. Dozens of emergency vehicles from several departments parked everywhere, and some still had their Mars lights flashing. The police car in which Daniel Rivera sat was surrounded by four police SUVs with their lights flashing. Daniel looked out at all the chaos down the street with an empty stare.

Marge Oberman, the assistant director of operations for the Veterans' Administration, was standing on a concrete street planter above the crowd and was already calculating an inventory of all employees. Wisely, she had each department head make a visual count of their staff, and used her cell phone to record the results. Bellamy and the group heard her diligent work on organizing the chaos as they came outside.

Selma went right up to Marge and inquired, "How we doing Marge?"

"So far, it looks like everyone is accounted for, double checking now," Marge replied without taking her attention away from her task.

"Outstanding work. Great thinking on your feet. I won't forget," Selma said.

Oberman smiled and nodded, still not looking up.

Bellamy received word that all the employees were accounted for and miraculously there were no injuries. He radioed to all who could hear the news, and then signaled with three blasts of the horn. The pace of the responders immediately slowed, and the urgency left the air.

The machine gun's powerful rounds didn't ignite any small fires or other combustion, but a fire engine's water cannon began spraying the blown-out corner of the building as a routine preventative. Another fire truck's hose soon joined that spray, and the showers of water traveled up and down the side of the building in precise rhythm from top to bottom and then repeated over and over. The corner of the building and its contents were reduced to such debris that the area resembled wet shredded paper. There was nothing left to indicate that these were functioning offices. The water soon soaked the debris that was left by the attack and the side of the building had a grey, chunky sludge that poured downward off the building.

There was strange quiet to everything and everyone at the scene. Emergency personnel walked about doing their duties, while some started to leave. Even though people were standing around looking at the carnage there were no loud voices, in fact, not much conversation could be heard. This is what shock and awe sounded like. In the aftermath hung an ominous atmosphere of fear and dread

CHAPTER 2

It Becomes Necessary to Dissolve the Political Bands

California was in the midst of its worst drought in decades. The dams holding in the reserves of precious water were being opened with a frequency that had the conservation experts sending crisis alerts to the governor's office daily. Governor Rich Herrmann was willing to try anything—even employing a part Native American shaman who claimed that he could find hidden underground reservoirs of water using nothing but a stick. The man had been walking around a field for the past hour mumbling to himself. Herrmann watched in anticipation on his phone.

People have always said Rich was born to be the governor of California. He was tall and good looking. His mixed background—African, Asian, European and Latino—blended together in a way that made everyone feel like he was one of them. But he had one huge thing going against him: He was a Republican in a deeply blue state. But Rich was a political savant and had won every election since elementary school. He had his finger on the pulse of California and its citizens hanging on his every word. On the campaign trail he had made one big promise: green grass. It seemed silly at first. His campaign manager thought he was out of his mind. But by promising a luscious lawn, Rich tapped into something very deep in every Californian's psyche: the California dream, where the impossible can happen. Rich had sensed that every dream included bright green grass on the front lawn right behind the white picket fence next to the Prius station wagon.

"Right here," the man said on the video as the stick pointed at the ground in front of him. The people around the shaman began to dig. Despite himself, Rich felt the excitement of a gold prospector. He knew it was silly, but he was desperate.

Just then there was a knock at the door. An intern Herrmann recognized but couldn't put a name to entered and whispered in the ear of Tom Huang, Herrmann's chief of staff and best friend since college. Tom, a fourth generation Chinese American, had spent his whole life fighting against every stereotype of an Asian male. He was tall and muscular and screamed jock more than skinny math nerd. But while many dismissed him because of his muscles, Rich knew that he was—most of the time—the smartest person in the room, even though his voice had a resonance like a California surfer stereotype.

Herrmann could read the look on Tom's face. It was the same look he saw when he was told that his mother had passed away. First, he worried that something had happened to his two little girls, Maggie and Kelly, or his wife, Toni. He even thought about his dog named Rabbit: Did he have another seizure? He wondered how much the vet bills would be this time.

By the time Tom had gotten to the Governor's side, Herrmann's palms were sweating. "Governor," Tom began.

But Herrmann cut him off. "Tom, how many times do I have to tell you to call me Rich?"

"Rich, you're gonna wanna see this."

"A terrorist attack?" Herrmann asked as he watched the CNN feed on the big screen in his private office with the rest of his senior staff. Herrmann couldn't believe his eyes. The CNN anchor expressed surprise to report that there had been no casualties or injuries. "There's only one word to describe it: a miracle," the reporter added.

"Thank God," Rich said.

"Don't thank *her* just yet," Tom warned him.

As if on cue, the anchor announced, "We are getting word that the alleged terrorist Daniel Rivera is a resident of Santa Maria, a small town located off the central coast of California."

Audible groans went up around the room like a Mexican wave. The expression cascading over Herrmann's body was like a punch in the gut. The terrorist was from his state. "Damnit, God Damnit! The country already thinks were a bunch of lib-radicals. This is not good. Not good." Then the consummate politician collected himself swallowed hard and became the charmer. "I miss the days when our terrorists were from the Middle East."

No one laughed. Not because it wasn't funny but because everyone in that room had the same exact thought.

Tom looked at his boss for any indication of what he should do.

"Call everyone together," Rich began. "You know we're going to hear from the President, and we'll need a game plan."

Almost as soon as the words had left his mouth, the entire room scattered back to their offices.

As Rich waited for the rest of his senior staff to arrive, he continued to watch the news. "Tom, am I overreacting here? Do you think the country will focus on the California connection?"

"Let's hope not, but ever since that crap in '22, the country looks at us like we're recklessly lawless."

Herrmann shook his head, "I warned them that the amnesty program would be looked upon as extreme."

"Clearing out the prisons did save millions and just about lost that election for you." Tom said.

"I'll admit it, that move shook up the prison systems," He paused and studied the monitor. "They're reporting that Rivera was protesting cuts in veterans' benefits. Maybe this is another wake-up call to Washington?"

Staring at the monitor, Huang nodded.

"I can't condone such horrible violence, but, damnit, we're abandoning our veterans. I get where this Daniel Rivera is coming from. Look at the policies enacted over the past year?" Herrmann said.

"Rich, something's gotta give here. The Californians, and a handful of other States, are being completely marginalized. In fact, the last time you went to D.C., the President refused to meet with you. Come on! Instead, he met with some low-level staffers who had come up with an excuse that there had been some emergency and that her boss was suddenly too busy to meet." Tom said.

"We never did find out what that "emergency" was." Herrmann added.

"Oh yea, we did. We did some recon and according to the President's social media feed, the only thing mentioned that day was throwing out the first pitch at a Washington Nationals game. We all wondered what we had to do to get the President's attention. I mean he professes to be a Republican and all and he won't say hello to a colleague from the same aisle? Come on." Tom's words shot out with anger and bitterness.

Herrmann was so deep in thought, he didn't hear Tom walk over to the desk and grab the landline that was flashing. "Gov..," his chief of staff began and then corrected himself. "Rich, the Prez is on the line." California and Herrmann was apparently high on the President's radar—but the body language in the room stated that this was not the attention Herrmann nor his staff wanted.

President James Matthews III had won an electoral landslide a half year before in the fall of 2024. But following a trend since the forty-fifth president, Donald Trump, he had lost the popular election by a historic amount: four million votes. It didn't shock anyone that the California governor was one of those who voted against Matthews. In fact, his state had voted overwhelmingly against him. If the exit polls were to be believed, ninety percent of the citizens of California voted against Matthews. To everyone's surprise, even the rural parts—which traditionally voted conservatively—cast their ballots against the President.

The current political joke was that James Matthews III was the love child of former president Donald Trump and a Republican version of John F. Kennedy. Someone who was idolized—outside of California, New York, and a handful of other states along the West Coast and North East at least—and a billionaire and successful strongman businessman who "told it like it was."

Before the attack on the Veteran's building, the news cycle was aflutter about the rumors that President's Matthews' was going to appoint another four Supreme Court Justices to the court so that they would overturn many of the laws that he saw as affronts to the moral fiber of the country. The pundits debated whether the President had the power to add justices legally, but the one thing Matthews had going for him was that he was correct when the media quoted him as saying that the United States Constitution did not spell out the number of justices there can be at any one time.

"I'll cut straight to the chase," President Matthews said when Herrmann put the phone to his ear. Before the California Governor could even respond, the President continued, "What I want to know is how you are going to handle this. Because we both know it would be best for the country if you and I were on the same page."

What the President was asking for was Rich's support to do whatever HE thought was best. This was pretty much how Rich knew the conversation was going to go. The President was a man who asked for people's loyalty without ever pledging his to anyone. But knowing that didn't make it any easier. "It's a pleasure to chat with you, Mr. President," Rich said in as an agreeable of a voice he could muster. His sarcasm was lost on the president.

"Ahh...Sure, good morning." Matthews responded with insincerity in his tone before he continued on his agenda. "I know you did not support my bid at the convention, Rich. Can I call you, Rich?" the President asked and without waiting for a response he continued, "But, we're fellow republicans and I need your immediate action on this Veteran's attack."

"Rich is fine, Mr. President." Herrmann's words seemed to be spitting out through clenched teeth. His friends got to call him Rich, not those he detested. However, politics was all gamesmanship and he played it well. Herrmann could hear President Matthews' smile as he began what seemed to be a well-prepared statement. "This is what you are going to do, Rich. You are going to find every illegal hiding in your goddamn heathen state and lock them up in jail. I do not care what doors you have to break down or who's feelings you have to hurt, but you will find every single one of them. The country needs a strong response to this morning's terrorist attack. Do you understand?"

Herrmann's mind raced with thought of all the things he wanted to say. Most of them involved screaming obscenities at the president. He considered slamming the phone down dramatically—but all Matthews would hear would be the 'click' on his end. In the back of his mind, Rich knew either option would not be helpful.

Herrmann shook his head to clear it. His wife, Toni told him he needed to be more in the moment. She called him the 'First Post-Modern Governor of California'. It was her way of saying that he was always looking at himself through the lens of history and not being present. *What would Toni do?* He asked himself.

The answer was obvious. "I'm sorry, Mr. President. I can't do that," he told the President. It was short and sweet. It took a moment for the President to respond. He was not used to people saying no to him. What Herrmann couldn't have known was that it was the first time Matthews had heard those words in months. "Rich," President Matthews began. "You just made the biggest mistake of your career. I promise you that I will do all I can to make sure you regret that you ever uttered a no to me." He then hung up.

Herrmann couldn't help the smile that appeared on his face when the line went dead. Tom Huang locked eyes with Herrmann and his smile was even bigger than his boss's. "Boom! That was a left jab to the jaw. It wasn't a knockout blow, but it was good."

CHAPTER 2

"Tom, I hate Goddamn bullies. When I was a kid, I went outta my way to fight them whether they were picking on me or a stranger. This ass is just the latest one." Herrmann said.

But as soon as the smiles had appeared, they were gone because the president would hit back–and soon. After all, he was the most powerful man in the country. Not just because of his position, but because he had managed to do what no president had done before him: completely subsume the other branches of the government under his control. The Republicans in the Senate and the House, who had super majorities in both, were completely under his spell. The joke amongst the Democrats about their colleagues across the aisle was that they couldn't go to the bathroom unless the President told them it was okay. And once Matthews stacked the Supreme Court with his cronies, he would be in control of all three branches. The checks and balances the Founders were so fond of would only be something people studied in school.

Staffers began to file into Herrmann's office. They could tell by the look on the governor's face that this would be one of those meetings that would last a very long time. When everyone finally arrived and were brought up to speed with the call, Rich looked around and asked, "Any ideas on what the President is going to do?"

Everyone around the long conference table had different ideas about how President Matthews was going to retaliate, but all agreed that the president was not going to back down. After just a few moments of heated debate, Herrmann saw the futility of trying to read the tea leaves. "Ok, Ok, this speculation has a purpose, but let's focus on how we should respond. I need to come out with a statement." Herrmann said.

"Nobody supports what Daniel Rivera did, but we are all growing more and more frustrated with what is coming out from the Beltway and especially in the White House. I need to come out strong against the attack but also speak out against the policies that led to Daniel Rivera doing what he did." Herrmann added.

Herrmann's speechwriter, Coryell Crockett, blurted out, "I'll start drafting the talking points right this second." She buried her head into her laptop. Michelle Shamblee, Herrmann's press liaison added, "I have your schedule fired up and I'll get the local media on board as to when you will be making your statement." The well-oiled machine's gears were moving, and the confidence Herrmann had in his team showed in how his body unclenched. He knew they would be prepared with an effective response.

An hour later, Herrmann was in front of a packed room of reporters and cameras. He was built for these moments. If he had been in politics fifty years earlier, Herrmann would have been a natural for the presidency. However, now the idea of a president coming from the state of California was deemed ridiculous. With the prison amnesty program, the extreme liberalism of Silicon Valley, and Hollywood's dominance in the media, a Californian had long been considered too left-wing to win a national general election anymore.

"Thank you for coming," Herrmann started off the press conference. "It is important that I say in no uncertain terms, that today's attack at the Veteran's Building in Washington D.C. was unacceptable…" Herrmann followed the script the rest of the way, reminding people of some of his state's grievances. He concluded with a plea for national unity and coming together in times of crisis.

Everything went pretty much the way Herrmann and his team had planned until the third question from a *Los Angeles Times* reporter was shouted out. "Your statement here seems to contradict the president's latest announcement," She paused as the room turned to look at her. Herrmann seemed confused, he obviously didn't know what she was talking about. "To quote the president, just moments ago, he said he would do what is best for the country, whether the Governor of California agreed with him or not."

"I haven't been informed of that statement from the president," Herrmann responded.

Eager to keep the spotlight, the reporter almost didn't let the governor finish, "President Matthews is issuing an executive order that will suspended all civil liberties of illegals and call for their immediate apprehension by law enforcement authorities by any means necessary". Herrmann's face turned red. The president had struck back.

CHAPTER 3

The Preamble

"Liar! Liar! Did you hear what Herrmann called you? That's treason!" Jad Stanton walked right into the Oval Office through one of the two doors angling the president's desk. He stopped in his tracks in front of the desk when the President held his right hand up. The President had an uncharacteristic laugh in full launch that was started well before Stanton's interruption.

"Jad, I just watched it," he said through his laughter. "Calm down. Do you think I care what that gnat thinks of me?" The President stood up and walked around to the front of his desk. As he arrived at the front of the historic desk, he grabbed a handful of shelled pistachio nuts from a crystal bowl. "What? Is he going to stop sending me my favorite treat? Shit, I'll get Macadamias from Hawaii. He's one state and one governor. I've got dozens of them." He threw the pistachios in his mouth and smiled. "I made billions, my fortune on toilets; you think his potty-mouth comment offends me or I haven't heard worse before?"

Stanton interrupted, "Mister President, your companies make more than toilets, why—"

Interrupting him, the President said: "Jad, my grandfather, made toilets; my dad turned it into a multi-million-dollar company by being ruthless and crushing the competition. I'm not ashamed of my upbringing." He paused and took another healthy handful of nuts. "You're new; let me remind you who I am, I'm not ashamed of where I've come from. I love this. Let him think he's insulted me. I crush people like him. But, unlike that idiot Trump, my two terms in the Senate taught me how to use the government to my advantage. Oh, we will make Herrmann pay. He won't know what hit him."

Stanton collected himself and put his hand on one of the two floral sofas facing each other near the door. "Just tell me what you want done, Mr. President."

"Jad, we don't react to the comment. People will forget about it. We just don't forget what side that fool is on," President Matthews instructed, beginning to walk back behind his desk. "Oh Jad, speaking of being new here. Don't just barge into my office. You've got something for me, have Peter buzz me before you come in. I may just be launching nukes or something," he said, smiling. "And, you don't stand over me in front of my desk."

Nervously, Stanton seemed reprimanded. "I just thought as your chief of staff I had access –"

"Jad, this isn't your grandfather's Senate office where you can play with toy soldiers under his desk," President Matthews said, flashing a fake smile. "Chief of staff. Hmmmm, in the old days your position was called secretary, but I guess that isn't politically correct." He stared at Stanton as if looking through him.

"Sir, chief of staff is your right hand," Stanton pleaded.

President Matthews raised his right hand. "I've got a right hand. Let me make clear, your job is to fetch things for me. If I say go get this or do this, you do it."

Stanton continued his mild pleas, "But, I'm not a gofer. Isn't that what Peter is for?"

"I'm glad we're having this conversation. You are what I want you to be."

President Matthews walked back in front of the desk and looked into Stanton's eyes. "I hope you realize that you only got this job because I did a favor for your father. I had a perfectly fine chief of staff or gofer for decades. You got this job to create a debt that I can cash in, plain and simple. You have no special privileges or access," his tone was firm.

"You get buzzed into this office…always," President Matthews added. "That's all."

Stanton turned and walked out. Head down and slumped shoulders, his face carried a pained look as if he'd just been taken out back to the wood pile and given a good whopping. President Matthews lifted the computer screen that was integrated into his desk and replayed Herrmann's press conference. He snickered again, then with another flick of some keys on the computer he summoned Peter McKenzie his head admin, "Peter, could you come in here?"

Within seconds, McKenzie opened the door to the Oval Office and stood right inside as close and as tight near the door as possible. "Yes, sir?" Peter asked.

"Could you get secretary Ellis in here as soon as he can make it. Something I want to plot out while it is fresh."

McKenzie had the president on speaker phone and signaled for his assistant to make the call to Ellis.

After the assistant completed the call, McKenzie was back to the President with his usual efficiency, "Mr. President, Secretary of State Ellis is in his office. He can meet in an hour."

"How did Mr. Ellis become the confidant of the president?" The assistant asked.

McKenzie smiled, "I just got an updated security file this morning. Here, and read it out loud. I want to make sure it has the detail. Just read me the section on the background with the president."

The assistant began to read aloud, "Albert Ellis gave up his position as CEO at General Motors to join James Matthews' cabinet as Secretary of State. Ellis' reputation in the auto industry was as a brutal competitor who would stop at nothing to crush rivals. He particularly aimed his dirtiest tactics against the foreign car makers. He was forced out of General Motors while an unprecedented class-action lawsuit was filed against him for unlawful trade practices. Participants in the suit were automakers from Japan, South Korea, Germany, China, and India. Ellis was accused of product 'dumping.' The product being automobiles that GM sold in these countries at ridiculously low prices to undercut the foreign automakers and weaken the auto industries in each of those countries. The strategy of flooding foreign markets with vastly cheaper alternatives to nationally made products is a role reversal of practices that U.S. industries had accused foreign countries of doing for decades. The biggest offenders using these product dumping tactics were China and India. It was alleged that Chinese and Indian manufacturers were supported by their governments to conduct these dumping practices and undermine U.S. industries by being unfair competitively. Ellis copied these practices after filing and winning several lawsuits against Chinese and Indian product manufacturers only to discover that winning these outrageously expensive lawsuits in U.S. courts did not stop the influx of cheaper non-competitive products into the U.S.

A furious Ellis countered these trade actions by somehow manufacturing a car made so inexpensively that it could be sold in these countries for half the price of the least expensive car in each country. That was saying a lot because India had a car it was selling like hotcakes for $3,330 U.S.D. His strategy worked and the automakers in China and India were greatly crippled by GM's cheap car. In fact, the Chinese and India automakers were so hurt by Ellis' tactic that their planned expansion into the U.S. with their inexpensive cars was halted as they scrambled to regain their market share in their own countries. Ellis' moves made him even more hated in the auto industry worldwide and even U.S. automakers hated him out of jealousy that they didn't or couldn't make the same auto.

One of Ellis' only fans was the two-term senator from Pennsylvania, James Matthews III. As the owner of a huge U.S. manufacturing conglomerate, Matthews delighted in seeing the foreign companies get a taste of their own medicine. Matthews came out on the Senate floor and in the press praising and supporting Ellis' genius. Soon after Matthews public support, the two met face-to-face and formed a strong alliance.

The diabolical Ellis didn't stop there. He copied the same strategy and manufactured low priced cars in Japan, South Korea, and Germany. He did that for no other reason than he could and that the plan made money insured that he could. The disruption to the auto industries in each country was devastating, and the ripple effect was that each of the foreign automakers' market share inside the U.S. fell drastically along with their worldwide share. General Motors became the world's largest automaker by a wide margin for the first time in sixty years.

With all the financial success that Albert Ellis rained on General Motors you would think that GM would brand him a hero and a titan inside GM, but his ruthless management style, manipulation of the GM board of directors and C-Suite, and his disregard for people by sacrificing them for whatever end goals he set made him hated throughout General Motors. He was seen by everyone there like Attila the Hun sending thousands of soldiers to their death only to enrich his land holdings. No one was sacred inside GM, and the C-Suite became a revolving door under his leadership. Matthews used this same style in his companies, and neither man appeared to have any friends in their personal life. Even toward each other, they, nor anyone commenting on them, used the word, 'friendship' to describe their alliance. But, an alliance they did form and when the federal lawsuit was filed and had compelling evidence, both Ellis and Matthews knew Ellis' days at GM were numbered. Matthews then tabbed him for his Secretary of State. The deal struck between the two was that Matthews would not only rescue Ellis from General Motors, but Matthews would end the federal lawsuit against him. It was a win-win for all concerned."

"Good, I asked Juarez to put more life in that section. His last draft read like a list of bullet points." McKenzie commented.

On the hour, Peter buzzed the President and announced Secretary Ellis' arrival. Ellis was immediately let into the Oval Office. The two did not shake hands or offer any form of greeting. They sat on the facing sofas in the middle of the room and got right down to brass tacks.

"Al, I've got a small situation budding here, and I wanted to bring you in right away and get your advice. This piss poor excuse of a Governor of California is becoming a pain in the ass. Like me, he's in office since January.

Already, every executive order I sign he has disobeyed," President Matthews started.

"Environment, energy, healthcare, social programs, agriculture, trade…" Ellis piped in.

"And now, my reaction on immigration after the attack on the veteran's administration. He defied me in the public forum."

"He called the President of the United States a liar," Ellis added.

"You know I don't give a shit about that. But his open defiance of his President is marking a pattern here that I want to stop dead in its tracks." President Matthews didn't show a lick of emotion.

"Should we bring in the Attorney General to this discussion?" Ellis asked.

"I guess this would all be his area and I guess protocol would say, yeah, I should, but I hardly know that guy. He was a favor I gave to his uncle who got me a good portion of the Bible Belt. I know you, Al, and I trust your opinion. That's why I called you in right away," Matthews added.

"I guess thanks," Ellis smiled. "First, I think you need to act fast. If the governor of California sits back all sassy and thinks he got the last word in that will just enable him for future battles. You need to slap him down, and I would recommend slap him down hard. And not in public. Don't start some juvenile name-calling or pissing contest. You do that, and he still comes out as standing up to the President. No, do something in your power to hurt him."

Matthews looked away from Ellis and considered his comments. Then Ellis broke the silence. "I've watched you do business over the years, James. I remember what you did to that eighty-year-old retail plumping company that sold your products up and down the east coast. That company made your plumbing division a lot of money for all those eighty years. What? About five hundred million a year? You found out that this company was beginning to sell your products online from their own website instead of directing customers to your brand site. You heard about that and that same day you pulled your products from their stores. Slap! Your companies get in line or get out of business. I doubt you had many other companies breaking the rules."

President Matthews smiled at Ellis' command of Matthews business dealings. "We temporarily took a hurt with that move, but it saved us billions in the long run." President Matthews looked off into the distance. "I see what you are saying, and I was thinking the same thing."

"James," Ellis' narcissism being the equal to the President's and their friendship gave him the rare license to call the President by his first name. "California is a subsidiary of the United States. A retailer, just like the Home Market stores. California sells the products that the United States provides. When are we going to treat the states like that, the retailers that they are? Federal control of the states has been eroding for years with administrations that have given them the power to make decisions independent of the federal government. But, whose country is it? Whose raw materials is it? California is a name put on a retailer that is cultivating, and I use that word ironically and purposely, the products that belong to the United States of America. Is California any different than the Home Market stores?"

President Matthews nodded in agreement, and then said, "I got it. I see what you are saying. So, let me brainstorm with you on some action that will slap down Herrmann."

"He's wildly popular in his state. Right there is a long-term problem for your presidency," Ellis said.

"So was Ned Cromwell who started Home Market. In fact, he was popular in ten states and he and my grandfather were close. Popular is not as powerful as respect. I have to get Herrmann's respect," President Matthews said thoughtfully.

"He ran on a campaign that promised green grass or lawn sprinklers or some such thing," Ellis said, chuckling. "Slap him right in the face of his popularity. Do something that blocks him from keeping his promise. Take away his popularity. What did you do to what's his name? Oh, Ned. You took away his tools to do business."

The President sat pensively. Then he stood up and moved to his desk and pressed a key on his computer and spoke, "Peter, can you get Nick Myers at EPA on the phone right now?"

Before he could sit back down, the desk phone rang. "Nick, talk to me about water, California water. What does the federal government control out there in that water system?"

President Matthews listened for quite a long time whilst jotting down notes on a desk pad. "Thanks, Nick and thanks for being so responsive," President Matthews said, ending the call.

President Matthews resumed his meeting with Ellis. "Well, I think I have the hand to slap that face. Nick was telling me that we control the Central Valley Project run by something called the U.S. Bureau of Reclamation. There are three major dams in that project among others. The Shasta Dam is the largest water storage facility; then there is the Folsom Dam and the New Melones Dam. I think we just might turn off those dams for a bit and nobody keeps their grass green."

The following day the operations of the three major dams in the Central Valley Project were shut down. At the same time, hundreds of federal immigration authorities began house-to-house searches in Hispanic neighborhoods throughout the state to check on the legal status of citizens. The immigration officers visited farms and detained workers to verify their residency. Scenes of people being questioned by teams of officials in ICE windbreakers appeared all over the Internet.

People all over the country were outraged and the ACLU immediately threatened lawsuits. But threats of lawsuits don't stop immigration officers from detaining citizens and the speed of the President's actions easily ignored all the verbal sparring from the ACLU and others.

The President dispatched thousands of federal officers bolstered by personnel from other states and even other departments in law enforcement to intensify the efforts in California. Federal officers took Hispanic citizens from their homes, often after physical confrontations, with hundreds of citizens taken into custody. There was property damage and scenes of family members of the arrested citizens attacking the immigration vehicles, often breaking the vehicles windows. The actions of the immigration squads and the physical damage in the areas of California where it took place were reminiscent of the 'Kristallnacht' in Nazi Germany in 1938.

California looked helpless to stop any of the federal actions. It seemed like everyone knew someone taken into custody for possible deportation. At the same time, Californians complained to the state about the lack of water. Tensions rose, and the California population seethed with anger.

Governor Herrmann didn't remain helpless. Two days after Matthews shut down the dams and sent in the immigration teams, Herrmann ordered an immediate stop to all tax money due to the federal government as well as any lease funds, or payments of any kind owed the federal government. This monetary action was able to take effect instantly, whereas Herrmann's action to stop the immigration detentions would have taken more time. He ordered the California National Guard deployed with the intent to block the federal immigration teams. Such a deployment could be made immediately but operationally it took days, possibly weeks to get the Guard on the scene. In the meantime, the ACLU did get a lawsuit filed within a week and a federal judge halted the detentions until a court date could be held on the legality of the detentions and arrests. But the damage was done. Within the eight days of the raids by the immigration teams, 300,000 people of Hispanic descent, mostly Mexican, were being held in federal lock-up facilities. Given the strategically placed bureaucratic hurdles that the administration put in place, it would take months if not longer to get these people released from their incarceration. Legal or not, Matthews' actions accomplished what he set out to do.

The outrage in the media throughout the country was overwhelming with many commentators calling the immigration officers 'The Blue Jackets' after their blue windbreakers with the huge ICE letters on the back. The conventional media and social media outcry not only made the Kristallnacht references but compared the Blue Jackets to the Nazi Brown Shirts of Germany in the 1930's.

The battle lines were becoming drawn in the sand or more accurately in the water between California and the administration of President Matthews.

CHAPTER 4

A Decent Respect to The Opinions of Mankind

"Thank God," Noah Murakami told himself once they entered California airspace. Noah was twenty-one years old, half-Japanese and half-Caucasian. He was the kind of *hapa*—the word that has come to mean half-Asian and half-something else—that neither looked Asian nor white. Most people thought he was just a tall and skinny Mexican kid who didn't speak Spanish. He had a boyish good look about him, but his eyes betrayed that he had seen more than anyone his age should have.

Noah was born and raised in South Pasadena, a suburb in LA. After consecutive tours in Iran, North Korea, and Afghanistan, this was the first time he had been back home for almost five years. He could swear the air in his home state felt different. The feeling made him think about his mother, father, and siblings. If he had more time, he would have loved nothing better than to head south for a day to see them because a visit was long overdue.

One of the new Texans, a prototypical blond-haired blue-eyed southern good old boy, in his squad, his name escaped Noah now, was staring at him.

"What?" Noah asked.

"You've been smiling ever since we've got into California airspace. "You do know why they're sending us here?" the Texan teased Noah. When Noah didn't answer, he continued, "To stop the libtards in your home state from destroying federal property." The Texan's words left an uneasy feeling in the pit of Noah's stomach. Noah looked at the others on the plane with him. Those that met his eyes were also from California, or from neighboring states that shared California's politics. They all had the same worried expression and thought: *what the hell were they getting themselves into?*

As soon as the plane touched down, they boarded transport helicopters and were dispatched to Shasta Dam to reinforce a battalion already there. By then, a large group of protestors had also gathered and the two sides were squared off like some bad Revolutionary War re-enactors.

"I didn't sign up for this," Noah told his best friend, Mark Perez, a five-foot four-inch Filipino American with brown skin and black hair who always said "bro" at the end of every sentence. Mark nodded in agreement.

There were already rumors of clashes between the protestors and the soldiers. The only orders command had given was not to let the protestors get within a hundred feet of the road leading to the base of the dam. What Noah didn't know was what they were supposed to do if the protestors refused to comply. Would they be forced to shoot indiscriminately into the crowd?

Noah figured out right away why the protestors had gathered and why they were sent there. All he had to do was the read the signs the people were holding. It was the first he heard of the water crisis. Noah never told anyone—including his best friend—that he didn't blame any of the protestors. In fact, if he had a choice, he would have been on their side holding one of those signs too.

CHAPTER 4

Mark leaned toward Noah as they set up their sleeping quarters. "It's ironic, they sent you here, don't you think bro?"

Noah was so in his head, he didn't follow.

Mark laughed at the look on his friend's face and then spelled it out for him. "You know, with your name being Noah and we being here because of water and all, bro. I hope it doesn't flood, I don't swim."

Noah smiled, but it didn't reach his eyes. Mark had been through enough battles with Noah to know what he was thinking. He tried to reassure him, "We're on the right side. And if we're not, we can just go AWOL bro."

This was put to the test the next morning when Lieutenant Colonel Erikson told them in the morning briefing, "We have been given authority from the Chief of Staff to open fire if the protestors broke the barrier and approached them." Everyone in the briefing knew that the orders had come from President Matthews himself.

Noah couldn't believe what he was hearing. He raised his hand. "With rubber bullets?" he asked after being acknowledged. The others in the room laughed, but he didn't care.

"Live ammunition," was the Lieutenant Colonel's answer. "We have intelligence that there are terrorists hiding amongst the protestors."

Noah didn't buy this but he knew better than to raise any objections. Besides, the commanders were already looking at him funny. Noah was scheduled to be at the front in thirty minutes. As he got dressed, his mind was racing. Could he really shoot a fellow American? It wasn't that he was afraid of shooting people. He had shot his fair share of enemy combatants. But he was no monster. His nightmares kept him up almost every night as proof.

But he knew he couldn't live with himself if he shot Americans—the same people he had sworn to protect.

Noah came up with a plan. During the shift change, he would get out of his fatigues and then slip into a crowd of protestors. From there, he would try to catch a ride out as soon as possible. He knew it was a bad idea to tell anyone, but he needed to give a heads up to his best friend. "I'm going," he told Mark. He hoped that Mark would go with him or try to stop him, but all Mark said to him was, "Good luck, bro."

Ten minutes later, Noah understood the moment he crossed into the protestors that he had just made either the most important decision or the biggest mistake of his life. He was fully aware that if caught it meant a court-martial and a long time in the brig—if not a military-style execution for desertion, which was legal during times of war. But knowing all this didn't stop him. He quickly found his way to a road and hitched a ride away.

Around the same time, Noah's mother, Tricia Murakami, was on her way to work by foot—not because she worried about climate change or wanting to keep in shape, but because she lived only a few blocks away from the school where she taught kindergarten, in the South Pasadena Unified School District.

Tricia had brown hair, hazel eyes, and much to her chagrin carried twenty extra pounds on her small frame. She had spent most of her youth trying to get rid of the extra weight but eventually accepted it as just part of who she was. Soon, it was the favorite part of her. She always told people that it just meant "there was more of her to love."

Tricia treasured the tree-lined streets and Craftsman homes of her hometown. It was a city that prided itself on being a small town despite being only ten minutes away from the hustle and bustle of downtown LA. Her morning routine was to listen to a podcast of the local National Public Radio affiliate KPCC. She had never been particularly interested in the news, but with the way politics was going she made it a point to be kept informed.

The KPCC reporter, who had a slight accent that Tricia couldn't place, announced, "A new California ballot initiative to repeal the clause in the state constitution that California is 'inseparable part of the United States' has gotten enough signatures to be on this November's election ballot." The reporter then interviewed Californians who were generally in support of the proposition, but Tricia's mind was on the red Toyota Camry parked in the drop off zone in front of the school. There was a long line of cars behind it. Tricia hated when parents parked there and was about to tell off the driver when she noticed a group of people already surrounding the car. At first, she assumed they were her fellow teachers, but something didn't seem right. Then she noticed the blue jackets with the words ICE written on the back. Tricia stopped. She had seen the videos of immigration officers arresting undocumented people, but until now she'd never witnessed it up close. Everything began to slow when she saw one of the officers drag a man through the open driver's side window and slam him onto the ground. And then another blue jacket pointed his gun at the driver's face. On the other side of the car, another immigration agent—a hulk of a man—had their gun pointed at the little girl in the back seat.

"Daddy!" the little girl screamed. Her voice jarred something in Tricia's head and time began to move at a normal speed again. She recognized the little girl as she exited the Toyota with her hands shaking in the air. The girl was Ava. She was a cute seven-year-old in a pink shirt with the school's name written across the chest. She had been in Tricia's kindergarten class the year before.

Without thinking about it, Tricia ran to Ava and hugged her. The huge man in the blue jacket told her, "Step back. You are interfering with federal law enforcement action."

Tricia looked the man in the eye and responded, "She's not a criminal. She's just a little girl." By this time, other teachers and parents had begun to gather. A few had taken out their cell phones and were recording everything.

The man in the blue jacket took a step toward Ava and Tricia. Tricia's mother's instincts kicked in and she put herself between the little girl and the hulking man. When the agent got closer, he stared at her and said, "You are interfering with a criminal investigation. I could have you arrested."

Tricia stared right back. "How is holding an innocent child interfering with a criminal investigation?" Tricia didn't know what had come over her. She had never even been on the receiving end of a parking ticket, never mind being arrested. But she had never felt more righteous before in her life.

Instead of answering her, the officer tried to reach around Tricia and grab Ava. Without thinking about the consequences, she raised her hand and slapped the immigration officer on the face. Hard. A slap that was heard around the world thanks to all the cellular phones recording it all.

For the briefest of moments, there was silence before a sudden burst of cheers from other teachers and parents.

The huge man was not hurt, just stunned. He could probably kill Tricia with one hand, and it looked like he really wanted to, but two of his colleagues escorted him away before he could do anything. Tricia's unexpected response appeared to confuse the blue jacket's ranks. They huddled, packed up, loaded into their vehicles and left. After all the blue jackets were gone, the outside of the school became eerily quiet.

Ava had been saved but her father was taken. Tricia tried to comfort her but what could she say? The only words that she could find were, "I'm so sorry." But the sadness on the little girl's face broke her heart. The image of Tricia hugging the crying little school girl in the pink shirt also went viral. There was a Madonna/child heart tugging reaction around the world at the still picture of Tricia hugging Ava.

The rest of the day was a blur for Tricia. She could barely concentrate on the five and six-year-olds in her classes. Her mind kept returning to the look on Ava's face. The other teachers called her a hero for standing up to the blue jackets, but she did not feel like one.

When the last bell rang, Principal Sloan, an uptight man in his fifties who wore a perpetual grimace like he had just smelled something rancid, summoned her to his office. Tricia assumed that, like her fellow teachers, he was going to tell her what a great job she did. But she should have known better. The two had a rocky relationship ever since he had come to the school. Sloan believed that Tricia coddled the kindergarteners too much while Tricia didn't think it was possible to coddle kindergarteners too much. The only explanation Tricia could come up was that he wasn't from her state. He was from Arizona. And according to him, they did things differently out there. The first sentences out of Sloan's mouth set the tone for the rest of the conversation: "What the hell is wrong with you? Those guys were just doing their jobs."

Tricia opened her mouth to protest but Principal Sloan continued, "And those illegals are breaking the law and should be in jail. We shouldn't be giving them a free education."

Tricia just stood there and didn't reply. She didn't want to hear any more and decided to leave. On her way out the door, Principal Sloan told her, "You are on indefinite suspension and if it's up to me you'll never set foot on this campus again."

Tricia spun around. "You can't do that."

With a smile, the principal responded, "I just did."

On her walk back home, Tricia imagined different ways to murder the principal. *A gunshot to the head? Too quick. Stabbing? Too bloody.* Of course, she knew she wouldn't really kill him, but thinking about it made her feel better. She knew she was mostly trying to distract herself from what she was most worried about: How would Rowan, her husband, take the news of what she did?

Rowan worked for the Jet Propulsion Laboratory or JPL for short. Most of his projects were with the federal government but after recent events their lucrative contracts were being canceled and given to states that were on friendlier terms with those in power. The two had spoken about what would happen if he got laid off. They had taken solace that the house was paid off—a gift from Tricia's parents—and the fact that she had a job.

Tricia considered calling Rowan to tell him what happened but figured it would be better to explain it

CHAPTER 4

in person later. Tricia was old school and still believed that it was best to tell bad news in person. She was still considering how when she approached her 1925 dark brown Craftsman.

With one hand, she turned on her phone and with the other she reached out for the door handle. But before she could grab it, it flew open. Her youngest daughter, Grace was standing there with a wide grin.

Grace had grown up so fast over the past year. And while Tricia had always struggled with her weight, Grace seemed to be perpetually skinny. Unlike her brother who looked more Hispanic, Grace appeared Asian. Tricia hated to say it and knew how racist it sounded but the perfect word to describe her daughter was "exotic." At twelve, Grace was already turning boys' heads. Seeing the look in young pubescent teenage boys' eyes kept Tricia up at nights.

"Mom," Grace began. "You're a meme!"

Tricia didn't know what her daughter was talking about.

"You're all over social media." When her mom didn't respond fast enough, she shoved her smartphone into her face.

Tricia began to watch the video and even she was surprised by how loud the slap was. It was almost like the crack of a wooden bat smacking a baseball.

"Look how many times it's been viewed," Grace said to her mom, beaming with pride. Tricia glanced at the bottom of the screen and saw that it had over two million hits and had been shared over five hundred thousand times already.

"You're Internet famous," Grace told her mom with awe.

Tricia sat on the couch. She needed to get her bearings. She flicked on CNN and her—or rather her video—was the headline story. Almost as if planned, her phone began to buzz with texts, voice mails, emails, and Facebook messages. It seemed everyone was trying to get a hold of her.

Tricia wondered what her husband thought of all this. She assumed he already knew what happened and was considering how to do damage control when he walked through the front door.

Rowan was the cliché Asian guy. He was short, wore thick glasses, had straight jet-black hair, and was awkward even with his own family. But the two things that Tricia loved about him was his intelligence and his loyalty—especially his loyalty. He was the most loyal person in the world and put his family above everyone and anyone.

"What the hell Trish, what the damn hell were you thinking?" Rowan screamed. After fifteen years of marriage, Tricia had never seen Rowan so angry. But before he could say anything further, their middle child, Ezekiel, entered the house. This way too skinny sixteen-year-old looked even more angry than usual, which was saying something considering lately everyone in the family had to walk around him as though he was some kind of ticking time bomb living in their midst. And it wasn't just the all black clothes he had started wearing six months earlier or the fact that he had stopped looking people in the eye anymore. There was something dark hanging over him.

Ezekiel was always the black sheep of the family. While his older brother was handsome and his younger sister preternaturally beautiful, Ezekiel somehow missed out when it came to looks. He wasn't ugly per se, just somehow off. And unfortunately, he missed out on his father's intelligence and his mother's social skills.

The only person in the family who wasn't afraid of setting Ezekiel off was his younger sister, Grace. She ran to her brother with her phone outstretched, "Did you see?"

Ezekiel nodded, but looked at his mom. "Why'd you do that?" he asked. And then mumbled something unintelligible. The only thing Tricia caught was, "You're so embarrassing." Before he stormed off to his room.

At that moment, the doorbell rang. Standing in the open doorway was a news camera and a reporter. "Mrs. Murakami, may we ask you a question?" the reporter shouted. Grace opened her mouth to speak but Rowan had the good sense to slam the door before she could say anything. Within an hour, the entire front yard was covered with local and national media.

Rowan paced in front of Tricia. "What were you thinking?" he kept saying.

Tricia gave up trying to answer him. She knew he was just trying to work it out in his head. He wasn't mad at what she had done, he was just worried at what it might mean for the family. "How are we going to pay the bills if I get laid off?"

"Let's not worry about that for now," she told him. "How about we sit down and eat dinner like a normal family?"

But with the commotion on their front lawn, neither honestly believed that anything would be *normal* for a long time.

An hour later, the whole family was sitting at the kitchen table. Tricia managed to cobble together a meal from the previous evening's leftovers and stuff she scavenged in the freezer. She brought a plate of food to Ezekiel's room and left it outside his door. He hadn't eaten at the family table for the six months. Tricia didn't like it but had given up fighting him about it.

Tricia and Rowan encouraged political conversation at the dinner table. One of the Murakami family traditions was debating the issues of the day. The topic tonight was the California proposition to leave the United States and form their own country. Grace was for it. Rowan was against it. And Tricia didn't feel strongly either way.

"It's like... they're a different country," Grace said, referencing all the other states outside of California.

"We always have been different, but I think every state has its own character," Tricia said.

"I agree," Rowan added. "I will say that California seems to have a target on its back in the last several years."

"What does that mean?" Grace asked.

"It's an old phrase, it means that others are against you," Tricia, always the teacher, jumped in and clarified. "I agree with your dad, it seems like more than ever in my lifetime Californians are looked at differently from those in other states.

Rowan cautioned temperance. "Winds change," he said. "Politics swing back and forth in history. Right now, California is looked upon as negative, but that could change in the next administration. Who knows?" He argued "There is no reason to do anything rash."

" Ya know, I think both of you have good points. It's so funny that I'm sitting between you both because Grace wants us to leave the union and dad says we should stay put. I'm right in the middle. I just don't know what I feel about this proposition to secede."

Tricia was about to elaborate on her opinion when she saw something out of the corner of her eye. Someone was climbing over the wall in the backyard. She assumed at first it was some overanxious reporter. But when she saw the head, she knew who it was right away: Noah.

CHAPTER 5

These Truths are Self-evident

After hellos and hugs with his family, Noah went to his room to rest. Noah was relieved that he wasn't asked why he was home. He was confident that would come out later. Just as he plopped his tired body on the top of his comforter, his phone rang and Mark's name flashed on the screen.

"Noah, you Okay, bro?" Mark was whispering on the other end of the phone call. "Did you make it home okay?"

"Yeah, I'm home. Where you at?" Noah asked cautiously. He had trusted Mark literally with his life in battle so there was no reason not to take his call. Still, he was being extremely cautious. He knew how the military worked and they would go to great lengths to get what they wanted, even ordering a friend to turn on him.

"We're just north of Oakland, bro. Got deployed right after Shasta."

"Tell me you didn't fire into that crowd like they said?" Noah asked.

"Our squad fired over their heads and the crowd dispersed. But, yeah, we did fire, bro. I hope the media reported it accurately. No one got hurt, but it was a fuck'n mess, man, fuck'n mess. The guys are all fucked over this. And now we're in Oakland because immigration is planning the next big push up here soon. There's word of a large demonstration up here tomorrow. Your governor refuses to call out the national guard, so we've gotta have the local police's back."

"This is bull, dude, bull," Noah said.

"I know, bro. Nobody likes this except the freak'n skinhead crazies. That fuck'n Tex asshole wants to kill people. Never been in a firefight—and he wants to shoot Americans! I swear this is going to blow up, bro. He's raging about California hippies and shit. He's going to kill one of these people here tomorrow I can feel it. Maybe more."

"Shiiit. I hated that guy; all white is right shit. Guy can't string two sentences together that make sense and he hates anybody who isn't a cracker." Noah's words spit out of a clenched jaw. His eyes were distant and piercing.

"You did the right thing, man. I'm thinking the same thing, bro," Mark's voice trembled. "I swear if this Oakland thing goes bad. I'm calling you for directions."

"No prob bro. I'm here for ya," Noah reassured him.

Oakland exploded. When Mark's platoon arrived with the other marines before sunrise in the North Oakland section of the city, the crowds of protestors had already set up their stations. As the marines jumped off their troop transports they saw a vast crowd made up of diverse ethnicities. Oakland being one of the most evenly divided areas in the United States with ethnic populations of White, Black, Hispanic and Asian people almost evenly divided in numbers. The crowd was well organized and large hand lettered signs indicated where certain groups were gathering. There were contingents from University of California Berkley, Kaiser Permanente, Ship Workers, Clorox, Auto Workers and Pandora Radio. Even at such an early hour the energy of anger steamed off the crowd.

The thousands massing for the demonstration stood shoulder-to-shoulder in Raimondi Park. There was no room for sitting or lounging on the grass with the numbers that showed up. In fact, the crowd poured onto the streets. Media trucks with their antennas sticking high into the air surrounded the park. Two news helicopters hovered overhead to capture the event. It was the largest demonstration ever amassed in Oakland—and possibly in the U.S.

The eight hundred marines were a pimple compared to the thousands upon thousands on hand to protest, but they were heavily armed and professional. Washington hoped their presence would contain the crowd as it did at Shasta Dam, but this crowd was different. People in Oakland had a long history of activism and their nature was very different from those at the Shasta protest. Oakland was a much more tough and grittier town than the communities around Los Angeles. The images of the football fans at Raider's games with their *Thunderdome* costumes are symbolic of the nature of the Oakland people. Those mean, monstrous looking fans decked out in spikes, armor and grotesque masks were statements by the people of Oakland of their inner selves. There were several of those costumed super-fans in the crowd clad in their game day regalia, including clubs with spikes protruding outward. The Shasta protest was about sending a message, the Oakland crowd that day was about action. The crowd was hell bent on doing something to stop injustice after injustice inflicted upon them. The crowd was surging with destruction. They didn't want to raise consciousness, they wanted to obliterate oppression.

Lieutenant Colonel Krall stepped out of his Hummer to inspect the eight hundred troops gathered in precise rows and columns according to their company and platoons as if on the parade ground. Krall addressed the marines, "Our intel informs us that these people plan to march to the shipyards at the Port of Oakland and shut them down for an indefinite period. Our job here today is to contain this crowd, corral them here at Raimondi Park and then to disperse them with the help of the Oakland police," Krall snarled in his southern drawl. "There will be no injuries here today to us or to them. The police commander will direct us to set up a blockade at the point of the crowd's march forward. We will hold our ground and not let the crowd move forward. I will be at the front of you directing our actions. My orders will be relayed to you by your company and then platoon leaders. There will be no action independent of my orders." He paused dramatically and stared down the eight hundred soldiers, then let out a loud yell, "Troops!"

With that, the eight hundred soldiers clicked their heels and yelled back in unison, "Boo Ya!" The clicked their heels and yells were their signal that they were ready and motivated. With the dry weather and lack of wind, the sound of their boots snapping together was almost as loud as their battle cry. Battle tested marines mixed with Marines fresh out of boot camp and hungry for action.

Mark and the Alpha Company of one hundred and sixty marines took their position at the front of the line that was blocking the Grand Avenue entrance to the Nimitz Freeway. Alpha Company stationed itself on the freeway entrance ramp with their troop carriers parked behind them horizontally to block the freeway entrance. Bronco Company and half of Easy Company stationed themselves in the same way at the 7th Street entrance.

The remainder of the battalion was stationed at the east perimeter of the park on Campbell Street.

Police intelligence told the military that the demonstrators were planning to march from the Raimondi Park staging area onto the Nimitz Freeway and then to the Port of Oakland. The crowd would strangle rush hour traffic on their route. The orders straight from the main man himself in the White House was to block the entrance to the freeway as the interstate roadway was federal property. President Matthews was using the same tactic, or some might say excuse, as he did at Shasta. His troops would be protecting federal ground. The police had another agenda but that was not revealed to Mark and his fellow marines. All the marines were told was that they were to be stationed on federal property and Washington is shutting this federal freeway down.

At 7:00 a.m. the crowd surged toward Grand Avenue, walking on Frontage Road and already blocking traffic in a typical rush hour.

As diverse as the crowd's ethnicities were, so were the causes that they rallied for that morning. At the front of the crowd were the shipyard workers who were angered at President Matthews and the federal government because of proclamations Matthews signed days into office aimed at breaking the shipyard workers' union. Matthews, like his big business friends around the country, had a deep hatred of unions for obvious reasons. The shipyard workers were a logical first target for union busting because of their relatively small numbers and their location in coastal towns. In Matthews' thinking, the bulk of the country wasn't immediately affected by any troubles the shipyard workers may suffer, so publicity-wise, union busting of shipyard workers wasn't going to alarm most Americans. For Matthews and his big business supporters, the shipyard workers' union would be the easy first domino to fall in the elimination of all unions in the country. Matthews frequently bashed unions in his presidential campaign in a way that worryingly turned many an average American against them. Besides, unions often voted strongly democratic—and Matthews loved to punish losers.

The second large contingent was led by the Kaiser Permanente employees and other health care workers. Kaiser Permanente was one of the largest employers in the state. It invented the HMO model and was a powerful influence in all of California. Matthews vowed to disband the fourth generation of what was originally called Obamacare. Although the National Healthcare Bill was revised four times since its adoption under the Obama presidency, now two administrations ago. Big business continued to hate the yolk it placed on their costs. The public loved it, but big business hated it. Matthews signed an executive order that took federal funding away from the National Healthcare Bill. He couldn't get the bill dismissed, but he could take away its funding, making it ineffective. The public, the medical field and the insurance companies were furious at Matthews' unilateral action.

The third largest group were those angered at Matthews' actions toward immigration. With the large Hispanic population being equally represented in Oakland, most of Oakland was touched by the raids by the ICE officers in Los Angeles and they vowed it would not take place there.

The crowd pushed out of Raimondi Park and snaked right, heading toward Grand Avenue and Nimitz Freeway.

Mark and Alpha company were given the command to be on immediate alert and stand ready. Half way between Raimondi Park and Alpha Company, thirty Oakland police officers in riot gear were staged and the crowd was on them quickly. The police barked orders to the crowd to stop and move no further. The crowd ignored the police warnings and marched on literally pushing past the bewildered officers. A few of the officers tried to stand their ground against the crowd but this was a big mistake: the crowd pushed the officers, punches were thrown by both sides, but that was only the start of the melee. An officer was hit with a wooden sign, another with a flag pole and the police were ordered to pull back. The police commander didn't want another national police incident so no orders for even the slightest use of force were given. The police commander counted on the marines just up ahead to stop the crowd. "Let them take the fall for any use of force," he told his men.

Mark stood side-by-side with his platoon. He watched what happened to the police ranks. All the marines had the same thought going through their minds: "What are we going to do when the crowd reaches our blockade?" Alpha company's bodies couldn't stop the crowd of thousands without brute force. The trucks parked across the roadway seemed more like a show now than any real deterrent. Why not just disperse now and take up positions in the shipyard and have the stand there? The marine officers didn't convey any new instructions. The marines and their leaders stood firm and waited for the crowd to arrive. It seemed like a paper barricade to all on hand.

The crowd, on the other hand, looked like a menacing mythical dragon slithering up Frontage Road. Those in the front of the crowd waved their signs, pounded fists in the air and shouted angry slogans—all of which added to the image of the head of the dragon snapping at the marines up ahead with its tail reaching back to Raimondi Park. The enthusiasm of the demonstrators was ignited by how easily they dismissed the police, but the marines up ahead would be an entirely different can of worms.

The crowd moved closer and still no orders from the marine officers. Slight movements from some of the marines belied a weakening of their usual rock-solid resolve. Body weights shifted, brows were wiped and shoulders twitched as the crowd inched closer. Clearly, the marines were grappling with the possibility that they might have to fire on fellow Americans.

Time ticked and there were still no orders. Then none were needed. Tex dropped down into a firing position, shouldered his M4 carbine and unloaded a magazine into the crowd. When that magazine emptied, he loaded another and continued firing indiscriminately. Two other marines dropped to one knee and joined in the shooting spree. The crowd panicked, turned and pushed backward completely changing direction. The officers finally barked a command "Halt your fire." As the crowd fled, dozens of citizens lay on the ground dead. There was no movement from any of the fallen bodies. The marines fired with skill and purpose.

Mark froze. He didn't know how to process what he just witnessed. He had killed hostile, evil people for his country, he had drilled into him the values and cause of a free society, but this was like being in a third world. No, he had been to the third world, this was some fourth world. He made a decision at that moment. A decision he would keep to himself for now.

The public outcry around the country over the shootings was thunderous and nowhere was it stronger than in New York City. Thousands took the streets in Manhattan in protest of the federal action in Oakland. The marches were peaceful and the police cooperated and even joined the rallies. The exceptions to this peaceful protest were the events in the areas that had Home Market stores. President Matthews' cash registers. Sixteen Home Market stores were scattered around New York City and the boroughs. Windows were broken and they were looted to the empty shelves. The massive store in lower Manhattan, touted by the pre-presidential Matthews as a model urban home goods store, was set ablaze. The fire was quickly put out, but the message against Matthews was loud and clear. Sales at the Home Market stores throughout the country were drastically down, practically non-existent. Business analysts proclaimed that this was the largest one day drop in sales by a store chain in any category in history.

The New York versus California rivalry is apparent in every aspect of American culture and commerce. But, as the two greatest economic generators in the nation, in actuality they share more in common and had more of a kinship than either state would admit. Cartoonists long drew maps of the USA with gigantic New York City on the east and enormous Los Angeles on the west and tiny dots for Chicago, Boston, Phoenix, Dallas and so forth. Even as the nation was on fire with divisiveness, New York's response to the Oakland tragedy and the protests in New York City took on a glimmer of one-upmanship. The Governor of New York State, Chris Haynes held a press conference the evening after the sixteen Home Market stores were destroyed in New York City.

"As governor of the state of New York, and in response to the illegal and inhumane actions taken by our federal government in recent months. Actions that violated the rights and traditions of the people of the United States to constitutionally live with liberty and justice for all in a free society. And, with strong reaction to the recent events in Oakland, California, I hereby proclaim that I am exercising my executive power as governor of the state of New York to call a special election to be held at a date to be determined and announced later. This special election will present to the people of New York a vote to secede from the union of the United States of America. It is a call to form a new republic of New York, independent and separate from the United States of America."

He paused, took a sip of water, and looked directly into the camera. The look and the silence punctuating the gravity of his statements. Then he continued.

"We have suffered too much in recent years at the hand of tyrannical leadership in the federal government. This tyranny is reaching a crescendo with the present administration. The future looks bleak for any change in the course of this oppressive leadership. I firmly feel that this action is necessary to protect the safety and well-being of the citizens of New York State and I hope that every citizen of this great state will agree with me that separation from the actions and influence of the federal government of the United States of America is the prudent and righteous course to insure our continued existence. Now, secession will be a gradual process. The first step is for each and every New Yorker to vote in favor of becoming a free state. After that vote, things will not happen overnight. This will be a safe and secure process. Further, given the federal actions of the past administration and now this current administration I, my staff, your legislators, and experts around the state will attest that separation from the United States of America will have immediate benefits for every New York citizen. What the federal government has taken from you in the last four and one-half years will not only be fully restored but will be positively amplified with the programs your new country can provide. We will be okay, in fact we will thrive in independence." Haynes held up a leather folder that prominently displayed the seal of the state of New York. He opened the folder to show a paper on one side of the folder. Then placed the open folder on the podium and began signing the paper. "As I speak to you right now, I am signing the executive order to place a vote of secession on the ballot for the to-be-announced special election. By the New York State constitution, this executive order must be seconded by the signature of ten thousand citizens of the state. Within a month, my office will be circulating petitions throughout the state to collect these signatures. Please take the honor of signing this historic document when asked. My fellow New Yorkers this is all I have to say to you today. I will not be taking questions at this time."

The governor ended his press conference and the shock waves were felt around the nation. New York State boldly took the first action in a modern revolution.

In Washington, President Matthews' anger raged. He was in a regularly scheduled meeting with his full cabinet when the news conference of Governor Haynes hit the airways. Peter McKenzie interrupted the meeting and the screens in the conference room played the live broadcast.

"Well, this is good, this is good, excellent," Matthews growled at the biggest screen. "I have California disobeying all the orders I send out and now New York wants to put together a vote to be independent. Well, bring it on! Let the country see where they stand and what they think of the rest of us. It's about time!"

He had insurrection in the two most powerful economic states in the union. If he had any doubt about the willingness of the states to draw the battle lines, that doubt was erased by that press conference. New York had been a sleeping giant and the Oakland incident and the looting in New York City woke that giant.

A jittery and hate-filled marine fired the shot heard round the world.

CHAPTER 6

All Men Are Created Equal

On the morning of the 9/11 attack, Tricia Murakami couldn't take her eyes off her television screen. She must have watched those planes going into the World Trade Centers a couple thousand times that day. It was the same for Tricia after the news broke a week ago that almost a dozen protestors in Oakland had been shot by the US army. But this time, because everyone had a smartphone, she could see the events unfold from every angle imaginable on YouTube. Every time she saw the video feed, it broke her heart and she teared up.

Rowan walked into the living room and saw Tricia crying and staring at her phone. "Please stop watching the damn video."

"I can't help it. I always thought we were an exceptional country and our freedoms were unquestioned. I've thought that since elementary school, but this has me questioning everything this country is about. Who are we?"

Tricia knew Rowan was right to admonish her with an uncharacteristic order. She put her phone on the bedside table. She had to get ready for work; an online petition started by the parents at her school had somehow managed to get her reinstated only a few days after she had been suspended. She assumed Principal Sloan wasn't happy about it. That thought made her smile, but she also knew that he would try to get back at her in other ways. But she didn't care. She was teaching again.

CHAPTER 6

Tricia looked at the clock: it was almost seven. She had to hustle. Breakfasts needed to be made, and lunches packed. Not to mention the fact that she had to take a shower and draw up a lesson plan for the day. She was almost out the door of her bedroom when she heard the phone buzz. A notification. For a moment, she considered not checking it. But curiosity got the best of her. She picked up the phone.

Tricia saw the headline: *President Matthews Promises to Pardon Soldiers.* She quickly skimmed the article and saw that the President had sent out a message over social media promising not only to pardon the soldiers who had fired and killed the protestors but to punish any marine who didn't support the shooters.

Tricia could not believe what she was reading. If this were a movie she would have pinched herself. Tricia had to sit down on the bed for a moment. Breakfasts and lesson plans would have to wait. For the first time in her life, Tricia felt the need to do something. Anything. What that something was, she wasn't quite sure. But she knew she could no longer sit idly by and do nothing.

"What's wrong?" Rowan asked when he found her still sitting on the bed five minutes later. Tricia assumed that Rowan would not understand. She quickly put her phone away and said, "Nothing."

The rest of the morning was a blur. By 7:50 am Tricia was out the door and headed to school. The only good thing that came from Oakland was that the news cameras and reporters now left her alone. Her front yard was totally barren of the media. The only signs that they had even been there was their discarded litter and some bald patches on her lawn.

On the way to school, Tricia mentally went over the kids in her class. She imagined their smiling faces and then said their names to herself. First the AM class and then the PM class. It was her way of learning her student's names but also to help calm herself down. The news that morning and the nervousness of going back to work was like a weight that made it difficult to keep walking.

Tricia made it to school before the first bell, despite her trepidation. Once she opened the doors and saw her kids, everything else was forgotten. She was back in teacher mode. It was a relief not to have to think about anything other than teaching how to read and count. But that all changed when the kids settled in their seats because the first thing they would do every morning was to say the pledge of allegiance. But Tricia did not feel like pledging allegiance to the United States anymore. Skipping over this, she asked the class, "Who wants to help with the days of the week?" She then glanced at the assistant teacher, Yvonne, who was frowning. She didn't know why they had skipped over the pledge of allegiance. Being an excellent assistant, Yvonne moved over to the calendar as though that was always the plan.

The first student raised her hand. It was a pretty little girl in pigtails and a fancy dress. Tricia didn't recognize her. She must have been a new kid that had moved into the district while she was on suspension. Tricia looked at Yvonne for help. Yvonne jumped right in, "Gina, thank you for volunteering."

But Gina did not move. Instead, she asked in the thickest and sweetest Southern drawl, "Why didn't we do the pledge of allegiance?"

Tricia did not want to bring politics into the classroom. Especially into kindergarten. She just smiled at the girl and said, "We're going to try something different today."

CHAPTER 6   63

Gina frowned. "But we have to do the pledge of allegiance."

Tricia was becoming frustrated. "We don't have to." She was about to call on another student to help with the calendar when the little girl started to cry. Tricia looked at Yvonne for help, but the assistant teacher was in as much shock as she was. This wasn't how she wanted her morning to go. She thought fast. "Honey, if you want to say the pledge of allegiance then you can."

The little girl instantly stopped crying and looked pleased. Tricia continued, "And if anyone else wants to, please feel free to do so. As far as I know, we are still a free country."

Gina stood and recited the pledge of allegiance with her right hand over her heart. Two other children stood up and mumbled their version of the pledge while they giggled and wiggled as if this was a game. When the little girl finished, she looked around at the others with a smug grin that instantly bothered Tricia. Tricia imagined this little human was reflecting the values and actions that her parents drilled into her since birth. A little Stepford in the making. She had never hated one of her students until that moment. She didn't want to feel so strongly about this little child, so she told herself again that the girl's actions were not her own, but those of her parents. *Direct your feelings toward the parents*, she told herself. She pushed all those thoughts to the back of her mind. She had a class to teach.

The rest of the class pretty much went as planned. They went through the food groups, and Yvonne had prepared an item from each of the five groups for the kids to try. "Even if it doesn't taste good to your tongue," she told her students. "it doesn't mean you shouldn't eat it. It could still be good for your body."

When class was let out, a group of people had gathered outside the door to pick up the kids. In South Pasadena, kindergarten was only three hours, so most working parents had to rely on daycares or nannies to watch over the kids until the afternoon. Many of the students would be picked up by a driver and then driven to a facility somewhere off campus. Mixed in the group were a few parents. Tricia saw Gina's mother right away. She didn't look like the other parents there: she was dressed up as if she were going to some debutante ball with her hair perfectly coifed.

As soon as Gina dashed out of school she motioned for her mother to get close. Leaning over, Gina no doubt told her what had happened earlier in the morning. The mom's eyes flickered toward Tricia with such intense hate that Tricia unconsciously took a step back.

A moment later, the mom was marching toward her with Gina in tow. "Are you some kind of bedwetting California liberal?" she screamed in Tricia's face. Tricia's first instinct was to fight back, but all the others were watching.

Tricia took a deep breath before she told the mom, "Calm down." It was the wrong thing to have said because it only seemed to make the mom angrier.

"Don't tell me to calm down, I knew we should have moved to Texas instead of this backward shithole."

Tricia imagined punching this woman in the face and ruining her hair. But she had the good sense not to do it. She liked her job too much. Instead, in the calmest voice she could muster, she said, "If you have a problem with something I did in the classroom, then you should bring it up with Principal Sloan."

The mom looked her over before saying, "Don't worry, I will."

The call from Principal Sloan came halfway through Tricia's afternoon kindergarten class. She was summoned to his office as though she were a truant student ditching class. As soon as she stepped into the office, Tricia already sensed how the conversation would unfold.

"Trish, have a seat." Without waiting for her to sit, Sloan continued. "I'm sure you know what this is about. We *say* the pledge of allegiance at this school. We say it every day and we say it with enthusiasm."

"Mr. Sloan, if I may, saying the pledge of allegiance is not a legal requirement for a teacher. It isn't in our employee handbook, either." Tricia's formality wasn't situational, every person in the school addressed him as, Mr. Sloan.

"Ok, well by the end of the day that *requirement* will be in the employee handbook. Every teacher, in every classroom will say the pledge of allegiance, *every* day. No exceptions and no fail."

Tricia handed him a sheet of paper. "I have already written a letter to the school board that outlines my objection to such an order."

Sloan looked at it dismissively.

"I would like it put on the agenda for the next school board meeting." She added.

Sloan put the paper aside, still keeping eye contact with her.

"Now, we have the issue of bullying the student. Absolutely reprehensible. This is also going into your personnel file." He paused, "You will verbally and in writing apologize to this student in front of your class and in private in front of her parents. You will send your written apology to the student and her parents by registered mail. And, this will be on your own dime, not the school's." He said.

Tricia handed him another sheet of paper. "I have addressed this in this report I also want submitted to the school board at its next meeting. I am also filing this report with the union." Tricia waited for his reaction. Sloan glanced at the report and put it on top of her letter, folded his hands and resumed looking at her. "Until I hear from the school board and my union, I will not take any action on either of these points you bring up."

"Well then, Mrs. Murakami. As of this moment I am placing you on suspension until we hear from both of these bodies."

Tricia stood up. "I…what…you can't…"

Before she could say anything further, Sloan interrupted, "This meeting is over." He watched as she leaned forward as if to continue the conversation. "You can exit the school, take your belongings, etcetera, etcetera. You know the drill." His eyebrows raised and he had a smirk on his face.

Tricia walked all the way back home in a daze. Once again, she wondered how she was going to tell Rowan that she was suspended on the first day back at her job. This time, at least, the news wouldn't be able to beat her to it. When she walked through the front door, Tricia found her oldest son vacuuming the living room. Noah insisted that while he was home that he would need to pull his weight.

One look from Noah was all that it took for him to know something wasn't right. He glanced at the clock and saw that it was just barely two pm—too early for school to be finished for the day. "What happened?" he asked.

Tricia sat down on the sofa and confessed everything, and Noah listened with great surprise. He had never thought of his mom as an activist. He, like every son, just thought of his mom as a mom. Although after what happened in front of the school the last time she was suspended, he figured he should have known better.

"That little girl sounds like this guy from Texas in my unit," was all he said after she told him the whole story.

Like everyone else in the entire world, Noah had seen the footage of the Texan gunning down those protestors in Oakland. Thinking of the Texan, made him worry about Mark. He hoped his best friend had been able to get away safely. He read online that desertions in all the branches of the armed forces had gone up by over fifty percent after the shooting. Soldiers from California, New York, and a few other states were dissertating in droves. The president had issued an executive order earmarking extra money for the FBI to hunt down these soldiers.

As soon as his mother had finished telling him about what happened at school, the doorbell rang. Noah nearly jumped out of his skin. Tricia looked at her son with dismay. Her oldest had always been the calmest of her children. But he had been on edge ever since he had returned. She quickly checked the camera feed on her phone to see it who it was. When she saw it was just one of her nosy neighbors, she decided it would be best if she didn't answer it. Instead, she turned to her son and said, "Now it's your turn, tell me everything."

Noah knew exactly what his mom was talking about. "I'm home on…" Noah started to deny there was anything to tell. But one look from his mom was enough for him to spill the beans about what happened at Shasta, his leaving his unit, and hitchhiking back home.

That afternoon Tricia and Noah realized they had a lot more in common than they ever thought. The two seemed to be on the front lines of a movement they couldn't quite put their fingers on but knew was important. But not everyone in their family shared their sentiments. Ezekiel, who had been in his room, had come down and heard the whole thing.

Ezekiel hated his older brother. But not because he was always the perfect sibling. Or because he was always being compared to him. He hated Noah because he didn't understand him. Noah was constantly trying to distinguish himself. Stand out from the crowd. Which was the antithesis of who Ezekiel was. If it could have been possible, Ezekiel would melt between the crack and disappear forever. That's why he hated his mom's celebrity status when the viral video of her and the Blue Jackets in front of the school went viral, launching her from cult hero to the left and villain to the right. He hated the extra attention he got at school. He blamed his mom for the uncomfortable questions he was asked in class for two weeks after it happened.

As his mom and brother kept talking, Ezekiel crept back up to his room. His brother had gone AWOL. He knew that there was a reward for anyone who turned in a missing soldier. He didn't want the money for the sake of the money. Wealth had never been one of his driving motivations. Instead, he hoped that if he turned his brother in, Noah would be taken away and his family would once again return to normal.

Ezekiel dialed the number he found on the Internet. "I'd like to report an AWOL soldier." He gave his address, number, and his brother's name. It was surprisingly easy.

The person on the other side of the line told him, "You're doing the right thing." Hearing these words made him suddenly question what he was doing. *Was he really doing the right thing?* He just wanted things to go back the way they were. Even though he hated his brother, he didn't hate his mom. He knew what he had just done would really hurt her. And he had no illusions that Noah was his mom's favorite. She would never admit it, but it wasn't hard to tell. He swore that she looked at Noah differently than she looked at him or even his sister.

A little while later, Ezekiel pushed aside the curtain when he heard a car screeching into the driveway. At first, he feared it was the FBI or the police, but instead he saw his father getting out of his car. When his father looked up at him and waved, Ezekiel quickly closed the curtains and waited. By then, he knew he had done the wrong thing.

Downstairs, Noah and his mom were deep in conversation. "There is a very large group being formed of people that want to leave the union. Not just radicals, there are politicians, soldiers, leading business people." Noah said.

"Oh my God, I didn't realize that this was becoming so organized." Tricia said.

"They are so organized they have a clever name for their organization, The California Movement for Secession or CMS. Dad would love that acronym." Noah said with a smile. "They have already approached me and they are trying to enlist former soldiers because of our experience."

"How did they find you?"

"I don't know and quite frankly, I don't care…I like the sound of what they are doing."

"I'm interested. I'd like to check them out. Maybe attend a meeting."

"Let me see what's coming up and let's go together."

At that moment Rowan walked through the door, "What meeting?" Rowan asked.

Noah and Tricia exchanged glances. Tricia had been married long enough for her to know what her husband's reaction would be. She told him what they had been talking about.

"Be careful," he cautioned them. "The Federal Government is too powerful. Somehow they will get you. In the last Civil War, the South had lost and was burned to the ground. So I don't think any state had a chance in hell of actually leaving the United States."

The conversation continued over dinner. After they ate, they sat in the front of the TV and watched the news where the President called New York's special election treason and ordered all federal funding to the state completely cut. Surprising everyone, Texas had come to the support of New York. The governor of Texas told the anchor, "States should be free to make up their own minds if they want to be part of the Union or not. They shouldn't have someone in the White House swamp dictating what they should or shouldn't do."

Tricia, Grace, and Noah were clearly all on the side of New York. They thought that California should quickly follow suit. Rowan was the voice of reason. "We must be patient. Although things are tough now, believe me, they will get better. I believe that things are cyclical and soon things would swing the other way."

"They want us to go back to the middle ages," Grace told her dad. "They want women in the kitchen having babies and African Americans as slaves."

Rowan was about to open his mouth to argue with his youngest daughter, but Grace continued: "And they are already locking up Muslims like they did to our family back in World War II." Rowan closed his mouth. The internment camps were something that still resonated in the Japanese American community, despite almost ninety years having already passed. Rowan's grandfather had been incarcerated in Tule Lake, Northern California and his father had been born in one. Rowan's father had spoken to him almost every day about it and commanded him that it was his responsibility to make sure it never happened again to anyone else.

Rowan was remembering his father's words when Ezekiel came down the stairs. The surprise of seeing his middle son out of his room was almost as shocking as the words that came out of his mouth. "Noah, you have to leave—now..."

CHAPTER 7

The Form of Government Becomes Destructive

Everybody knows that angry people with time on their hands are the most dangerous. Tricia's suspension was into its second week. Whether it was a sense of *been there, done that*, or some other form of apathy, this time the parents didn't rally to form a protest demanding Tricia be reinstated at the school. She remained out of work, but certainly not idle.

Without letting any of her family know, Tricia contacted the governor's office and volunteered to help out in any capacity with plans for the secession movement. Simultaneously, she researched the California secession movement and found the most reputable and organized group that was working for the cause of secession. The group that intrigued her the most was the California Movement for Secession, the one Noah mentioned to her. And, as he said, they cleverly went by the acronym, CMS (Content Management System), the standard business software term. To the President Matthews' of this world, CMS was just boring business jargon and, no matter what the Google's algorithm was, Internet searches of all kinds would pop up the movement on the first page. It also didn't hurt to sway Tricia's affinity for the group that a large number of the California elite were endorsing the organization. The usual group of Hollywood stars gave ringing endorsements of the organization, and it seemed millions of dollars. Impressively, this list of Hollywood elite was from both liberal and conservative ideologies. CEOs from the major California industries were also listed on the CMS webpage of backers as well as politicians, police, educators, universities, religious leaders, athletes and maybe most critically, the Silicon Valley tech industry. This group had legs. CMS was also closely aligned with the California Republic Military (CRM), which was a grouping of military and police already forming a state militia. It wasn't evident in her research whether CMS begot CRM or who was the chicken or the egg, but these groups were clearly partnered, sharing resources and power. It was no coincidence that both groups shared not only similar acronyms but could be mistaken for business terminology. CRM stood for Customer Relationship Management in the jargon of the corporate world. Both acronyms popped as a not so subtle slam to the businessman president. The feeling building across the state of California was, 'fight fire with fire.' And, everyone knew that that ideology would draw Matthews like a moth to a flame.

Tricia attacked her involvement with the secession movement in the same way she always hunted for teaching jobs, leave no stone unturned and apply to the best and brightest. She also employed the strategy that you throw yourself at all the places you want to work at regardless if they had openings or not. She contacted Gordon Newton directly, the chairman of CMS and former lieutenant governor under four-term governor Jerry Brown.

Tricia was elated when Newton personally contacted her a day after she reached out to him. "Mrs. Murakami, this is Gordon Newton, I understand you want to talk to me?"

"Mr. Newton, I ahhh…almost didn't answer the call…a strange number came up."

Newton was monotone and to the point, "As you can imagine, security right now is on high alert. That's why I didn't respond to your email with an email. I would like to talk to you in person. Can you come to our offices?" Newton asked.

Later that same afternoon Tricia went to meet with Newton and the administrative staff of the California Movement for Secession. She was excited at the opportunity to meet the people at the heart of the secession movement, but her enthusiasm was tempered by her curiosity as to their integrity. She couldn't help but question if this was all real.

Tricia was led into a conference room, and Newton and his staff greeted her enthusiastically, "Mrs. Murakami, it is such a pleasure to meet you." Newton's tone was very different than the monotonous voice on the phone that very morning. "Your brave action against the blue jackets has seemed to have rallied a besieged nation. We have been following you since that day and know you have paid a heavy price for standing up against tyranny. You lost your job, and quite frankly you're not going to get it back. Let me get right down to it. We want you to work for us, here. We will pay you double your teacher's salary."

Tricia was shocked by the instant offer. "What will I do?" She asked dumbfounded. She gulped at the enormity of the possibility. Her eyes drifted away from the group. She was suddenly afraid. She was going to become even more fearful in seconds.

"We, the movement that is, need a spokesperson, a face that can represent us. We think you are the natural

CHAPTER 7   75

choice. Your video slapping the blue jacket went viral, so without so much as some focus group or analytics, you in some sense have already become *the* face of the movement," Newton paused and made sure he maintained piercing eye contact with her. "And, I'm not only talking about California, you've rallied New York as well."

"I don't know if I can do this. I was just panicking about having a job here, now you're spinning this even bigger. What will my husband say, my kids?" Her voice cracked.

"Tricia, you're over-thinking this right now. You leave the logistics to us. We've been doing this longer than you. Let's bring you on board, get your income back and once you are here, you can see what we have planned. Just let it incubate a bit," Newton said.

A tall, handsome African-American man spoke up. He was one of those men who was so fit that his clothes showed off his physique. "Hi, I'm Jaleel Henry, communications director. Tricia, I respect you digesting all this, but, we would like you to make a statement or public appearance on the Oakland murders."

"Please, J, please, give her some time," Newton said. "Tricia, really, you think this over—but things are moving fast, and we do need you."

Tricia paused and took in her surroundings. She hadn't been introduced to all the players at here but yet she was being asked to be their collective public face. She didn't read any of the faces as objecting to Newton's offer.

She broke the silence: "I remember when my husband, his name is Rowan…" Everyone nodded as if they already knew that. "Was offered the job at the Jet Propulsion Labs. He was as scared as a cat about this big leap in his career. You know what I told him?" She stopped and waited as if someone would answer the rhetorical question. No one did, instead, they all waited in silence for her answer. "I told him to jump at the opportunity because smarter people than you and people above your pay grade are saying you are right for the job otherwise they wouldn't have made you the offer." A sheepish smile filled her face. The comment opened up a cacophony of chuckles, "great comment" "yeps" and all around good cheer.

"I believe in the movement. Mr. Newton, I believed in you when you were in office." She paused again. "I would be a fool not to help in any way I can. If you all think I can help in this way, I would be a hypocrite not to join your team here…I accept your very complimentary offer, right and here and right now. When do I start?"

The group stood and shook her hand. They were so exuberant that she almost expected them to if they weren't all well past teenagers, to have cheered and pounded fists in the air; they were truly that jubilant with her on-the-spot decision.

Newton spoke up, "J, here, ahh, Jaleel, our communications director would love to work with you immediately to create a video statement coming out on the Oakland murders."

Everyone introduced themselves individually and said their welcomes. They then filed out of the conference room with only Jaleel and Newton staying behind.

"Can I ask you a couple of questions?" she asked.

"Absolutely," they replied in unison.

"First, besides my fifteen minutes of social media fame, why me?"

Jaleel was eager to respond. "When you reached out to Gordon, that put the idea in our heads. May I speak candidly?" He paused. Tricia nodded. "You represent what is great about this state. Your family is ethnically diverse, you're in a profession that is the bedrock of society, you are socially aware and your actions were not only heroic but were, well, hands-on. Excuse the pun. And, as long as I am being candid, you're a woman. And a mom."

"Oh," She gulped. "But wouldn't Mr. Newton be the logical choice as the face of CMS?"

Newton jumped into the conversation, "Tricia, look at me. I'm a, ahem, middle-aged white guy and a politician. Sure, a percent of the population is OK with that. You're fresh, a citizen, with no history of activism…"

Jaleel interrupted, "You see, we immediately did our due diligence on you. We did a complete background check once you went viral."

"No, Tricia Murakami, you are perfect for stirring the emotions of this state. As you so clearly pointed out, people more expert than you have chosen *you* to be the one," Newton quipped.

Everybody agreed, the general consensus was Tricia was a natural for her new position in CMS. It took only two takes for Jaleel and his staff to create a slick video that featured Tricia making a statement condemning the shooting in Oakland. In the video, as she spoke, images of the shooting ran in the background. With a 3D technique, the wallpaper of the video had the Constitution of the United States scrolling down the screen. It was well presented, but not overly produced. But most importantly it would have the desired effect of stirring emotions.

The highlights of Tricia's two-minute, heartfelt statement stated: "My son volunteered and served in the Marines with three tours of duty in the Middle East. He served his country proudly, but when his marine battalion was ordered by a tyrannical administration to duty at the Shasta Dam, a domestic assignment that was *not* in the charter of the United States Marine Corp, he could not in good conscience continue to serve a president that would order citizens to soldier against fellow citizens. He rebelled against such tyranny and left the Corp and his brother marines. My son's platoon was the front line at the Nimitz Freeway in Oakland where new recruits fired upon American citizens exercising their constitutional right to protest unjust executive orders from a demigod leader. Had my son not followed his conscience, he would have been on that front line. We can no longer pledge allegiance to a leader who will abuse his power to pit us against each other. History has seen the result of such leadership and it has brought the world to the brink of annihilation several times before. I join my son in good conscience and I proudly announce my allegiance to the California Movement for Secession. I urge you to examine your consciences as well."

Tricia Murakami had her third viral video. And with the help of Jaleel and his team, this one had four times the hits as the 'Slap Felt Round the World.'

Noah watched his mom's statement when first posted. A buddy of his texted him to alert him that a posting was being initiated in a few minutes and his mom was going to be on it. Noah interpreted that text to mean his mom was going to be in the background in the text or the footage of the slap felt around the world was being replayed. Noah had the time, so he sat on his bed and scrolled with his phone to the link his buddy directed him to. He had no warning for what he was about to see. He watched it alone

CHAPTER 7

in his room as he wasn't sure how his dad would react if he knew about it and he wasn't about to alert him that mom was an Internet star again. Noah was confident that dad wouldn't see it coincidentally because he wasn't that plugged in as one would think an IT guy would be. Ezekiel was somewhere tantruming and Noah doubted he would be pleased with their mom's table comments now being viral pronouncements, while Grace was probably over at a friend's house basking in the glow of what she thought was a celebrity mom. But he was confident that Grace knew about it as fast as he did.

Once the video began and mom was in the forefront making her statement, he instinctively jumped up off the bed and stood at attention as if on the Marine parade ground. He stopped short of saluting. His heart pounding so hard with pride it hurt his chest. He was fully in. He would do whatever California needed of him, and what mom needed of him.

He called his mom's cell immediately after watching it. "Mom, great video. I didn't know you were a part of the movement. What, the what?"

Tricia's broad smile transmitted through the call as a soft hum. "Noah, this happened all so fast. I'm excited, but I'm concerned about how your dad is going to take this. And your brother and sister," she said.

"I know, mom, but dad will be OK and Grace will think you're the coolest. Zeke is the one we have to watch. You sure he isn't a Matthews?" Noah quipped

"Smart ass. I was there, back at ya." Tricia paused. "Listen, let me tell dad and the others at the right time."

"Got it." Noah hesitated as if he was going down his mental list of all the things he wanted to ask and say to his mom. "Mom, I want to get involved in all this. I have skills..."

"Noah, I know. Come with me tomorrow. They are assembling a state militia or army called the California Republic Military. You'd be perfect and they could use you. I'll get you in front of the right people. I have to run now so I can be home for dinner. Talk later." Tricia's cadence picked up.

"What? This is a nine to five rebellion?" Noah quipped.

Fueled in part by how keyed up she was, Tricia burst into laughter. "Where'd you get that snarky humor side? It sure isn't from your dad."

"Mom, go, see ya later. I love you and I'm proud of you."

The next morning Noah accompanied Tricia to CMS headquarters in the Harvard Park section of LA. CMS occupied a huge abandoned warehouse on West Gage Avenue, smack bang in the middle of the Harvard Park neighborhood. The huge facility ran from South Western Avenue to South Normandie Avenue. It was several stories tall and its beige brick exterior shined as if it was recently sandblasted clean. The generous number of windows all seemed newly replaced by the dark brown steel frames and thermal pane glass. It was retrofitted to meet all the communication and staffing needs of the CMS and its divisions such as the CRM. This site was chosen for a number of reasons, not the least of which was that Newton's political platform when he was lieutenant governor to revitalize blighted areas. A LA site also made sense because many of the movement's early leaders and supporters were from the locality. Finally, the headquarters had to stay apart from Sacramento until after the secession.

The long-term plan was that the current state capital would naturally become the capital city of the Country of California after it officially broke ties with the US. An additional very strategic rationale for CMS's location seemed idealistic at first, and a bit Hollywood-ish, but actually proved prophetic. Harvard Park is a heavily gang-infested neighborhood. Newton hired the gangs as security for the headquarters and their marriage worked perfectly. Getting paid a generous salary by CMS, the gangbangers had no problem showing zero mercy to any federal agents snooping around Gage Avenue. Newton took particular pride in the residual effect of this strange bedfellow partnership. Crime rates and the drug trade drastically lowered in the area and even in the surrounding areas of Chesterfield Square, Vermont Slauson/Knolls/Square, and Manchester Square. CMS had not a single security issue since the time it opened its doors.

Noah met with officers of the CRM in a very well-appointed conference room on the second floor of the CMS headquarters. A captain, two majors, and a lieutenant all dressed in dark blue fatigues sat at the conference table and interviewed Noah.

"Mr. Murakami, thank you for meeting us today." Noah smiled and nodded toward the group. The CRM officers sat clustered together at the opposite end of the table. "I am Captain Murphy, this is Major Diaz, Major Percevel, and this is Lieutenant Garcia. We are the review board for former US armed forces personnel that are inquiring about enlistment into the CRM. As you can imagine, we have to be extra diligent in accepting US personnel into our ranks. We have separate procedures for those Californians enlisting that have never served."

"I understand," Noah said.

Captain Murphy lifted a dark blue file, "You have a commendable record with the US Marines. That's all here. We won't be questioning you about details on that. After this interview, if we determine to proceed with your enlistment we conduct a civilian background check, you must submit to a drug test and physical and we send you a questionnaire to complete. In your case we are forgoing the aptitude test and the family and friends' interviews."

"I understand." Noah said.

"If you agree with all these procedures, we will proceed with our interview. Do you want to proceed?" Murphy asked.

"I agree." Noah responded.

Major Diaz took over the interview, "Mr. Murakami, I echo Captain Murphy's statements. We have no concerns about your ability to be a soldier. You have proven yourself an outstanding military man. Our interview here is quite simple and maybe short. We want you to explain your desertion from the US Marine Corps."

There was a silence, then Noah spoke, "Should I start into that?"

The entire board responded an affirmative.

"I love my country and I love the Corps. When I was told to deploy to the Middle East, I didn't question my orders. I put myself in harm's way to serve my country. But, at the Shasta Dam incident, when my commanding officer gave us orders that we may fire on civilians exercising their right to protest, I could not obey an order to kill innocent civilians."

"But, if this rebellion goes as far as it might, you may be given a similar order to fire upon citizens of the Unites States. Can you follow that order, son?" Major Percevel barked.

"Those citizens will be wearing uniforms or spies who are following their orders to do harm to me, my family, and my fellow citizens of California." Noah said.

"What if there is ambiguity as to the identity of those whom you have been given orders to strike against? Would you follow orders when you, yourself were personally uncertain as to the allegiance of those you are up against?" Lieutenant Garcia asked.

"In a state of war I will follow my orders given by my superiors. I did that in the Middle East and I can and will do it in my home state." Noah said. "So many years ago, in the US's first civil war, brother was pitted against brother, cousin against cousin, and so forth. If your brother or sister, mother or father happened to be on the other side of this conflict, could you execute your duty as a soldier of the CRM?" Captain Murphy asked.

"I will do my duty." Noah's answer was firm and resolute.

"Mr. Murakami, you swore an oath when you were made a Marine. You have now broken that oath. How can we trust that you will not break the oath you take to the CRM and to California?" Diaz asked.

"I have always been a loyal Marine. I am still being loyal to the country and the Marine corps in the defiance of a federal government has been and continues to be oppressive, violating the constitution and therefore anti-American." Noah answered.

"Fellow officers of the board, do you have any other questions for this applicant?" Murphy asked. The other officers shook their heads.

"Mr. Murakami, we thank you for your time and interest. You will be hearing from us in a very short time." Murphy added.

The next day, Major General Curtis Brown, chief of staff for CRM, called Noah. Brown offered Noah an officer's commission in the newly formed California Republic Military. He would join the CRM as a lieutenant. He would be protected from the U.S. military and his status as a deserter. The general gave special mention to the need for his experience and skills to lead new recruits. Noah was given instructions to report to the CRM base outside of Los Angeles as soon as possible. Brown was concerned about his safety if he was anywhere else but at the CRM base. He was right, of course.

Alone in the house, Noah began packing his gear to report to CRM. A couple of loud knocks disturbed the previously silent house. Noah grabbed his Beretta M9 pistol, loaded a full fifteen round clip and walked slowly down the stairs towards the front door. The knocking continued. Noah's head swiveled to check out the house. At the bottom of the stairs, Noah paused and stared at the door, looked left and right, tightened his grip on the pistol and listened. There wasn't a sound coming from outside the door. He wasn't filled with fear, he was filled with training. It was a rare moment since he returned home that he was alone and no one else around to answer the door. That wasn't something he would typically do given his status. The knocking began again. He walked to the door. "Who's there?"

A deep, commanding voice answered back immediately, "Lieutenant Murakami we are sent from Major General Brown as your guard and escort."

Noah hesitated, then responded, "You have ID?"

"Yes sir," the voice answered.

"Put them up to the peephole," Noah commanded. It would be his first order as an officer in the new army.

The soldiers followed his order and each put up a CRM ID. Noah recognized it as official based on his visit to the headquarters the day before. Still cautious, he opened the door to see two soldiers in dark blue uniforms.

Noah ordered the guards to station themselves at the front and back door. He then sat in the living room and waited for his family to return home from school and work.

Ezekiel was the first home. "What's up with the storm troopers? They find you?"

"When everyone gets home I'll explain everything. Can you hang around until then?" Noah asked his brother who was spending less and less time around the house.

"Sure," Ezekiel said, going off his room.

Grace was home not long afterwards. Predictably, her reaction was the opposite of Ezekiel's. "This is so, so dope. We have our own guards and they open doors. I feel like a princess. I can't wait to post," Grace effused.

"You know you can't post anything to do with me or mom, silly bug," Noah reminded her of house rules put in place since the upheaval.

"I know. But can I shoot a video and save it for later when this all dies down?" Grace was quick on her feet when she had any idea that would get her increased popularity with the social group.

"Ahhhhhh, no!" Noah said firmly. "Listen this won't be here long. When mom and dad get home, I'd like to talk to everybody then I'll be leaving."

"You going back to the Marines?"

"We'll talk when mom and dad get home. 'Bout another half-hour or so."

Grace plopped on a living room chair, her backpack thrown off to the side.

"Want something to drink while we wait?" Noah asked.

"Sure, the usual." The usual was a mineral water and lime, which Noah fetched for her.

Always close, Grace and Noah had no problem chatting up while waiting for their parents. They discussed superficial stuff because Noah deflected any political topics for the moment.

About forty minutes later, Dad walked through the door.

"Son, you being taken back?" were the first words out of his mouth, His voice cracking with worry.

Noah explained that the guards were safe and not there to return him to the U.S. Marines. He deftly deflected getting into details promising to reveal all when mom came home. Rowan went into the kitchen, got himself a beverage and brought out a few snacks for everyone.

Whereas Grace was excited about the upcoming news, Rowan's mood was grim. He didn't join into Grace and Noah's small talk, and a worried look dominated his face.

Another twenty minutes later, Tricia entered the house. She was calm but looked right at Noah as she walked into the living room. She had a, 'what's going on here?' expression that was zoned into her son. His eyes widened and a half smile communicated back to her, 'I got this, don't worry.'

Tricia settled into a chair. Noah rose up and yelled out for Ezekiel who promptly came down to them.

"I guess I have some explaining to do," Noah started. "I've been given an officer's commission in the California Republic Military."

Ezekiel looked like he was just about to crawl out of his skin; his face turned red and angry. Grace flashed the biggest smile possible. Rowan's *Eeyore* look became more defeated, if that was possible. While Tricia appeared intrigued.

"I met yesterday with a group of officers of the CRM and a few hours ago, a General Brown offered me an officer's commission. I accepted right away and I leave now. The guards were provided to protect me from the Marines or any of Matthews' agents."

Rowan spoke up, "This Republic Military…geezus… we have an army now?" The question was taken by all in the room as rhetorical. "I don't know how I feel about this, Noah. In one way, I think it's all game playing and posturing, but, on the other hand, with this guy in the White House, he's bound to do anything. This could be worse for you than the Middle East."

Noah didn't respond and Rowan went on, "Noah, you're an adult, you make your own decisions, but this secession thing is getting a life of its own and it could be dangerous for those so closely aligned."

Tricia couldn't hold back any longer. She had not told Rowan or the younger kids yet about her new role in the rebellion and she felt compelled to do so now. "Well, I don't mean to take away Noah's thunder here, but I've taken a job with the rebellion too, as you call it."

Rowan's and Ezekiel's eyes widened. Like many fathers and sons, their shocked expressions were carbon copies of each other. The tension in the room was as thick as San Francisco fog.

"Now, before anyone says anything let me explain. You know I have been looking for work, well I contacted the secession movement and they offered me something immediately. I'm working in their communications department and will be giving speeches and appearances and things like that. I am also the one who put Noah in touch with the right people."

Ezekiel stood up to leave, but both parents insisted he stay put. Rowan spoke, "Tricia, we didn't discuss all this and now you're laying this bomb on me? I'm all anti-Matthews, but this is all going a bit fast, isn't it? Do I get a say here? Time to process any of this?"

"Rowan, it's more than a job—it's doing something I believe passionately in. Besides, it is more than double my teacher's salary. Same benefits and all that. We both believe in the California cause. They put things on the table and I scooped up an opportunity. I've been there all week. I just needed a chance to tell everyone. Noah knew of course." Tricia's eye contact with Rowan spoke volumes about how she wanted his support here.

"Ya know, we see these pictures of embattled countries and you feel for what it must be like for your home to be torn apart. We've contributed money to causes, marched in protests, spoke up in conversations. But you never in your wildest dreams think that the United States could be torn apart like those other places. Now it's here. I am afraid. I do admire both of you following what you believe in. I love you both and will support your decisions. But give me time to examine my own position in all this. If you are looking for me to jump into the fray here, I can't at this very moment. Forgive me but I am confused, a bit shocked and very angry at that ass in Washington, who is ripping this country apart. I hope he doesn't do the same with to our family."

CHAPTER 8

Organizing its Power in Such Form

The room was quiet for a few moments after Rowan's speech. Tricia was disappointed. She wondered what had to happen before her husband would join the movement. But, as frustrating as it was, it was also the reason she loved him. She liked that he was steady. Never jumping head first into anything. In fact, it took almost ten years for them to get married. And they only did so when Tricia got tired of waiting and asked him herself. She even had to get the rings.

Tricia opened her mouth to speak but at that exact moment the giant picture window next to them shattered. Tricia had heard the old cliché that time slowed to a crawl during an emergency but had never believed it. That is, until that moment. She stood still for what felt like minutes but what probably was only seconds. It wasn't until her oldest son yelled, "Get down!" did time return to normal.

The entire family obeyed his barking order and were all splayed out on the ground when more bullets tore up their living room. Rowan crawled over to Tricia and selflessly shielded her. Noah did the same for his sister.

"Ezekiel!" Tricia yelled as she thought of her middle son. She tried to get up to go look for him and make sure he was okay, but Rowan held her down.

"I'll go get him," Noah said, as he began to crawl towards the stairs. It's hard to believe that anybody could ever get used to being fired upon, but Noah had been in so many firefights it didn't faze him. He actually had the opposite reaction. He got a high. He just wished he had a gun, a knife, even a bat. Anything. When Noah got to the stairs, he ran up and made his way to his brother's room.

"Ezekiel," Noah half-whispered. "Are you okay?" He feared the worst when there was no response. Now, he really wanted a gun. No, an RPG. He tried the doorknob. Locked. Worried that his brother was bleeding to death, he kicked it down. The room was empty and the windows had been blown out. Then he saw blood and followed the trail to the closet. He slid open the mirrored doors and found his brother huddled in the corner cradling his arm, with tears streaming down the face.

"I'm dying," Ezekiel told his big brother. He said it in the same voice he used to use when he was just a cute kid. Before he became a brat.

"You're not dying," Noah looked Ezekiel over carefully and found that the blood was coming from a large cut on his arm.

Noah bent down and was about to touch his brother when Ezekiel backed away. "What?" Noah asked. Without looking at him, Ezekiel answered, "I peed in my pants." Noah looked at him sympathetically. "Don't worry," he began. "The first time I was in a shootout, I did the same." Ezekiel looked up. "Really?" Noah nodded. "Now let me look at your arm." As Noah checked his brother, he heard the sirens and footsteps running up the stairs.

"You'll be okay," Noah told his brother. "It really looks like some glass grazed your arm. It's a big scratch, you weren't shot or anything."

CHAPTER 8

The CRM soldiers were with them moments later, quickly followed by Tricia, Rowan and Grace. Tricia was about to go to Ezekiel, but Noah held her back with one arm and raised his free arm out to block the others. "Everything is okay," he told them. "Give us a sec." And as quickly as everyone had entered, they were gone.

Ezekiel was thankful that he could change in peace without anyone knowing what happened. After all, this was his fault. If he hadn't turned in his brother, they would not have known where he was. He couldn't look his brother in the eye. "I'm sorry," he muttered under his breath. Noah laughed. Not the reaction Ezekiel had expected. When Noah looked up, his brother was looking at him with a big smile.

"You don't get it. I'm not apologizing for my pants." Ezekiel gulped and fought back choking, "I called you in."

Noah stared at him. Then, he shook his head as in disbelief.

"You're not mad at me?" Ezekiel asked.

Sure a part of Noah was angry. His brother of all people had ratted him out to the FBI, but a bigger part of him couldn't believe his brother had actually apologized and felt bad about what he had done. He liked this version of his little brother. "No," he lied. And almost as soon as the words left his mouth, Ezekiel hugged him. For the first time in a long time, the two were brothers in more than just name.

An hour later, the Murakami family were relocated to a safe house, which was located in what used to be called South Central. The same South Central that N.W.A. and Dr. Dre had made famous in the 80s and 90s. The Latino gangster who opened the door for them warned them, "I wouldn't leave the house wearin' red or blue."

Tricia nodded, mentally thinking about which clothes she would no longer be able to wear. Seeing Tricia, the gangster started to laugh. "I'm just fuckin' with you. There ain't no gang wars anymore. This isn't the 80s. Besides, we got a real war to fight now." The first thing Noah did when the Latino gangster left was to check all the doors to make sure they were locked. Then he brought all the shades down. Next, he turned off the porch lights and warned everyone to stay away from the windows and never to open the door for anyone. For their protection, a CRM soldier was stationed outside the house and two more were in an unmarked car on the street.

Ezekiel had been a good sport about the move--until he and Grace started to fight about which room was going to be theirs. Rowan, on the other hand, did not look at all pleased. He glared at his wife, who did everything she could to avoid his gaze. Tricia knew he blamed her for this. And they both realized that their lives would never be the same. "Let's try to look at things positively," she told him. Rowan's eyebrows raised. He was curious how she could spin this. Tricia thought. Then thought some more. Her mind raced for something. So, she said the first thing that came to her mind "At least we're not dead." It was not what Rowan had expected. And despite himself and his mood, he laughed.

A short while later, Tricia and Noah were in a low rider speeding through the city. A peculiar limo and even strange for an Uber, but an unwritten law of urban life was no one would mess with this chrome and red chariot. They had to get to work. Rowan wasn't happy about having to stay in the safe house and hide, but he hugged his wife and oldest son and told them to 'be careful." Tricia was going to the California Movement for Secession headquarters while Noah was headed to the California Republic Military base. Both looked out their respective windows wondering what their futures held.

Tricia was dropped off first. She was ushered through the quiet offices into a makeshift conference room by Jaleel Henry. On the way, Tricia tried to ask Jaleel what the meeting was about, but the CMS' communications director wouldn't tell her. Tricia was momentarily confused when she only saw her boss, Gordon Newton, speaking to someone on a computer. She had expected a room full of people. And because of the angle of the screen, she couldn't even see whom he was talking to. The Chairman of the CMS invited Tricia to take the empty seat next to him. Jaleel sat next to her.

It was only when Tricia was in the chair did she notice who was the screen: The California Governor, Rich Herrmann. Seated next to him, but out of Tricia's view, was Rich's chief of staff, Tom Huang. Gordon introduced Tricia to the governor. "Rich, this is Tricia."

"Governor Herrmann, it's a pleasure to actual get to meet you," Tricia said.

"The pleasure is all mine. But at the moment, please call me Rich." Then in a mock whisper, he told her, "I'm off duty." He went on to explain how he couldn't be associated with the CMS but since Gordon and he were old friends, he wanted to make sure his office kept in close contact with what they were doing. But he made it clear that when the time was right, they would work together.

"The reason I called," the governor continued, "was that we just got word that our friend in the White House is going to be blockading all major federal highways into New York."

Neither Gordon nor Jaleel were surprised, but Tricia covered her mouth.

"We were hoping you guys would help organize some response."

Gordon nodded and then told both Tricia and the governor, "We're planning a protest here in Los Angeles. Near the federal building in downtown." He then turned and looked directly into Tricia's eyes. "We want you to say a few words."

Jaleel interjected. "I wrote up some..." he started to say as he pulled out an already prepared speech. But Tricia shook her head. "I want to write my own words." The communications director glanced at Gordon to get his reaction. He nodded. Tricia was thankful that Gordon believed in her. But there was one major problem: she had no idea what she was going to say.

The moment Noah got to the base, Major General Brown was waiting to greet him as he got out of the car. "I have a surprise for you," the general told him. Just as Noah wondered what it could be, he saw his best friend, Mark Perez, standing off in the distance.

"You made it out!" Noah said as he ran to him and gave him a hug. He was glad to see his old buddy. Then the two caught up over a cup of coffee.

Noah wished he could spend all day with Mark, but he was soon taken to a control room in the middle of the base. Seated around the table were General Brown, a Navy fleet admiral, an Air Force general, and a half-dozen officers from various branches of the military. Noah took the empty seat and the meeting began. General Brown brought up a map highlighting the resources that were located in California: The San Diego Naval Base, Edwards Air Force Base, Camp

Pendleton, Fort Irwin, nuclear installations that were known by the general population and those that weren't radar sites, and more. Brown detailed the weapons and machinery and the number of men that were located at each site and how difficult it would be to take control of them.

As General Brown detailed each location, Noah began to wonder if they were going to go on a mission that very night. He asked the general, "What is the time frame on taking over the bases?"

Brown frowned and then answered, "That's why I gathered all of you here. If we move too early, we can set off a war we might not be ready to fight just yet. But if we move too late, we risk losing the element of surprise."

There were murmurs around the room. Some wanted to strike right away, others were more hesitant. Noah was all for taking action, but he didn't want to rush headlong into a suicide mission. Finally, General Brown held up his hand. The room quieted instantly. "We are working on infiltrating each location to make sure we have eyes and ears on the inside," the general said. "I'm telling you all of this to give you the big picture. If California has any hope of surviving, it will depend on us. We will be working and coordinating with civilian leadership at CMS. For the time being, we need each of you to begin training our new recruits." General Brown then dismissed everyone except for Noah.

When the room was empty, General Brown motioned for Noah to take the seat next to him. "How is your family?" he asked.

"Fine, sir," Noah responded.

Brown waved his hands dismissively. "I don't want to hear any of that 'Sir' shit when no one else is around, understand?"

Noah was about to say, "Yes, sir," but stopped himself and nodded instead.

"Good," Brown smiled. But then his face turned serious. "I have a mission for you and your men."

Later that night, Noah was meeting his troops for the first time. He thought the word "troops" was a bit generous—they were a ragtag group, most of whom had little fighting experience. A few had been in the military at some point in their lives, some were police or correction officers, there was even a person who used to be a Civil War re-enactor. In other words, here was the militia version of the Bad News Bears. Noah and Mark's eyes met. *These are the people who are going to be defending California?* He asked himself. At least he had Mark. The two had been in so many tough situations he knew that he could count on his friend to watch his back.

Noah wished they had at least been issued uniforms. It would have made them look less ragtag. But Noah assumed it was to give the allusion that they weren't a real army in order to allow them to stay under the radar longer.

Noah wanted to give a rousing speech to his men—and one woman. Something that would inspire them and get them to rise above their potential and do the impossible. "Just remember one thing. The American revolutionaries were just a bunch of farmers and they beat the British, the best trained, best equipped, and most professional army in the world." Noah was a history buff and knew it wasn't exactly true. The Americans weren't a bunch of hicks as many believed, but from the flickers of hope he saw in a few of the recruits' eyes. He figured a white lie wouldn't hurt.

The next morning, Noah's troops gathered back at the base. Just like himself, none of them looked like they had gotten much sleep. He'd twisted and turned all night with fears that he was leading his men to the slaughter. His only female soldier, Justyice, raised her hand to speak. Noah quickly looked her over. She appeared to be hapa, or half-Asian and half-Caucasian, like him. She was tall, athletically thin and fit and exceptionally beautiful. Her jet-black hair pulled tight into a ponytail and her equally black pupils piercing in her study of Noah. In any other circumstance, he would have been interested in getting to know her better on a personal level, but that was out of the question in such circumstance. He nodded to her, and she asked what everyone had on their minds. "Are we going to be issued weapons?"

Noah had asked General Brown that very question the previous night. Noah repeated the general's answer to him, "No."

Justyice's eyes opened wide. He hadn't liked the answer either. Noah knew all his troops were listening, so he made sure he spoke loud enough for all of them to hear: "We are there to protect our fellow Californians not to engage in a firefight with the federal troops." That didn't make Justyice or any of the others feel better. Nevertheless, each person climbed on the bus.

The ride downtown was silent and too quick. Noah was thinking about how suddenly his life had turned. He chuckled at the thought that he was now officially a rebel. He looked at the others on the bus and wondered what their stories were. He was especially curious about Justyice. *What was her story? Where had she come from?* As he was looking at her, she turned toward him and caught his eye. Noah quickly looked away, his face turning red.

They arrived at the multi-story red hued federal building to find a scene already in chaos. Protestors from all over California had begun to gather all morning. On the other side of the protestors and in front of the building was a whole contingent of the United States Army. Between the two groups a stage was being built.

Before stepping off the bus, Noah handed out black bandanas to each of his troops to cover their faces. Noah's instructions were simple and clear: "Make sure no harm comes to the people of California and don't get yourselves killed." As Noah led the group through the protestors, everyone stopped and stared at them. The black bandanas gave them an ominous look and the crowd was quick to get out of their way. Noah lined up his men between the protestors and the army and linked arms. Mark held a pole with the California flag. They were ready.

At the same time, a half-block away, Tricia and the CMS leadership were in a parked van. She had a notebook open in front of her and a pen in her hand, still trying to figure out what to say. Also inside the car were Gordon and Jaleel who kept anxiously looking at her. Tricia considered asking Jaleel for his prepared speeches but didn't want Gordon to think she couldn't do it herself. She had five minutes before she was scheduled to go on. Tricia knew this was a pivotal moment because the world's media would be zoomed in to watch her. But just thinking about this gave her a splitting headache. *What the hell am I doing?* She asked herself. *I'm just a kindergarten teacher, not a politician and definitely not a revolutionary.*

"It's time," an aid whispered Gordon's ear loud enough for Tricia to hear. Everyone on the bus began to stand. But Tricia remained seated. Gordon looked at her. A flash of worry in his eyes. "Are you ready?"

Tricia took a deep breath. She wanted to tell him no. But before she could speak, Jaleel placed one of the speeches in

CHAPTER 8

her hands. As Tricia was about to protest Jaleel interjected, "Most politicians don't write their own speeches."

There were people out there who could write better speeches than her. After all, only a few days ago she was dealing mostly with five and six-year-olds. As she resigned herself to read Jaleel's speech, Tricia was quickly brought to the side of the makeshift stage. The next few seconds were a blur. A Hollywood celebrity that Tricia recognized but couldn't name was introducing her as the "mom who fought the Blue Jackets." The crowd cheered and she shakily made her way to the podium.

Tricia was not afraid of public speaking, but she had never been in front of so many people before. She looked down at Jaleel's words but when she opened her mouth to read them, they didn't feel right. They weren't her words. She couldn't say them. She closed her eyes.

From the front row, Noah watched Tricia. "C'mon, mom," he said. He could see her hand shaking. "C'mon, mom, c'mon," he repeated like a mantra. He prayed for his mother to give the rousing speech he knew they all needed to hear.

Images from the last few weeks flashed before Tricia's closed eyes. And then she saw it, the little girl with the Southern drawl from her class. Her standing there reciting a pledge to a fascist country that had turned their back on her and the people of California. Her people. Tricia opened her eyes and knew exactly what she was going to say. She then found the flag that Mark was holding, put her hand over her heart and began, "I pledge allegiance to the Flag of California and to the Republic for which it stands, one nation, indivisible, with liberty and justice for all."

CHAPTER 9

The Right of the People to Alter or Abolish It

"No, no, no! I can't take this...I can't take this!" Ezekiel pounded both forearms on the dinner table over and over. "All you people talk about is diss'n the life. We had a good life before all this."

Rowan held down his arms on the table in a firm but gentle way. "Zeke, calm down. We know this is hard…"

Tricia interrupted, her voice filled with obligation-the teacher, "It's the dictators who have been in Washington changing our lives, not us. You're in high school, you have to see what's happening?"

"Hey, something good is coming from all this. We've been in this safe house for two weeks and you're sitting down and eating with us!" Rowan said.

"Yeah, nice dinners, always freak'n yell'n about California against the country. Ezekiel ranted. "I'm not do'in this anymore."

"Ezekiel, you've been sitting at this dinner table each night and not said a word, why didn't you tell us these discussions bothered you?" Tricia's tone softened as she leaned in closer to her son.

Ezekiel's flood gates were wide open and his pent-up frustration poured out. "I've been sit'n here every night and you all blah, blah these theories on what will happen and who's make'n the next move. I don't give a shit. Anybody think of that?"

"Zeke, this is often the only time we get to talk, but I understand buddy, we've been pretty vocal at dinners about what's going on." Rowan also leaned toward Ezekiel. "We get to go to work and school like normal."

Dad's last word inflamed Ezekiel again. "Normal, what the F. We live with guards up our ass, we've got zombies bringing us to school and then they hang around in the hallways all day. This is complete shit."

"I think it's like we're celebrities." Grace added.

Ezekiel just scowled at his sister's comment.

"They're supposed to give you space and keep a far distance so you can lead as normal a life as possible," Tricia said.

"Well, that's not happening. They're always just a little bit away from me," Ezekiel said.

"I like my bodyguard." Grace added.

"You don't have a life." Ezekiel raged. "How am I supposed to get a girlfriend, or any friends for that matter with a zombie on my ass all day?" Ezekiel's head fell into his hands and he grabbed two fist fulls of hair and growled, "I need a life! I need privacy! I don't care about U-S-A or Cal-i-forn-i-a. I want this all to go away from me!"

The next day at school Ezekiel and Savanah, his girlfriend of a few weeks, sat at a lunch table by themselves. Savanah was a preppy dressed blonde girl with an accent from outside of California that Ezekiel couldn't quite place. She was slim, bordering on skinny and totally non-athletic. They usually had more of their crew at the table, but the twins, Caleb and Clayton, were out with the flu, Payton was invited by her new boyfriend to another table,

Alex was vaping somewhere off grounds, Sean and Tess, were out and about trying to find a secret corner to hook up for a quickie.

"I'm so sick of home," Ezekiel spouted after jamming a bite of burger into his mouth. "California this, California that. Fuck'n swear they we're all fuck'n California. FUCK CALIFORNIA!"

At the outburst, other students turned and looked at Ezekiel before resuming their own agendas. In the hectic pace of the lunchroom, a stupid shout-out gets a head turn, spilled food gets a stare, and a fight gets a stand-up. Priorities in the only unstructured time in the school day.

"What the hell? You're becoming a downer. I mean we have a long-term thing here, but I'm in this to have fun, not hear day after day about your mommy and daddy. When are you going to put the big boy pants on and do something? You ain't going to have more of this whining about all that mess at home?" Savanah, his perky cute girl, shrugged.

"They're my family. When I went to the FBI dude that almost got us all killed, me included." Ezekiel begged.

"Your mother, she's the B, she started this whole thing. I mean when she was a teacher she embarrassed my little sister real bad. She made her cry and everything. I mean she's only a little kindergarten girl, so frilly and proper and your mother let loose her political shit on her. She's in kindergarten, that's not right. Something's not right with her," Savanah stated.

"What, the? I didn't know anything about that, I swear."

"It's true, my sister cried every day she had to go to school since then. She only stopped crying when your mama got fired. You have to do something about those people. And, from what I hear about your little sister…she thinks this is all a play game. She's like a little Tricia in middle school, all riling up those little kids." Savanah was locked and loaded for the Murakami's and wasn't letting go. "You did right by your brother. He *is* a deserter. Don't you think bad of telling on him? Now, what are you going to do about the rest? Before they hurt other little girls." Savanah demanded. "And, your dad? He allows all this? What kind of man, father, whatever, allows his family to behave like this? In the South, a man is the head of the family, and we obey the man. That's the man *I* want. Someone who takes charge and does the right thing for the country. I did not know you people were like this." Savanah finished her rant as if she laid down her manifesto on Ezekiel.

The glassy stare in Ezekiel's eyes belied how tight he was wrapped around Savanah's pinky finger. He may as well have been her puppy at that point. Whereas his family's debates were all idealistic and conjecture, Savanah's logic was straightforward. His mom hurt a little girl, his brother deserted the Marines, his little sister is play acting mom, and his dad is a eunuch.

Savanah had stripped down the Murakami family, roasted them on the backyard spit and laid them out to dry in the noon day sun. Ezekiel lapped it up like a dog that hadn't had a meal in a month. Ezekiel's blind devotion to Savanah's take on things was helped by the fact that she was the embodiment of what happens to those toddler beauty pageant queens when they become teenagers. She was porcelain pretty, confident, brainwashed on the America-the-Beautiful religion, self-absorbed and knows how to wrap it all up in a bow and use it all with a male. A fine-tuned grooming handed down from one southern princess to another.

As Ezekiel went back to class that afternoon, he was turned. If he was rebellious toward his family's mission in the past, he was hell-fire and brimstone on a vendetta now to sabotage whatever they were about. Savanah had thrown new coals on the fire of adolescent rage that was cooled down after the attack on his family. All he could think about now was contacting the FBI and showing his parents the error of their ways. Of course, he would impress the hell out of his southern bell along the way. He imagined himself a great patriot by undermining the budding rebellion by taking down its figurehead—his mom. He would have Savanah throwing herself at his feet and her father would take him in as his own son and bestow great riches on him. His mind spun and spun all afternoon as teacher after teacher droned on about some inconsequential nonsense.

Then a troubling thought interrupted his great plans: how was he going to contact Agent X, as the FBI man called himself when he had called the hotline? He was on this lockdown with his family in the safe house. In the two weeks that they were all there, he hadn't been allowed to go out except for school. The family each received a new cell phone, those embarrassing flip phones. He kept his in his pocket all day because the other kids would laugh at him. Agent X gave him a phone number and a code to get through to him, but, of course, that was in his old phone. The teacher blabbed on about some trigonometry problem, but he had real world problems to solve. He could ask his parents to see if he could get his numbers from the old phone, but they might want to screen all the numbers. No go. The trig class ended and the mad rush into the hall seemed even more furious than normal. Ezekiel got up slowly, still pondering his dilemma. As he was almost at history class, he thought he spotted Savanah make a right turn down the crossing hallway and out of sight. Then it came upon him: Savanah could be the messenger! She could call the LA FBI office and leave a message. Who cares who takes the message, Ezekiel was sure if it had his name on it, it would find its way to Agent X. And he would stay on Savanah's good side by showing her he was taking action. Brilliant! Done. But, he still had the problem of how to meet with Agent X when he was on such a security lockdown. He had to figure out how to ditch his bodyguard. And that's when school actually served a purpose.

Ezekiel walked into history class late, as if he cared, but he almost missed the solution to his problem. The teacher started the class with announcements and right as Ezekiel hit the doorway he heard the teacher make an impassioned plea for students to join his history club that meets after school. The teacher's tone sounded desperate. He emphasized that the club focused on current events, and they would have guest speakers, to be arranged, of course. That's it! He could get away with staying after school by saying he was signing up for the history club. Found time. Once Savanah got in touch with Agent X, she could have him contact Mr. Pearson, the history teacher, and be the guest at a meeting. Ezekiel would suggest next week's meeting. That would be the hot spot, because being the first meeting for Ezekiel, he would have less to explain to his guard/chauffer for being super late. Let Agent X make a short presentation to the class and then the two of them could meet and plot strategy. Perfect. Savanah was going to love this and he would score extra by having her directly involved. He gloated how good he was at this.

After the last class of the day, Ezekiel rushed out to wait for Savanah by her locker, with his security guard watching from a distance. The guard felt sorry for Ezekiel that his little teenage love affair had to be put on ice by his seclusion. Ezekiel gave her the plan and her reaction was more than he expected. She bounced on the balls of her feet and kissed him deeply. As their lips and tongues parted, Ezekiel saw out of the corner of his eyes the bodyguard make the hand signal that it was time to go, followed by whirling his index figure in circles indicating, *"Wrap this up!' Dumb Asshole*, Ezekiel thought. Savanah pressed her hips tight into Ezekiel's and they kissed one last time, taking their time.

She whispered, "Done." And with that Ezekiel walked toward his bodyguard and his ride.

Two days later, and much to Ezekiel's surprise at how fast this all went down, the history club moderator and history teacher excitedly introduced a guest speaker for that day, "Ladies and gentlemen, I know I hadn't given enough time to advertise this or we would have more students in attendance, but we have our first guest for the club meeting." He paused as if allowing more of an audience to form, then as not to inconvenience such an austere guest he continued, "Brian Fellows, is an FBI field agent. He was or is shall I say, the inspiration for the TV show and movie of the same name, *The X-Files*." Fellows was imposing. He was tall and built like a bodybuilder. His physique was powerful looking even through the dark blue suit that covered his upper body.

Ezekiel didn't need the double entendre to know that this was Agent X whom he had spoken with previously.

CHAPTER 9

It was all too coincidental that the first guest was from the FBI. He did appreciate the irony that surely Agent X planted for their benefit.

As planned, Agent Fellows spoke uninspired for about a half-hour and didn't take any questions. He walked alone out of the room. Ezekiel waited a few seconds and then walked out after him. Seeing each other in the hallway, Brian Fellows motioned to Ezekiel to join him in an empty classroom. They walked passed Ezekiel's bodyguard that was stationed outside the classroom. Maybe it was seeing Ezekiel and this adult exit from inside the classroom together but, the bodyguard didn't flinch as Ezekiel and Fellows passed by and entered the empty classroom. They pushed two desks together and began to talk. "Zeke, may I call you Zeke?" Fellows asked.

"Sure, you did last time we talked and most people do."

"Zeke, I know this is very tricky business for you. I mean with your family involved in this secession movement and all. But, your country needs your help. In fact, we don't have anyone as close to the inside of this very misguided group as you. They are like a secret club or cult even. I am so afraid for your family being brainwashed by the angry hate this group is directing at our United States." Fellows looked impassioned as he locked eyes with Ezekiel.

"How can I help, Mr. Fellows?" Zeke's tone and body language was as eager as a puppy with its tail wagging.

"Call me Agent X, Zeke. My name isn't Brian Fellows. I just used that to make contact with you." Agent X paused to see how this lie was received by his protégé. "After all, in the spy world, you sometimes have to fight fire with fire." He slowed his speech down and emphasized the word, 'spy' also to judge how that label would play on the vulnerable teen. It had the desired effect of giving an identity craved teen a purpose he never had before. "Oh, back to your question. I'll always answer your questions and be right up front with you, always, Zeke." Brick by brick Agent X was grooming Ezekiel with the expert skill of any other predator. "So, you ask, how can I help. We'll get to that. We'll get to that. I'm foremost concerned about your safety and your family's safety. Have these people in that cult hurt you or your family in any way?" Agent X asked with a stilted sympathetic manner.

"No. I mean they took us away…ahem…kidnapped us from our house and they have us locked up. They drive us around in cars with windows so black that you can't tell where you are. But, they don't hit us or anything and the food is OK. I can take anything, I'm pretty tough for my age," Ezekiel explained.

"Good, good. Just be careful. It is an old technique to treat you well at first, then suddenly they turn on you. The element of surprise is really effective when they want something from you. There is also something called the Stockholm Syndrome. Have you heard of it?"

"No, I haven't. I haven't had health or gym. They were cut from our requirements a couple of years ago," Ezekiel naively retorted.

"Stockholm Syndrome is when you actually start to like your kidnappers. You feel sorry for them. Be careful of that if you find yourself sympathetic to these people who have so much anger and hate inside them. They want you to like them. Your parents will even want you to like them and their cause. If you fall for it…BANG! That's when they can snap you and torture you the most. Oh, they are capable of it." Agent X looked at Ezekiel and made sure it was all sinking in with him.

"Fuck, oh I mean, sorry, I didn't mean to…" Ezekiel turned red and felt for a moment back to being a little boy.

"It's OK, you can speak any way you want to me and say anything to me. As an agent of the federal government, all our conversations are secret, you know, confidential. There's a law about that. It's called the law of confidentiality. It covers our talks, even our actions. We agents can't be prosecuted for any crimes." Agent X was firm and slow. He chose his words very carefully and watched how they fell on the boy.

"I have been meaning to tell you it was very courageous to contact me. And, you were very smart to use your girlfriend's phone." He kept pumping up the fragile ego of the boy.

"Thanks, but cuz we are honest with each other, I have to tell ya, I lost your number cuz they gave me stupid flip-flop and took away my phone with your number in it. Actually, all my numbers," Ezekiel explained.

"Well, OK, good thinking then. Here, give me your phone. I'll put my direct number in it." Ezekiel handed him his phone and after Agent X typed in a few numbers and pressed other keys, he held the phones together in one hand until a tone rang. He not only paired the phones, he obtained complete access to Ezekiel's phone and it now was a tool at the complete disposal of the FBI. If this had been the only accomplishment of Agent X at this meeting, it would have been an enormous win for the feds, but the agent was accomplishing more than he could have imagined.

"Speaking of your girlfriend, she is incredibly proud of you. I'll tell you something man-to-man, something your dad probably wouldn't tell you. As you keep working for us..." he snickered a chauvinist's chuckle. "...you'll have that young lady in the palm of your hand. She'll do anything for you." He leaned back in his desk chair as if he was impressed with his own revelation. "Wow! You are one lucky bastard. Luckeeee bastard!" He laid that on the boy with a laconic, 'awww sucks' homespun feel. He then put his fist out and they bumped fists. Ezekiel had a huge smile on his face. "You just remember that my friend. This is why we are superheroes for our country. We get the best babes. Don't forget that."

Still smiling at his fantasies come true, Ezekiel was hungry for more. "So, what is the first thing you want me to do?"

"I don't have anything right this second, sir. Us getting our old team back is just happening a bit too fast, even for the bureau. But I have your phone number now. So, I'll contact you in a few days. Here's our code. If I call, you have to be in complete privacy, not even that hot babe you're dating can be around. If you don't pick up, I'll know that you can't talk. Then call me back as soon as you can. In fact, get out of whatever you are doing and call me back immediately. Assume everything we do is super urgent. I will never leave a message, OK, so if someone leaves a message, it's probably the bad guys from that cult. It won't be me. Believe me, we'll get you working right away. I don't know how much we can pay you but believe me, you'll be taken care of, and more than any bagger at a grocery store makes." He chuckled dismissively.

Agent X played Ezekiel so well he surprised even himself. In his brief sit down, he hit on every piston that pumped inside that adolescent boy. He whacked him starting with respect, independence, rebellion, privacy, identity, idealism, sex and lust, notoriety and fame, money, belongingness, secrecy, and even the whole Agent X identity seemed right out of a video game. The only thing missing was the cool soundtrack. He could tell that Ezekiel's head was spinning and he had a puppet for whatever purpose he chose.

Ezekiel went back to the history club and finished the meeting. No one at the meeting blinked an eye that he was gone so long. It was an after-school club, so kids were free to come and go as they pleased. When the meeting time was close to the end, Ezekiel's driver and bodyguard made his presence known by lingering in the hallway outside the classroom where the meeting was held. Whereas Ezekiel's reaction in the past was anger when the bodyguard appeared, he now looked at the appearance of this person as part of the elaborate game he was now a key player in. He even looked forward to it because it brought his new fantasy to life. He was really in the thick of a vital mission to save the country.

He quickly called Savanah before he had to meet his bodyguard. She picked up immediately. "I just got done with my meeting with the man," He began, careful not to reveal any secret information over the phone.

"How'd it go?" Her voice was shrill with excitement.

"Good, I'll give ya the details tomorrow at lunch."

As promised, the next day in the school lunchroom Ezekiel and Savanah took a table away from their usual lunch table. Whether it was the high Ezekiel was on as a result of his meeting with Agent X, or Savanah did something different, but she was looking her southern belle cute big time. Short skirt, knee-high socks, color coordinated cashmere sweater and in her hair a color-coordinated headband. She was ringing all the bells with Ezekiel. His new position as a junior spy was paying off already without her saying or doing anything.

"So, tell me all the details?" she anxiously asked.

Ezekiel gave her a blow-by-blow account of what Agent X said with the obligatory male ego embellishments. Savanah was giving out so much excitement at his new 'job' with the FBI as he bragged, she might as well have jumped across the table and gave herself to him right there. She did interrupt when he mentioned his mother, "My sister is still so scarred by your mom. She cries and even talks in her sleep about it. My parents talked about calling child protective services before your mom got fired."

Ezekiel didn't react. He would never tell Savanah, but her precious little sister was a brat to the max. He couldn't stand being around her during those tag along dates all boyfriends have to endure.

"So, have they given you the first assignment yet?" Savanah asked.

Ezekiel shook his head. "Girlfriend, it's only been twenty-four hours. Like Agent X said, they have some planning to do. I'm their most valuable asset right now. By the way, when they say 'asset' it's like a VIP," Ezekiel explained.

"I have an idea how we can blow this whole thing apart and get back at your, mo…" Savanah caught herself from throwing Tricia too far under the bus. "…the revolution, rebellion or whatever they are calling it. This whole thing is so stupid and wrong, wrong, wrong. This is America." Her anger seemed disingenuous, prissy, as if she got the wrong sugary concoction at the Starbucks. "I want to help you with this and be part of the team," she added.

"I'll see what my superiors say, but I think I can make that work, but, you can't break up with me then," he said confidently.

"Now, why would I do a thing like thaaat?"

She kissed him.

CHAPTER 10

Life, Liberty and the Pursuit of Happiness

Tricia watched the footage from her speech as she sat in the CNN studio doing a live interview. Her speech in front of the federal building had gone viral. If she wasn't the face of the California secession movement before, she was now. She was making the rounds on all the news shows, making her case for her home state to leave the Union.

When Tricia's speech finished on the monitor, the good-looking news anchor turned to her and asked with a wry smile, "Why do you hate America?"

Tricia was by now used to such an aggressive opening question. It was pretty much how every interview was started. Tricia offered a warm smile and joked, "It's like I told my mom and dad: given the acrimony between both parties, I think it'd be in the best interest of everyone if we split the family up."

For the rest of the interview, Tricia made the case for independence with the scripted answers that she'd practiced earlier with Jaleel. The most important point to be made was the simple fact that California and the rest of the country were so far apart politically that it didn't make sense on either side to remain together . This was nothing new. There have been rumors of California leaving the United States since President Trump was elected in the fall of 2016. It was the impotent leadership of Trump creating one impetuous executive order after another and the states' blatant rejection of these decisions that undermined the authority of the presidency and gave root to the independence movement. But now what was new was the fact that there was an intelligent, guileful president and the states' defiance needed to be stronger. But Tricia had her ace up her sleeve in the face of these questions. She looked at the anchor in the eyes and said, "But most importantly, no more taxation without representation."

The anchor looked perplexed. He asked the natural follow up, "Would you please explain that statement?"

Tricia was ready for this. "The voters of California have been disenfranchised." She paused to let that sink in. But before the anchor could ask for clarification, she continued, "Our thirty-nine million votes are worth less than those voters who hail from smaller states. Therefore, we do not have fair representation in the Electoral College and the Senate… This despite the fact that California continues to be the largest contributor to the federal government."

Glancing off to the side, Tricia saw Jaleel giving her a thumbs-up. The two had become closer over the last week. Tricia wasn't sure what she would have done without him. Jaleel was savvy with the press and had a knack for always knowing exactly what they were going to hit her with. She continued, "We demand that we get fair representation, if the President isn't willing to do this, then we have no choice but to begin the process of leaving the United States."

"What would you say to President Matthews if he is watching tonight?" the anchor asked.

Tricia paused, giving the illusion that she was thinking, but in reality, Jaleel had already fed her the answer to this one. She took a deep breath before saying, "I would tell him to do the right thing and allow the people of California to decide if they want to be part of the United States or if they want to be independent."

The rest of the interview went as expected. Tricia explained at one point, "If California were an independent country, it would already be the sixth biggest economy in the world—right ahead of France and India and California has had the highest GDP growth of any state for the last half-decade." She went on to add, "Because of the size of the population, the geography, and the coastline, California is well positioned to stand alone." The side of her mouth cracked a wry smile at her last comment.

A few minutes later, the interview was done and Tricia was being ushered out of CNN's Los Angeles headquarters via the side door. Wherever she went, she and Jaleel were surrounded by security who kept everybody at bay. Most of her interviews were from various undisclosed locations around the Southern California area. She had been invited to New York City and Washington D.C. to appear in person on various programs, but none could obviously guarantee her safety. It wasn't just the federal government that her security team was afraid of—they feared *everyone*. Because, according to the FBI's current top ten most wanted criminals, she was number one. There was a rumor about a ten-million-dollar reward for her arrest, but the Bureau would neither confirm nor deny it. Matthews instructed the FBI not to post a reward attached to Tricia's post, thinking it would place a higher importance on her insurgency. This was consistent with his style of belittling opponents to strip away their power in the public's eye.

"Great job," Jaleel told her as they sped away.

Tricia asked, "Can I have my phone back?"

But before they were even out on the freeway, Jaleel was already holding it out for her. "You have five minutes," he warned, handing it back to her.

Taking Tricia's phone was something they did during every interview. People have the bad habit of calling when they see folks they know on TV. There is nothing worse or more distracting than a phone buzzing live on TV.

Tricia saw the fifteen missed calls from her husband. She wasn't surprised that he had not left a single message. He had stopped leaving voicemails a few days ago. It wasn't that she was intentionally missing his calls. She was just busy. But that didn't mean she didn't miss her family. She missed them terribly. She hadn't seen them in over a week. CMS now had to keep her sequestered for her own safety being the FBI's most wanted. She'd barely spoken to any of them except for rushed calls between appointments—like now.

She looked at the clock. She had four minutes left. She returned Rowan's call. "Hi…" she began. But just as she began to speak what was on her mind, her words died on her lips when she heard Rowan crying. "What's wrong?" Tricia asked.

"I can't do this anymore."

Three minutes, Jaleel motioned with fingers raised and tapping his watch. Tricia glanced at Jaleel. He was already looking rather impatient. "Do what?" Tricia asked.

Rowan was quiet for a long time. Two minutes, Jaleel motioned. "THIS…," he said, but then stopped. He was thinking about how he was now hiding inside a stranger's home as his oldest son and wife played revolutionaries, his daughter was trying to imitate her mom to get her attention, and Ezekiel was hiding in his room planning only God knew what. He couldn't tell his wife that he had been fired from his job. His wife's fame had become a liability and with the security following him around it was difficult to explain on the few interviews he's gone on. Needless to say, he had not been offered a single job.

Tricia knew that Rowan had been fired. She was told in a briefing she had gotten a few days ago, but she was waiting for him to tell her on his own terms. She also knew about the interviews and how he had begun to drink at night. Not an excessive amount, but more than before. A bottle or two more of beer. That's not a lot for most people, but for Rowan, it was a bad sign.

One minute was Jaleel's latest signal. Tricia glanced at Jaleel who was now motioning for her to wrap it up. Tricia nodded, letting him know she knows the clock is running down. "Can we talk about this later?" she paused, hoping Rowan would let her off the hook. When he didn't, Tricia continued, "I miss you. I love you." Rowan didn't reciprocate. Instead, he just hung up the phone.

Tricia didn't have time to worry about Rowan. She figured their marriage had weathered bad times before and that they'd make it through this rough patch too. A small part of her wondered if Rowan was just jealous because she wasn't just this plain vanilla kindergarten teacher anymore but a hero. Not only did people recognize her, but they also respected her. This wasn't just something in her own head. She had been getting emails and messages from people around the world.

Jaleel and Tricia were taken to a nondescript office downtown. Half the time, Tricia wasn't sure who they were meeting with before arriving. But this one was different.

CHAPTER 10

This time she knew. She was going to be meeting live with the California governor. She was nervous and excited in equal measures. She told herself to relax. She wasn't some young fan girl.

As Tricia walked in, she was surprised to see an Asian man, instead of the governor. Tom Huang noticed her look of surprise and smiled at her. "I'm obviously not Governor Herrmann," he said as he quickly gave her the up and down. She was prettier in person than on TV. He shook the thought out of his head as he held out his hand for her. "I'm the governor's chief of staff. I was with the Governor on that video chat the other day. Nice interview on CNN by the way."

Tricia wasn't used to the idea that people knew who she was before she had introduced herself. It would be a while before she got used to it.

"The governor didn't think it would be wise to meet in person yet," Tom began.

Tricia eyed Tom. He was young and handsome. Very handsome. Tall. Well-dressed. He had a confidence that she found incredibly sexy. She wondered if she just thought that because it was the opposite of her husband. Suddenly, Tricia realized everyone was looking at her. She was so deep in thought that she had lost track of the conversation.

Jaleel quickly covered for her. He took the lead and began, "We are here to let the governor know that we are going to be starting to gather signatures for the petition to leave the United States."

Tom and Rich had figured that CMS was moving in that direction. "When?" Tom immediately asked.

"Now," Tricia answered.

Tom raised an eyebrow. "I thought you were going to wait for President Matthews…" Before Jaleel or Tricia could respond, Tom raised his hand. "I'm kidding." Tom took a deep breath. "You know Governor Herrmann would not be able to support a ballot initiative at the moment."

Neither Tricia nor Jaleel were surprised.

"What's the rush?" Tom asked.

As Jaleel opened his mouth to answer, Tricia jumped in: "Every day we wait is one more they have to prepare to keep us from our independence. The ballot initiative is just for show."

Tom was surprised by this answer and her honesty. He looked her over again. He was even more attracted to her than before. But what was most sexy about her was her strength. If he wasn't already working for the governor, he would want to be working for her.

"He was flirting with you," Jaleel teased Tricia when they were back in the car. Tricia couldn't help blushing. And she hated herself for it. She felt like she was in middle school all over again. "He was not," she insisted as she unconsciously touched her wedding ring.

Jaleel smiled. "You like him."

Tricia blushed even more. She forced herself to say, "I do not." But even she didn't believe the words coming out of her mouth. She was too long in the tooth and too married to have a crush on anyone. But just as she thought that, she began to imagine what it would be like to kiss Tom. It was the first time she'd fantasied about another man since she was married.

Jaleel began to sing, "Tricia and Tom sitting in a tree, K-I-S-S-I-N-G. First comes love, then comes marriage, then comes baby in the baby carriage, sucking his thumb, wetting his pants, doing the hula, hula dance!"

Tricia and Jaleel laughed. Probably because of the constant veil of tension they lived under, the silly limerick burst through their staunch, determined public images. They laughed until tears began to stream out of their eyes. They laughed so hard their driver and the security guard turned around to make sure they were all right. When they eventually got a hold of themselves, Tricia asked, "Thanks, I needed that. But please tell me we're done for today."

"One more," Jaleel said sympathetically.

Tricia sighed. She was exhausted. "Who? Please tell me it's not another interview."

"It's not. It's with El Presidente de Méjico."

Tricia looked at her. "Did you just say the President of Mexico? What does he want?"

Jaleel shrugged. "She! And she didn't say. She just wanted to meet," he paused for effect before saying with great emphasis, "You."

The car pulled over to the side of the road. A man waiting on the corner came to their window and passed a folder to the security sitting in the front passenger seat. This was not unusual. The CMS base usually provided intelligence reports about the people Tricia was going to meet with. That's why she didn't think it was unusual when security handed her the folder. She assumed the envelope would contain information on the president of Mexico.

Instead, it was about Tricia's family. Tricia quickly scanned the document. According to the report, there was a strong suspicion that someone in her family had been compromised. She sucked in a breath when she read the word, "compromised." *No!* she thought. There was no way this was possible. Her own family? Working against the movement? She took a deep breath and reread the report, slowly. Hoping her eyes were just tired and that she had just misread it.

But she hadn't. The report clearly stated that they have picked up chatter that someone in Tricia's family was working with the FBI. But they could not be sure who it was. They wanted Tricia's permission to confiscate all cell phones, computers, and move her family to another location immediately. Even though the report made clear that they weren't sure who was working with the enemy, Tricia was sure she knew: Rowan. Her husband. She replayed every conversation they've had over the last month. Then she remembered Rowan's own words, "But, give me time to examine who I am in all this. If you are looking for me to jump into the fray here, I can't at this moment. Forgive me, but I am confused, a bit shocked and a whole lot angry..."

Rowan clearly made his decision. Suddenly, she had the same feeling for her husband that she had for the President of the United States: Hate. She quickly signed the order, put the documents back in the envelope and returned it to the security personnel, who handed it back out through the window.

"Everything okay?" Jaleel asked, looking at her funny.

"Fine," Tricia said through gritted teeth.

She remained silently fuming for rest of the ride. A half-hour later, they were taken to the Mexican counsel's residence where they were ushered into a meeting room. On the screen, the Mexican President, Maria Gonzalez Barragan sat waiting. As Tricia took her seat and the room was cleared of all the staffers, including the Mexican Consulate General, she looked over the president. Strength and power oozed off from her every pore, even through the screen. Before Maria opened her mouth, Tricia knew she was going to like her.

"Mrs. Murakami," Maria started.

Tricia interrupted, "President Gonzalez Barragan, please call me, Tricia." The president smiled, "Only if you call me, Maria."

Tricia nodded her approval.

"Good," the president said smiling. "Tricia, thank you for coming on such short notice. As you can imagine, this is a very sensitive conversation." She glanced at Jaleel, who got to his feet and left without saying a word. Jaleel was used to being asked to leave, so it didn't bother him anymore. Besides, Tricia would update him later.

When Jaleel was gone, Maria continued, "I've seen your videos. You've caused quite a stir. How much is the bounty on your head now?"

"Ten million."

"It'll be a lot more than that by the end of the year."

Tricia didn't doubt that.

The Mexican president continued. "I want you to know that I am an admirer of yours. I believe that your cause is just." Tricia waited for the "but." "But, publicly, at the moment, we are not able to support you. I hope you can understand."

Tricia was not surprised. She'd had this same conversation with the Canadian Prime Minister a few days earlier. The Canadian one was a blow to the movement because some in the CMS believed that the best course of action was for all the Western Coastal states—Washington, Oregon, and California—to succeed from the United States at the same time and then join Canada. They figured that the sheer landmass of such a union would secure their security.

However, no country was willing to back the secession movement so early. They assumed that there was absolutely no chance it would actually happen. And if they put themselves out there too early, it would destroy any future relationship with the United States forever. The only country that had offered their support to the secessionist movement was North Korea. And frankly, the CMS wasn't sure they wanted it.

Tricia nodded. "We understand," she told the president. "However, Maria, what I would like to know is that when things start to happen, who's side of history are you going to be on? Theirs or ours?"

The president looked off camera and then shook her head slightly. Whatever she was about to say wasn't what her staff wanted her to say. The president then looked back at the camera—and seemingly into Tricia's eyes—and said the words Tricia was hoping to hear, "What I can promise you is that when the time comes, we will be open to having that conversation."

For Tricia, that was as good as a "yes" as she could have hoped. All the way back to headquarters she was all smiles. She was so distracted by how well the meeting went, she didn't check the caller ID when her phone began to buzz in her hand. "Hello?" she answered.

She was stunned when she heard Tom's voice. "Miss me?"

CHAPTER 11

It is Their Duty to Throw Off Such Government

The streets of the Elysian Park neighborhood surrounding Dodger Stadium were packed with posters that showed Tricia in a dark blue CRM beret resembling the iconic image of Che Guevara. Her headshot in the poster even had the defiant look off into the distance that resembled Che. Jaleel was the mastermind of the poster. He knew that the image would invoke an unconscious association for so many Californians who held Che up as a godlike figure in the Latino community and beyond. It didn't hurt that Tricia looked particularly attractive, perhaps even sexy, in a beret and she was comfortable with the image. The local hip-hop artist, Lil' Cool G was commissioned to design the poster. His graffiti art framed the colorful picture of Tricia in the beret. Symbols of California pride and urban anger popped in the background of the poster. The word, 'Free' in stylized, black lettering burst from what looked like an explosion running along the top of the poster. A closer look showed that the artist drew the smoke of the explosion in the shape of the state of California.

The usual 56,000 seating capacity of Dodger Stadium bulged to 80,000 with spectators standing on the field in front of the stage. Many in the crowd held up the iconic poster attached to wooden sticks. They waved it or pumped it as they shouted any number of slogans that were becoming attached to the movement: "Cali Free!"; "Free!"; "Cal Country!"; "Independence Now!"; "No taxation without representation!" and "Trish."

Tricia did not let the crowd wait a minute past the time announced for its start. She walked out onto the stage behind a double-file line of CRM soldiers in their new blue camo uniforms and dark blue berets. They all had side arms, but no rifles. The line parted and flanked each side of the stage. They stood in the 'at ease' military position with arms on their sides and legs spread for the duration of the rally. The presence of the new California military filled the stadium with awe and pride. This was the first live display of the CRM, and the crowd's cheers were directed as much to these soldiers as they were to Tricia. Scattered around the stadium more CRM soldiers patrolled. They all wore SWAT gear over their blue camos, bullet-proof vests, elbow and knee pads, dark blue helmets, heavy gloves and they carried automatic rifles.

The crowd and the CRM military were the largest and most impressive of the gatherings supporting the rebellion thus far. It was covered by every media outlet imaginable. Drones and helicopters filled the sky above the stadium and were perceived as either benign or menacing by the very few spectators that even bothered to pay any attention to them. Whatever their purpose, the air traffic was ignored by most of the crowd that directed their energy toward the stage. It was a coming out party, and the spirit of the Californians at the rally seemed to be, "Come and get us."

And come and get them was exactly what United States President James Matthews had in his crosshairs.

Minutes after Tricia and her honor guard marched out onto the stage, the sky cleared of the small air traffic that buzzed around the stadium. Just like small scavenger birds scatter at the presence of a bigger bird of prey, the helicopters and drones dashed out of site as three silver Airforce F-16s screeched from the south and did a very close flyover of the stadium. Their thunderous noise and power drowned out both the crowd and any possible speech that Tricia or the CRM could deliver. Tricia and the crowd looked skyward with a defiant, 'so what' smirk. Seconds after the F-16 flyover, the sky was still clear. The choppers and drones didn't reappear. The crowd cautiously continued to fix their attention on the vast sky with its the emptiness speaking volumes. Something was brewing, and the 'Come and get us' attitude of the 80,000 instantly turned into, 'What's happening?' The crowd didn't move, but you could see the look on many of the faces as if they were thinking, "Is it time to rush for the exits?"

Then, the next ball dropped. From the west came three Navy Super Hornet fighters. Their fly-over crisscrossed the contrails that still hung in the air from the F-16s. The disruption was a frightening show of power. Matthews was playing hardball with these rallies. His tactics were meant to spank them all back into subservience.

Tricia grabbed the microphone and looked out into the crowd. Standing right in front of the stage and to her left was her family, minus Ezekiel. Rowan stood uncomfortably; he looked limp and frail with a forlorn face. Noah stood military proud, his chin up and an unwavering smile filled his face. He stood out with his blue CRM uniform on, now decorated with dark blue officer's insignias. Grace looked on, acting as if she was at a pop star concert; she pumped up and down the wooden stick that held her poster; she cheered her mom individually and occasionally a CRM slogan, but mostly she cheered her mom's name. Officials of the CMS and CRM surrounded Rowan, Grace, and Noah. CMS and CRM personnel then filled the left side of the stage well into the standing crowd.

To the right of the stage were other CMS and CRM leaders. In the front of this group were members of the California gubernatorial administration and legislature. California's two senators and all their congress representatives made up the front lines of this crowd. Standing prominently as if a beam shined down on him was the governor's chief of staff, Tom Huang. While the chaos ensued, Tricia and Tom made frequent eye contact and smiled. Time froze in those moments. Neither had another agenda at the time, so they enjoyed the view of the other.

The moment then became scattered with yet a different cataclysmic sound. It was a few decibels lower than the fighters but more rhythmic. Ten Navy attack helicopters appeared, probably from the same San Diego carrier as the Super Hornets. The choppers didn't do a fly over like the fighters. Instead, they hovered over the stadium, circled it, split up and executed a crisscross maneuver gridding the stadium. They performed these maneuvers over and over. The helicopters flew so close to the people in the stadium that the deep bass roar of the engines lifted many of the crowd off their seats. The protesters standing were swayed in the same way. They continued the maneuvers over and over, crisscrossing, hovering, circling. It was clear that they weren't leaving until the rally was extinguished. Matthews' display of power was not going to let this rally proceed.

CHAPTER 11

But Matthews wasn't one to be all smoke and flash. The audience was peppered generously with undercover federal agents from multiple agencies. There were hundreds of them. They worked the crowd with a rehearsed precision. Their disruption took many forms. Some yelled at the CMS supporters, shouting, "Don't you love your country?" Or, "Traitors." Others were more aggressive and threatened, "Traitors are shot on site!" Or, "We're coming for you!" and, "Death to traitors!" Still others became physically aggressive with the crowd. They pushed and shoved, they put their faces right up into Californian's faces and shouted angrily, threatened death and even torture to them and their families. They goaded the audience, they taunted the audience, they wanted fights to erupt, they flashed weapons. Their goal was to make rallying against the United States uncomfortable, if not downright dangerous. Scare people, make them cower at the power of the United States. Make them go home and never be a part of this treachery ever again. That was Matthews' rally, the anti-rally, the antidote to the poison that Matthews saw as the rebellion.

Matthews watched the effectiveness of his infiltrators from a monitor in the Oval Office with McKenzie and Ellis. Satellite feeds zoomed in on the action so close that they could see individual agents as they tried to disrupt the rally. "Good, good, now that's how you break a movement's spirit," Matthews said. McKenzie and Elis smiled and nodded. "Californians, like all Americans are soft and if we make these gatherings painful, they'll end all right, they'll end."

Gloating over what they were seeing, Ellis added, "Oh, they bark a good game but take them away from their fast food and convenience stores and they'll run back home grab for their clickers and watch someone else be rebels."

"Let them get punched in the face and we'll see how many jump up and down for independence," McKenzie said.

"Whoa, look at that guy! Two blows right to that fat lady's head," Matthews pumped his fist at the monitor. "Yea, stand up to us. We'll sit ya right back down."

On the stage at Dodger Stadium, Tricia moved away from the podium, put her hands on her hips, spread her legs and looked skyward. She smirked defiantly. Her head unconsciously tilted into the same pose as the iconic Che image.

Jaleel came from the back of the stage, approached Tricia. The helicopters drowned out any conversation, forcing Jaleel to go right up to Tricia's ear and almost shout, "Don't worry. We're going to get great traction from this. This plays right into our hands. This effort is not wasted." Tricia smiled and nodded. She walked to the edge of the stage, put her hands out as wide as she could as if embracing the entire crowd. As she looked out into the crowd she saw pockets of frenzied activity. Those pockets looked as if the crowd was converging on itself in spots. They were very noticeable by the circular pattern they created when the majority of the crowd faced the stage. They were like the images of wormholes in space. It was apparent that fights of some form broke out in these pockets by the increased activity level directed at the center of each pocket. She could see hands and arms thrown toward the center of the circle.

When Tricia stretched out her arms, the seated audience stood in response to her embrace. Their clapping, of course, was drowned out by the helicopters violent whirl. But the standing ovation meant more than any cheers or claps. She needed to communicate more to the audience, so she thought on her feet. She grabbed two of the posters with her image. She motioned furiously to Jaleel and his staff at the back of the stage for something to write with and they immediately interpreted her gestures. A staff person ran to her with a thick magic marker and more posters. Turning over the posters to their blank side, Tricia wrote as quickly as she could and covered five large posters. She motioned for several of the CRM soldiers to come over and help. She and the guards held up the five posters. They read:

WE ACCOMPLISHED WHAT WE CAME FOR GO HOME

CALIFORNIA FREEDOM THANK YOU!

After waving of arms, jumping up and any show of elation, the crowd began to disperse. Tricia and the soldiers stood fast holding the signs. Tricia held the poster that said California Freedom, occasionally shaking it up and down. It was her new instant viral video.

Suddenly, shots rang out from somewhere in the audience. They were aimed at the stage. Tricia ducked as the soldiers that flanked either side of the stage reacted immediately. In a movement like a Venus Flytrap, the two lines of soldiers ran together and engulfed Tricia and those holding the signs.

A large pocket of the crowd swarmed on the shooter and swallowed up what looked like a man holding a shiny, double-barreled pistol with large scope or targeting mechanism sitting above the two barrels of the gun. His arm was being held high in the air, so the pistol protruded out from the tight crowd around him. CRM soldiers, easily spotted with their blue uniforms, rushed toward that spot, as well as the other spots where the crowd swarmed the troublemakers.

In the scrum that controlled the shooter, the crowd's anger swelled and punches began to land on the shooter, then kicks, then slaps from belts. The crowd turned bloodthirsty and soon the shooter was on the ground. The shooter's FBI badge that was fastened to his belt glistened in the sunlight. It was clear who he belonged to. One of the crowd took his gun that had slid on the stadium concrete when he fell to the ground. The young man took a quick look at the pistol and then pointed it at the shooter. The crowd began to chat, "Kill the blue jacket! Kill him! Kill the blue jacket!"

The CRM soldiers arrived at the scene and bear hugged the young man in order to prevent him from shooting the FBI agent. One of the soldiers barked, "He's more valuable to us alive than dead."

Another soldier remarked, "He's dead anyway."

The federal agent rocked on the ground in pain, his arms covered his face to protect him from more kicks and blows. The glimpses of his face that could be seen revealed a bloody pulp with large chunks of flesh dangling loose. His jacket and shirt were almost kicked off his body and his back was black with bruises and lacerations. As the crowd was pushed away from the limp body by the CRM soldiers, a person in the crowd shrieked, "Put him out of his misery."

Out of nowhere a team of EMTs arrived with a stretcher and they lifted the agent onto the gurney and he was taken away.

That scene was repeated in the other areas of the stadium where other agents disrupted the crowd. The sheer numbers of the crowd overwhelmed those agents and they were subdued. Many of these agents were also beaten. The CRM soldiers rushed to each of these areas and quickly controlled the crowd. Other federal agents were taken out by stretchers once CRM soldiers arrived. Small groups of CRM soldiers corralled as many of the federal agents throughout the crowd as they could identify. Most of those agents had been assaulted in various degrees by the audience. In each case, the CRM soldiers halted the assaults, controlled the crowd and took the federal agents into custody. Seventy-four agents were taken into custody and an untold number slipped out of the stadium. Matthews disrupted the rally but had not won the day.

Backstage, Jaleel and his staff, along with other officials and soldiers, huddled around Tricia. Tricia had plopped onto a steel-folding chair and felt like she was having a panic attack. Her breathing was heavy, her body shook, and her pupils were as wide as saucers. She was brought a bottle of water and given room around her chair. She slumped further into the chair. Her family was nearby. They had rushed backstage immediately after the chaos started.

Jaleel spoke up, "Trish, are you all right?"

Tricia just shook. She didn't answer his question. Noah knelt in front of his mom and held both of her hands. "Mom, you're OK. All the shots went wide of the stage. The crowd was on the shooter before he could take aim. He was one of Matthews' FBI zombies. We've got him. It's safe." He rubbed her hands. He knew to be silent and she would calm down. Tricia was strong. Her breathing slowed. Noah got up, walked behind her and massaged her neck and shoulders. "Take deep breaths mom. You're safe, we're going to keep you safe."

Tricia recovered, "I'm good. Thanks. Was anyone hurt?"

Tom Huang stepped up, put his hands on her shoulders, leaning over, he said, "None of our people, not even anyone in the crowd, although there were federal officers scattered in the crowd to make trouble and maybe do harm. They didn't fare so well. A couple was beaten pretty badly by the crowd. They and Matthews probably figured that Californians would just lay down and give no resistance. This was a huge victory for us."

Everyone within earshot noticed that Huang, a member of the governor's administration was using terms like, 'us' and 'ours.' It signaled to everyone in CMS how the governor and his people thought of the rebellion, though they weren't able to make their feelings and support known publicly yet. Several of the CMS people standing off to the side whispered to each other the pronouns Huang used. They felt affirmed. The day couldn't have been more of a victory for the rebellion in all aspects.

The only one who wasn't feeling particularly victorious was Rowan. He stood off to the side, feeling helpless. He loved his wife, but his scientist brain had difficulty sending signals to his frontal lobe to be the sensitive, supportive partner she's been needing now that she was front and center for the rebellion. Her segregation from the family, their differences about the amount of participation in the movement, and Ezekiel's anger, all contributed to Rowan and Tricia's marriage to be on tenuous ground. Rowan was concerned and to see his son step up before him and then Tom Huang force an intimate moment distanced him even more. Tricia was too consumed by her ever-increasing role in the rebellion to put any energy in their marriage and Rowan was increasingly an afterthought. The Murakami's unity crumbled along with the country's.

The CMS spun the events of the rally more effectively than Matthews' people. The images of the dirty tricks of those embedded agents and the shots fired at the stage were positioned to highlight how the federal government acted with deliberate force to harm citizens who were exercising their right to assemble. Even the futuristic, sinister gun aimed at the stage gave the CMS cause support. Blogs lit with debates on what that weapon was and how menacing it looked. It certainly wasn't built to fire blanks. The FBI was unleashed to use deadly force. CMS had established a large following on all their social media formats, so the news of the rally reached around the world instantly.

Governor Herrmann had to speak out on the travesty. He called a press conference hours after the Dodger Stadium rally dispersed. His tone was angry and stern, "Today, in Los Angeles, the federal government of the United States conducted an egregious act of aggression upon the people of California. Purposely and calculatedly, the president of the United States of America ordered the powerful machinery of war to act violently against a peaceful assembly of citizens that came together to exercise their constitutional right to meet and discuss issues. The actions today of this president show a distinct pattern of violent punishment against people that oppose the building dictatorship that he is attempting to create in Washington. To attack citizens of a free society for coming together to discuss democracy is a fundamental violation of the constitution of the United States. When a president uses his position and power in this manner, this is an impeachable action. I call upon Congress to act immediately to begin the impeachment process against President James Matthews III. Further, I call upon Congress, the Supreme Court, and all the citizens of this country to call for the immediate suspension or resignation of this president while this impeachment is taking place. To continue the presidency of this man that acts criminally against the citizens of this country cannot be tolerated by a free society. This country does not exist in freedom while a president can act as we have seen in these last months. First, he orders troops to fire upon protesters at the Shasta Dam, then the murder of citizens at Raimondi Park, and now warplanes and ground troops attack an assembly of citizens meeting in a peaceful gathering not even allowing for their agenda to begin. Where was the need to control or punish this crowd? Why such extreme measures? What indication was evident that this gathering needed infiltration by hundreds of federal agents? What law was or would be violated by those attending this rally at Dodger Stadium? There is no justification for this president." He paused. "California will not wait any longer for their brothers and sisters across this country to do the right thing and remove this president and his associates from power immediately."

Herrmann's message was clear. California was demanding immediate action against the president. It was a new dimension to the rumblings of secession being debated by California, New York and now other states. Was he saying that secession could be halted if the United States removes James Matthews? Could such action bring the country back from the brink of division? Herrmann's speech gave an alternative and an ultimatum.

CHAPTER 11

Matthews was compelled to respond. An hour after Herrmann's speech, a hasty rebuke was delivered by President James Matthews III. He used a different strategy than Herrmann and demanded network airtime by all television outlets. Whereas Herrmann was confident that his press conference would make it into the homes of most Americans, Matthews's action of seizing airtime, when he wanted it, came across as bullying and 'Big Brotherism.' He was already losing the media battle.

Matthews' strong suit wasn't public speaking and particularly speaking without his remarks being extensively prepared by a speechwriter. He opened his broadcast disingenuously with the affirmation coined by more popular presidents' decades ago: "My fellow Americans. I love this country. I love all this country stands for and I love the freedoms that we all enjoy that have been obtained by the blood, sweat, and tears of our ancestors over hundreds of years. Do I become angry when I have been given solid information that these freedoms are being threatened? You bet I do. Do I become protective of my beloved country when I have been given solid information that a very large group of radicals who intend harm toward this country are gathering to plot this harm? And these radicals, these criminals are allowed to plot their crimes in open public without restriction, without censor, without control? You bet I do. The job that I swore to do and YOU elected me to do is to fundamentally protect you and your families both within our borders and beyond our borders. I admit the actions taken today against this evil assemblage. I admit it was my orders to control and contain this anti-American meeting. Would you want me to do less? Is this not what you voted for me to do?"

He took a deep breath, part of trying to look forlorn. He tilted his head and lowered his eyebrows as if to soften the tough tone of his previous remarks. "My fellow Americans, I am not the criminal here as Governor Herrmann has accused in his speech of earlier today. I am your protector, your father, providing a safe house and a good meal on your table." His tone returned to the anger and defiance of his opening remarks. "In fact, Governor Herrmann's words are the ones that are criminal. His statements were treasonous and I am calling on my attorney general to process charges against him as an immediate and first step to be removed as governor of California. I am also instructing my attorney general to include his entire staff and administration as I know he did not act alone in preparing his statements and supporting this illegal assembly. This leadership in California is full of traitors and criminals. This poison cannot be allowed to spread. I would ask my attorney general to include the senators and congressman from California for, like a virus, I have no idea how much these people have been infected with this poison." He tried to soften his tone again, "I love this country and I love each and every one of you." Then modulating back to a stern warning, he ended, "I am your president, James Matthews III."

Matthews' broadcast came across like a dud, even to his supporters. He might as well have pounded his fists on the desk, became red faced and yelled threats. His waffling in emotion between tough-guy and over-the-top sensitive, using phrases like, "I love you" words that no president or politician had ever stated to the public, came across as bizarre and uncomfortable. Further, calling himself, "…your father…" narcissistically equated himself to George Washington. Instead of stirring affinity from the public, it came across as delusional. What was clear was that Matthews now had an even stronger vendetta against California and like the idealized "father" he saw himself, he was going to punish the rebellious children. But, like a psychotic parent, he wasn't just going to punish the children, he was going to eliminate them.

Tricia Murakami, Gordon Newton, Jaleel Henry, General Curtis Brown, Noah Murakami and a room full of CMS staff watched Matthews' broadcast at the CMS headquarters in Los Angeles. The mood of those in the room was best described as ambivalent. Matthews's demeanor, his threats, his awkwardness, all did not surprise anyone there.

Newton reflected on the broadcast with a smile, "Jaleel, we didn't even get a mention." Those in the room chuckled. He continued, "There's not much new to comment on. All I can say is… Here we go." He looked around the room reading the body language and judging the resolve of his closest colleagues. He stood and dismissed the group, "Let's get back to work."

CHAPTER 12

He Has Excited Domestic Insurrections Amongst Us

As soon as his family left their latest safe house to go to the protest at Dodgers Stadium, Ezekiel was going to leave. He hadn't seen Savanah in over a week because he no longer went to school with her. He was now homeschooled. He was given a new cell phone every day, not allowed to check his email, or log onto any other social media. In other words, he was isolated from the real world. Security told him it was for his own protection, but he felt like a prisoner.

Ezekiel desperately wanted to see Savanah. He swore he could still smell her perfume on his clothes—the ones he was wearing when she had kissed him. He had been daydreaming about that moment ever since it had happened. He wondered if she still thought of him like he thought of her. At night, he imagined what it would be like to marry her. Deep down he knew it was silly, but the romantic in him didn't give two hoots.

Ezekiel had been waiting for the day that his entire family would be gone. It was typical for his mom and older brother to not be home, but his baby sister and dad always seemed to be around. He knew this was his one chance to get away. He needed to act fast. At first, he thought he would poison the security detail, steal their car, and drive to Savanah's house. However, he couldn't figure out how to poison the guards without actually killing them. He rummaged through the kitchen cabinets looking for some formula of ingredients to slip to the guards, but his hands began to shake and he clenched his teeth in anger. The realization came over him that he couldn't hurt anyone. He cursed to himself and wondered why they made it look so easy on television and in the movies.

Ezekiel looked out the window and saw the two security guards who had been assigned to him were out in the front of the house talking and smoking. They were supposed to look inconspicuous but always managed to stand out. They screamed "security guards" with their tight-fitting open collar pastel shirts and windbreakers with large bulges. Their clear plastic earbuds in their right ear added to the picture as if one needed any more confirmation. The guards were having an animated conversation. Ezekiel couldn't hear what they were talking about but assumed it was about the rebellion. That's all anyone ever seemed to want to talk about anymore, he thought, rolling his eyes.

He knew this was his one chance. He grabbed his duffle bag, which he hadn't bothered to unpack, and dashed toward the back of the house. He hoped that he could get far enough away before they noticed that he was gone. He quietly exited through the glass sliding door, closing it gently behind before, before making good his escape by hopping the small fence.

Ezekiel ran for ten minutes before he stopped on a street that he did not recognize. It didn't bother him though. He was just happy to be out of the house and on his own. But when he looked up to get his bearings, he saw it: the poster of his mother. "Fuck you, I hate you," he yelled at his mom's image. And then he glanced around to make sure no one was watching and tore it down.

It took Ezekiel a little while for him to figure out where he was: Boyle Heights, East LA. Luckily for him, he wasn't too far from his hometown of South Pasadena. He knew hitchhiking was dangerous, but he didn't care. He was willing to take the risk that some pervert would pick him up. That's how badly he wanted—needed—to see Savanah. He didn't have to wait long. Cars stopped to give him a ride because it was so unusual in this day and age to see someone hitchhiking—especially someone so young.

When Ezekiel arrived at Savanah's house, he had to stop himself from running up the front steps and knocking down the door. "Calm down," he told himself as ambled up to it. He rang the doorbell and waited. When no one answered, he give it a hard knock with his fist. A second later, he heard footsteps approaching. Ezekiel braced himself to see the love of his life. Instead, Gina, Savanah's mom, opened the door.

Gina did not look pleased to see Ezekiel. After looking him up and down, she asked, "What do you want?" Gina's angry tone threw Ezekiel for a moment, so when he opened his mouth to respond he couldn't seem to put a coherent sentence together. The only word that came out was "Savanah?"

Gina turned and headed back into the house. She called out, "Savanah, your chink boyfriend is at the door."

Chink? Ezekiel thought. He'd never been called chink before. He had lived in a bubble and never felt the sting of racism in his entire life—at least that he aware of. But what made him the angriest wasn't the fact that she had called him that but that she had used the wrong racial slur.

He was half-Japanese, not half-Chinese. *Jap* would have been more accurate he thought to himself.

Ezekiel opened his mouth to tell Gina, when he saw Savanah coming toward him. The sight of her made him forget what her mom had just called him. Nothing mattered anymore. He had made it. This was the happily-ever-after he had been dreaming about for the last few weeks.

"What are you doing here?" Savanah asked,

The rhetorical question confused Ezekiel. He was about to tell her, "To see you of course" but before he could get the words out of his mouth she's turned on her heels and walked back towards where she'd came from. He stood there a moment unsure of what to do before following her into the living room where a large television was on. She had been watching the rally at Dodgers Stadium. They were replaying footage of the FBI agents being beaten by the crowd, intercut with images of Tricia standing on stage like a feudal warlord from another time.

During a commercial break, Savanah turned to Ezekiel and glared at him. It didn't take a genius to read her thoughts. She was telling him without words that this was all his fault! That he could have stopped it but had not.

Ezekiel said the first thing that came to mind, "I'm sorry." He felt like it was all his fault. She was right, he could have done more. He could have stopped his mother. If he had only done something. Anything, he thought.

"I'm moving," Savanah interrupted Ezekiel's thoughts.

Ezekiel turned and looked at her. He saw tears forming in the corner of her eyes. He wasn't sure he had heard her correctly, "What?" he asked.

"We're going to Texas," Savanah said slower so Ezekiel could understand.

Ezekiel had heard that people were leaving California. Especially those who didn't agree with what was going on. But he never considered that Savanah and her family would be one of them. "It's not safe here anymore," Savanah continued. "The American flag on our porch was taken down and set on fire on our lawn. My daddy had to use a hose to put it out."

Ezekiel's eyes narrowed and the frown on his face seemed to droop lower than his jaw. Savanah kept detailing her family's angst, "We can't wear anything with the American flag on it and my dad has been spit on and pushed by those traitors." Tears dripped down her cheeks and she paused to catch her breath through the tears. "While we were going to shop at Trader Joe's we weren't allowed to enter because my mom refused to sign a petition to leave the United States."

This was the last thing Ezekiel had expected. He had so many things he wanted to say. But the only thing that came out was, "When?"

"Tonight," Savanah told him. "I tried to message you on Facebook, but your account was deleted."

Ezekiel wanted to explain how the security detail had deleted all his accounts and wouldn't even let him play on the computer, but didn't think she wanted to hear it. He had so much he wanted to tell her. He considered—briefly—the idea of asking her to marry him so she wouldn't be able to leave but then dismissed it as silly. She would never say, "yes." Or would she? He couldn't think of any other way of keeping her from leaving. And then an idea occurred to him. He suddenly knew a way. "I'm coming with you," he declared.

Savanah's eyes widened. The tears suddenly gone. "You would go with me? Leave your family and never see them again?"

Ezekiel nodded, not trusting that his voice wouldn't break if he answered out loud.

"Would you do anything for me?" she asked.

Ezekiel nodded again.

"Would you risk your life for me?"

"Yes," Ezekiel said, finally finding his voice.

As soon he said that, Savanah kissed him, this time on the mouth. It was Ezekiel first real kiss and he told himself to remember every second of it because he was convinced it would be one of the best moments of his entire life.

He was so caught up in the moment that he didn't hear the footsteps coming down the hall. In fact, he didn't hear anything until a man cleared his throat. The sound startled Ezekiel but not Savanah. Because she turned toward the man and said, "Daddy, he wants to help."

It took a moment for Ezekiel to recognize the man. He had never met Savanah's father before. He knew he worked for the government but wasn't sure exactly what he did. Now he knew. He was an FBI agent. He was Agent X. Ezekiel's body reacted fiercely to the revelation. His heart pounded like being punched in the chest, he couldn't feel his legs and his hands were shaking. He held on to the arm of the sofa and struggled not to pass out.

#

Tricia entered the safe house first, Rowan by her side. None of their kids were with them. Grace and Noah had gone to the CRM base for a social gathering. Tricia and Rowan had not said a single word since the chaos in the stadium. Even though their bodies were close in proximity, their minds weren't.

Rowan was thinking about what happened at Dodgers Stadium. He could still hear the shots ringing out. He wanted to run and protect his wife, but his legs wouldn't move. No matter how much he willed them to. He felt so weak and hated himself for it.

Tricia was also thinking about what happened at the stadium, but not about Rowan. It was all the violence. And it wasn't just being shot at, it was everything. She has just assumed that California could leave the USA with very little or no bloodshed. Now she saw how silly that idea was. There was going to be a lot of deaths, especially if what happened earlier was any indication of what was to come. President Matthews wasn't going to let them leave without a fight. For a moment, Tricia wondered if she had the stomach for it. It wasn't her death that she was worried about—but everyone's else's that weighed heavily on her. She wondered how she would be able to live with herself if something happened to someone in her family.

"Ezekiel?" Tricia called. She allowed him to stay in his room all day but needed to check in with him periodically to make sure he was still breathing. Tricia frowned when Ezekiel didn't come down the stairs. She called again. Then a third time.

Tricia looked at Rowan with concern etched across her face.

"I'll go check on him," Rowan told his wife, his first words to her in hours. But he stated it without actually looking at her. He hadn't been able to look her in the eyes since Dodgers Stadium. "He's probably sleeping," he said as he went upstairs.

But something was wrong. Tricia, still a mom, with motherly instincts, knew it. She went over to the security guard on duty. "Have you seen, Ezekiel?" she asked.

The guard shook his head. "He hasn't left the house." But just as he finished saying it, Rowan appeared by her side. Tricia knew by the look on her husband's face that Ezekiel was gone before he said it. "He's not in his room."

The guard immediately got on the radio. A moment later, a half-dozen guards and Rowan were searching the house for him. But there was no sign of Ezekiel anywhere. Tricia sat on the couch and began to cry. The tears were mostly because she was worried about her son, but they were also because of everything else that had happened that day.

Tricia wiped away the tears and got a hold of herself. Her sobbing wasn't helping anyone. She knew she was going to be the only one who would be able to find her son. She went to his room and started to look around. The first thing she noticed was that his duffle bag was gone. It was a sign. She knew what it meant, that he had gone on his own. No one who was trying to kidnap him would bother to take his luggage with them.

Tricia began to tear apart the room. She looked in the closet, under the bed, looked for loose floor boards, everywhere. It wasn't until she flipped over the mattress did she find something. A notebook. She was about to yell out to the guards that she had found it but then stopped. Something told her to look through the notebook first.

It was immediately obvious to her that what it contained wasn't good news. Tricia was surprised by her son's anger—especially at her. She knew that her work with the CMS was hurting her family, but she was shocked by how angry her middle son was about it. She could have handled the anger, but she was unprepared to find out that her son was the one working for the FBI!

It hadn't been Rowan after all, as she had originally assumed. She immediately felt bad for thinking her husband betrayed her so quickly. But the duplicity her own child was much worse. She didn't have the words to describe how it felt to be deceived by someone she gave birth to and raised. Ezekiel had always been difficult, but she loved him as much as she loved all her other children. She always passed off his attitude as a prototypical teenage boy. She had been saved from that angst when Noah zoomed through his teens as he consistently had his sights on a military career. Having a passionate goal and an early identity gets one through the adolescent years quite efficiently.

"Find something?" Rowan asked from the doorway.

Tricia quickly closed the notebook as though she were caught doing something wrong. Rowan eyed the book suspiciously and asked, "What did you find?"

"Nothing," Tricia quickly lied. She wasn't sure why she kept Ezekiel's secret. Why she didn't tell Rowan or the security. She told herself it was because she needed time to process it, but it was deeper than that. She couldn't betray her son without talking to him first. She needed to find him more now than ever.

Her prayers were answered because as Rowan was about to ask to see the notebook, there were shouts from the front of the house. Tricia and Rowan ran down the stairs and to the front door where Ezekiel was standing there with his duffle bag. Tricia's first instinct was to strangle him, but she ran to him and hugged him instead.

CHAPTER 13

A Long Train of Abuses and Usurpations

President's broadcast to the nation
President Matthews called for prime-time on all the networks, meaning that for the first time ever he would be appearing on the major cable stations as well as the traditional broadcast networks. He announced that he was going to address the country on what his spokesperson described as "The California Crisis."

At precisely 8p.m. Eastern Time, all the TV screens flashed a red, white and blue background and in flame red italics lettering, the title "Presidential Address: The California Crisis" burst on top of the patriotic background. The letters became brighter and brighter until the title page left the screen and the next image was of President James Matthews III seated behind his desk in the Oval Office with his hands clasped together on top of the desk and a serious facial expression.

"Good evening," he began. "All of us are aware of the rampant criminal activity that is going on in the state of California. There are riots taking place, violence, subversive behavior, looting. There is lawlessness throughout the state. I have asked the governor of California to mobilize the national guard several times, but he has ignored my pleas. His actions show support for these criminal acts. I have no confidence in the ability of the government of the state of California to keep citizens safe. A nation cannot stand together when a part of that nation disregards the law and allows people to violate them. For this reason, I am tonight declaring California in a state of federal emergency. I have placed federal agents from multiple agencies in California to attempt to control the lawless behaviors. Furthermore, my cabinet, along with the military joint chiefs of staff are preparing a coordinated plan to use even a stronger military force to control the state by whatever means necessary. Such a plan will take time to mobilize, but I assure you that California will be returned to peace and safety. The federal agents already in California will do their best to maintain the peace and enforce the law until I am in a position to declare Marshall Law in the state and have the military presence to enforce it. I have also instructed attorney general Adam Reed to file charges against the leader of the California lawbreakers, Tricia Murakami. I will be directing federal agents in California to arrest Mrs. Murakami and bring her to justice. I am asking for all my fellow Americans to pray for peace in California and to work with me and your public servants as we strive to calm the state of emergency and bring much-wanted peace to the citizens of that state. Thank you. And God bless the *United* States of America," he concluded with great emphasis on the word, 'united.'

Ezekiel smiled as he stood on the front porch of the safe house flanked by the security guards. Tricia and Rowan were so unaccustomed to Ezekiel smiling these days that they actually burst out in nervous laughs and then their eyes welled up with tears. They both lurched toward the boy and hugged him. The guards politely turned away from the family reunion.

Not letting go of their boy, Tricia and Rowan ushered him into the latest safe house.

"How did you find us? We just moved to this house a day ago?" she asked.

"I wanted to come back, so I started to ask questions of almost everyone I could and then that led to someone who knew someone and they got me here." Ezekiel's tone was low and slow. His head hung and his eyelids were almost shut. He looked exhausted from his adventure.

"We're not going to lecture you on your escapade. Let us show you your room and you get some rest," Tricia insisted.

Rowan smiled and shook his head in agreement.

"I'll take him upstairs," Rowan asserted, and put his hand on Ezekiel's back as if to guide him off the chair, and up the staircase.

Tricia went into the kitchen to fix herself a cup of tea. She looked through the cupboards for supplies and was delighted that the staff stocked the coffee and tea shelf with the family's favorites. As she microwaved the water, the doorbell rang. It was Jaleel and two members of his staff.

Jaleel didn't hesitate giving her the bad news: "Tricia, I'm afraid you're moving again,"

"Come on! We just got here," Tricia protested.

"Didn't you hear about Matthew's broadcast to the nation tonight?" Jaleel asked.

"No, we've been dealing with a family situation here. Ezekiel…"

Before Tricia could finish Jaleel interrupted, "Matthews laid down another of his gauntlets. You've been specifically targeted as public enemy number one. Right there on national TV. You were named as the leader of the lawless, out-of-control Californians."

"You have to be kidding? What the hell!" Tricia reacted.

"The move is necessary. It's for your family's safety. We have a place where you will all be safe for a longer time. But our intel is saying that this location is compromised and with Matthews naming you for arrest, we have to move you all," Jaleel explained, apologetically.

"Can we do it after Ezekiel rests?" Tricia relented.

"Let me make some calls and see what we can do. It's late tonight, maybe we can push this to the morning, I don't know." Jaleel already had walked away from her and took out his cell phone. He went into a small sitting room next to the living room, closed the French doors and talked on his phone.

Rowan came back down the stairs and Grace was with him. "What's happening?" he asked.

"We have to move—again! Matthews announced live on TV that I am a criminal and there's going to be a manhunt for me," Tricia explained. "They want us to move again. They say it is a safer and hopefully more longer-term place."

"Crap, Trish. This family is being split apart here. They've got you in the crosshairs, Noah on the front lines, Ezekiel running away, Grace and I are the only stable ones here," Rowan complained. He looked down at Grace who appeared disappointed that she was left out of the action figures in the family.

"What do you want me to do? We've gone down this path together—all of us in this family. You want me to turn my back on all the people? Should I not do what is right? I don't want to go all teacher on you, but what if our founding fathers all said, 'Gee, I've got a nice roof over my head, a warm fire and plenty of food. Why should I leave my comfy hearth and fight for independence?'" Tricia barked back.

"I just don't know how much more of this I can take," Rowan added.

"*You* can take? Come on Rowan. Matthews is positioning himself to be dictator of the U.S. If we don't stand up to this, then the whole idea of this country will disappear. At least California will carry on the dream of a free republic. You're either with us or against us," her tone was emphatic.

"Whoa! That's goddamn strong. With us or against us? So, if I decide to stay out of all this, that means I'm against…you? Our marriage? Our family?" He looked down at Grace who was studying both of them in this, now a full-fledged argument. Grace leaned her body against her mom's.

"That didn't come out right. I didn't mean anything about our family, or our marriage. I'm just emotional right now. There is a lot of heavy weighing on me. Can you just support me for a little while longer? I'm sure once the CMS and the state declare the intention of secession, any number of new figureheads will emerge for Matthews to sling his hate toward." Tricia put both her hands on Rowan's shoulders, but he was unresponsive. He couldn't give her eye contact. Grace moved away from the two of them.

Jaleel returned and, after polite hellos to Rowan and Grace, he announced, "It will be OK to stay here until the morning, but we are tripling the guard. We'll move your personal things out tonight. First thing in the morning you'll move to the more permanent location."

Rowan and Tricia nodded. Jaleel opened the front door and a team of workers came in and started to pack up the house. A new security guard walked in behind the movers and promptly stationed himself on an easy chair. Tricia and Rowan looked over at him and didn't need to ask.

#

President Matthews called a meeting of his military joint chiefs of staff, his chief of staff, and his Secretary of State. Notably absent in this meeting were any members of Congress, his own Secretary of Defense, the Vice-President and any number of people that traditionally and logically should be present at a planning meeting of that magnitude.

"You undoubtedly know why I have assembled you here. Let me get to the point. How quickly can we mobilize a force large enough to control and stabilize California?" Matthews said, without looking up from some documents that he was leafing through.

The Chairman of the Joint Chiefs of Staff, four-star general Jonathan Tuttle responded with precise, immediate cadence, "Mr. President, we have no models for such an operation. We would have to build the logistics, train the forces, plan the operation. In short, this is a massive undertaking."

"Some time ago, your people defeated Sadam Hussein who had the third largest army in the world and you did that, in what, a month? I need California under control immediately. Now, we have troops in bases, planes in airfields, and a large naval fleet all stationed already in that state. What could take so long, General? Tell me?"

Matthews' voice barked the last two sentences as he looked directly at Tuttle.

"If I may, Mister President, although to the media that operation appeared to be over quickly, the planning of it was years in the making and the logistics to accomplish it were also being assembled and shipped to bases for years. Models for fighting a Middle East war had been debated in our military academies and at the highest level for decades. Further, the coordination between the different branches was intricate and took time." Tuttle responded firmly.

Mathews interrupted with contempt in his tone, "Is there anything else on your list of why we can't mobilize this force immediately?"

"Franky, yes, Mr. President, you are talking about our troops taking action against their own people. When I mentioned training, this is going to take intensive and highly specialized training, you might want to call it re-training of the mindset of our troops. You saw what happened when you used troops to defend that dam. We had hundreds of desertions from the ranks. The troops are not mentally prepared to do combat with fellow citizens. We don't have any reference for such training, we've never even thought of such a scenario. To rush into this quickly would be chaos among the troops. This is a total restructuring of the military."

"So, this can't be done—is that what you're telling me?" Matthews demanded. "Do you all agree with General Tuttle?" He looked around at all the military chiefs who all nodded in agreement with Tuttle's assessment.

"Can I at least count on Seal teams or special forces to be prepared immediately?" Matthews yelled.

Tuttle, in complete control, continued to speak for the others, "As I said, Mr. President, we would have the same problems in mobilizing special ops troops to act on fellow citizens. Look at it this way, there is a high probability that many of those troops are native Californians. You're asking something that is right out of the *next civil war*. Brothers against brothers, cousins against cousins. Our military is just not the same as 150 years ago. Our society is not the same as it was 150 years ago. These special forces are not robots."

"Then get me robots, damnit. We have the largest state in the union planning to split off from this country and you are all telling me that there is not a damn thing we can do about it. I am the one being preemptive here. I see this coming down to a battleground and I will control and stop this. This is my destiny." Matthews fumed so aggressively, he had to pause to catch a breath. "That's enough. I want you all to leave and prepare for the inevitable. I don't care what it takes, we need a large, brute force to invade California. And at that point, the enemy will not be citizens of this country—Tell that to your troops, the enemy will all be traitors and saboteurs. I want robots!" Yelling hoarsely, he waved his hand and dismissed the meeting. After the room emptied, Matthews called in Peter McKenzie, "I want the FBI and the CIA directors in here in an hour."

The new safe house for the Murakami's was quite accommodating. It was located in a rundown section of West Adams in LA where the mansions of the silent film stars long ago were abandoned and left to decay. The area was slowly being re-gentrified, so rehabbed mansions stood surrounded by completely abandoned houses in complete shambles. One of the old pale pink beauties was entirely rehabbed by the CMS and refitted with state-of-the-art security and technology. When the Murakami family was moved to the house they all were quite impressed, even Ezekiel. It was a compound, with stone walls surrounding it, metal gates at the front and a pool in the back. The Murakami's had never seen anything like it, not even on their best vacation. They had 24-hour security and the live guards protected the entire perimeter of the home, not just stationed out the front door as at the last safe house.

Tricia and Rowan let Ezekiel's runaway be forgotten in all their enthusiasm for this new home. Ezekiel made a beeline for the pool after a quick, approving check of his new huge bedroom. He even made the comment, "Mom, you can protest all you want if this is what we get out of it!" Grace also loved her room, and there was even a room set aside for Noah for when he could visit. The house presented itself like a playground to the family. Rowan and Tricia had a sound-proof study big enough for both of them to have separate spaces to work and fully equipped with desktops and 32" monitors. For a moment, the Murakami's were a family again, but that moment didn't last long.

After a morning of settling in, Jaleel paid a visit to the 'ranch' as Ezekiel dubbed it because he was told by one of the guards that an old cowboy actor had built the property in the 1930s.

Jaleel came to inform Tricia that she was needed again for a rally. They talked alone in the study so that no one could hear, not even Rowan. The plan was that she was going to be flown to San Francisco for a large gathering. This rally was a pure recruiting function, the first of a new concept that CMS devised. It was a program of staging pop-up rallies, just like the pop-up stores were becoming the rage in retailing. CMS was going to hold these pop-ups all around the state to solidify support for the rebellion, recruit for the CRM and other newly created staff positions needed in the infrastructure of a new country. They wanted Tricia on a private jet that afternoon for an early evening rally in San Francisco.

Right on schedule, Tricia flew into San Francisco International in the late afternoon. The spontaneous travel and the bang-bang mechanics of the trip didn't sap Tricia's energy. She was excited to take the message of the rebellion to northern California and eager to gauge the feeling of the Californians there.

As her motorcade approached Giants Stadium, the response of the northern Californians became abundantly clear. A quarter mile from the stadium and the streets were filled with people almost shoulder-to-shoulder. Tricia and Jaleel in their SUV were downright joyous at the site of so many people in the streets so far away from the stadium when just hours before CMS announced the pop-up rally for all interested. If this many people gathered this far from the stadium, the stadium must be packed. They assessed that this was a great success already. The SUV had to slow to a snail's pace to navigate through the crowd. Smartly, Jaleel and his staff had allowed plenty of time to arrive before the rally.

The crowd was in a frenzy, and the shouts from the crowd could be acutely heard inside Tricia and Jaleel's car. The chants were even angrier than other rallies. The crowd shouted: "Throw out USA!" "Leave Our Land!" "We Don't Need YOU Uncle Sam." "Uncle Sam-You're Not in MY

FAMILY" "Uncle Sam-We're disowning You!" The iconic poster of Tricia was everywhere. As they inched along the streets toward the stadium, no one in the crowd identified Tricia in her car, even though all the vehicles had the CMS seal prominently displayed on the doors, because of the dark tinted windows. The crowd recognized that the vehicles were part of the rally, but they could have been carrying anyone.

"Do you think we should open the windows and greet the crowd as we drive?" Tricia asked Jaleel. She was visibly enthused by the energy of the crowd and excited to get the event underway.

Jaleel thought for a moment, but he was distracted by his phone ringing with several calls all at once. "Hold on a minute. I'm getting some news here from someone up ahead. I'll check on when we should let our presence known. We want to make sure we have the maximum impact." Jaleel listened on the phone. "Really poor reception. Maybe too many people on their phones in the area. Can't really hear what they are trying to say. But let's wait on opening the windows…we're almost there now anyway."

"The enthusiasm is so powerful. I can't wait to be with them," Tricia enthused.

Their car turned onto King Street in front of the stadium and they saw that they couldn't have been more wrong about the mood of the crowd and the reason so many people were in the streets around the stadium. Many trucks, vans, SUVs, and cars with prominent markings labeled, FBI blocked the gates to the stadium. The entrances to the stadium were bedlam. Everywhere she looked she could see nothing but people pushing and shoving. No one had been let into the stadium. The federal government was blocking another massive rally. FBI agents on loudspeakers shouted at the crowd and the crowd shouted back with their own bullhorns and other devices. Punches were thrown, people were falling down, words such as 'Arrest' 'You will be hurt' 'Disperse' were heard coming from the FBI loudspeakers and bullhorns. People were being grabbed by agents and handcuffed and thrown into vans. Stones were flung at the agents. It was a violent, out of control mob on both sides. The difference being that the FBI had weapons and seemed poised to use them any moment.

And then the inevitable happened. Shots were fired. It was hard to determine from which side, but once the first shots went off it had a domino effect . The FBI barked through their loudspeakers, "You will be arrested if you stay here. Go home. Do not attempt to rally here. We cannot guarantee your safety" Their warnings were repeated over and over. An FBI agent was seen being shot in his bullet-proof vest and then falling off a car roof. The FBI returned fire at the spot where they thought the bullets rang out. The crowd pressed on rather than heed the warnings of the agents. Like at the Dodger stadium rally, the mass of the crowd and the hesitation of the agents to release the full fury of their gun power, overwhelmed the agents. But this time, rather than being in isolated pockets, the federal agents stood in groups and hung stronger than at Dodger Stadium. More shots rang out from the agents into the crowd and the crowd rushed the agent's positions. Sporadic gunfire from the crowd rang out toward the agents.

All the while Tricia, Jaleel and the staff in the other three SUVs in their motorcade watched in horror at what was taking place in front of them. Jaleel gave the word to the driver to back out of the area and leave, but the crowd was too large. The drivers had to open their windows and make sure of their identity as being with CMS or the crowd would have turned on them. The markings on the vehicles weren't enough to keep the crowd at bay.

It didn't take long for the crowd to identify that these SUVs were carrying Tricia to the rally and chats of "Tricia" and "CMS" rose to a roar with the crowd. The crowd's affection was unfortunate as it drew the FBI on the motorcade like hungry dogs. A large team of blue windbreakers headed right for the four SUVs. As they got closer to the SUVs, they stopped and began to fire at the cars. Their hesitation of earlier was lost on these prime targets and they fired with abandon.

Jaleel yelled, "Down! Down!" Because the cars were not bullet-proof, bullets ripped through the sidewalls of the SUVs with a sound like a can opener on a tin of tuna and ended in a slap of metal. A bloodcurdling scream was heard and then Jaleel realized Tricia was hit. With her blood quickly soaking her clothes, he couldn't make out how many times she was shot. "Tricia has been hit, get to hospital, now!" Jaleel screamed to the driver.

With that, the drivers honked their horns furiously, increased their speed and the crowd cleared a path for them to exit. The crowd screamed 'Tricia' and pointed at the cars trying to exit and the crowd parted for them to leave. The FBI tried to chase after them, but the crowd converged on those agents on foot and closed up the path. The crowd put obstacles in the way of any FBI vehicles trying to follow Tricia's motorcade.

Helicopters appeared overhead and military style vehicles arrived on the outskirts of the crowd. The crowd again cleared a path as the vehicles had the markings of the CRM. The CRM vehicles drove directly toward the FBI positions. The FBI was grossly outnumbered and the CRM soldiers ordered the agents to drop their weapons. They did as commanded and the soldiers jumped from their armored vehicles and surrounded the agents at each of the entrance gates where they were stationed. The CRM soldiers took the federal agents as prisoners.

Now, a distance away from the stadium, the SUV with Tricia and Jaleel sped toward a hospital. With all the blood covering her, Tricia looked seriously hurt to Jaleel's untrained eye and time was critical.

The events of the day were broadcast live on the networks. As the action around the stadium was well under control by the CRM soldiers. Governor Herrmann appeared on the broadcast. "As you can see unfold here today in San Francisco, California suffered yet another egregious attack by federal authorities trying to block our constitutional right to assemble and free speech. Further, Tricia Murakami was seriously injured trying to arrive at the event and was rushed to the hospital in serious condition. We will keep you posted on her status as we have news."

Herrmann paused to make an announcement, "I am ordering all FBI offices in the state, all CIA offices in the state, all ICE offices in the state and all DEA offices and all officers assigned to these offices to evacuate the state of California immediately. Within 24 hours, our state police with the assistance of the national guard and I have asked for the support of the California Republic Military or CRM to inspect each and every facility of these agencies and ensure that all federal personnel has evacuated their posts in the state of California. Any federal agent continuing to work for the federal government within the state of California will be taken into custody by this combined force."

Herrmann's statement was most significant in uniting the CRM, an arm of the CMS, with the resources of the state of California. The governor held true to his commitment and 24 hours after the San Francisco event, an event that was now being called the Battle at the Bay, teams of CRM, bolstered by national guard and state police, swept through federal buildings all over the state to clear out any agents working out of those buildings. The buildings were locked and in the days that followed these teams did follow-up raids on the residences of federal agents to ensure they had either left the state or surrendered. The media had full coverage of the raids to the suspected agents' homes. Some of the images showed CRM teams breaking down doors of homes only to find them empty, but other images showed federal agents being taken into custody. The response of the citizens of California to these images was widely supportive.

In those next several days after the Battle of the Bay, there was no news of Tricia's condition.

One of Jaleel's assistants showed up at the Brentwood safe house, 'the ranch,' to personally tell the Murakami's the news of Tricia. Noah was there as well to support his dad and siblings. The assistant, Kerry Calee, let them all know what she could, "I don't know the specific nature of Tricia's injuries, but it looks like she will be OK. She was struck by several high caliber bullets, but miraculously, no vital organs were hit. She is safe, under 24-hour guard, she is conscious. Unfortunately, we can't risk any of you visiting her at the present time. She will need to stay in the San Francisco area hospital for some time. I will personally keep you all immediately updated as I know more."

"How could the feds have mounted such a strong presence at a pop-up event like that? It is impossible for them to mount such a coordinated action like that in such a short time. They must have been tipped off," Noah remarked with a mixture of sadness and anger.

Kerry responded, "That's what we were thinking, but no one knew about the rally prior to it being announced except for a small circle. We are looking very, very closely into that."

"No one here even knew where she was going. I thought she was just going to the headquarters for the afternoon," Rowan added.

"Yes, I know that. Still, someone tipped them off. We'll find out." Kerry closed.

CHAPTER 14

Right Ought to be Free and Independent States

"We can't confirm nor deny whether Tricia Murakami is dead or alive," Jad Stanton, the president's Chief of Staff, reported to the full cabinet seated around the large conference table in the White House. "No one has seen her since the incident at Giants Stadium."

This was not the news that President James Mathews had wanted to hear. But it soon got worse. The director of the CIA stood next. He reported that the California ballot proposition to leave the US would win by a landslide. Worse still, the analysts in the State Department predicted that such an event would trigger other states with similar leanings to follow; namely, New York, Washington, Oregon and Hawaii. Ironically, most of the South didn't care if California left or not. They hated California with the same passion they hated the Yankees. Maybe more. But Matthews knew how important the west coast state really was. Not only was it one of the biggest contributors to the federal budget, but the natural resources and location also made it one of the states the country could not afford to lose.

"Out," Matthews screamed, not yelling at anyone in particular. The entire cabinet rushed out the door. No one wanted to be on the receiving end of the president's wrath. The only one who stayed was Peter McKenzie, the president's chief administrative assistant, and in reality, his true chief of staff. Peter had been with Matthews since his first political ambitions and was his most trusted and devoted staff person. It was Peter's idea to name Jad Stanton his chief of staff in order to gather political favors. Peter had no interest in titles or protocol. McKenzie was also Matthews' chief strategist and speech writer in all of his political campaigns.

When the room was cleared, McKenzie told the president what he already knew. "Your numbers have gone way down since this all started. They think you are weak and aren't handling this very well."

Matthews slammed his hand down on the table. "You don't think I know this, Peter? I want to do something, but my hands are tied."

McKenzie smiled.

"You have an idea?" the President asked hopefully. When McKenzie didn't answer right away, Matthews quickly grew impatient. "Don't just sit there smiling at me—tell me."

As the President waited for a response, he looked his confidant in the eyes. McKenzie had always known what to do and when. After all, it was pretty much McKenzie who got Matthews elected when everyone else thought it was mission impossible. The President had no illusions about him though. He figured more than half of what he did was illegal or so close to illegal it was hard to tell where the illegality of his actions began.

"I can't exactly tell you," McKenzie told his boss. This was not the response that President Matthews had expected. Matthews was about to ask what he meant by that when McKenzie continued. "Plausible deniability. The less you know, the better."

CHAPTER 14

The President wasn't used to not being in the know. In fact, he prided himself on knowing every facet of what was going on in his administration at all times. Only McKenzie knew this, but he had bugged every office and cell phone of any person who worked for him. But for the first time in a long time, President Matthews felt like everything was going to work out. Matthews had complete faith in Peter McKenzie.

"In the meantime, I've arranged a speech for you tonight in front of the full Congress," McKenzie said. "We're going to reassure the nation that they are in good hands and that your hands are the only ones that can do it."

President Matthews and McKenzie began to write the speech right away. Matthews knew it would be the most important one of his presidency—maybe the most important speech in the history of the nation. McKenzie reminded him that he needed to sound strong in an effort to win over the population. Their aids made sure they did not use the word "war" but instead "rebellion"—since rebellion was part of the vast presidential powers and wars were under the jurisdiction of Congress. In a few hours, he was sure that he had written the best speech of his life.

In mid-morning that same day a white late model work van with the blue and red District Department of Transportation (DDOT) logo on its side doors pulled to the curb on Northwest Drive near 1st Street NW in Washington DC. On the roof rack where two black plumbing pipes. The van's hazard lights began to flash and two workmen exited the cab of the van. They placed orange cones around the truck in every direction. In no hurry they began to rope off a square section of the grass and spray painted the edges of the square. Approximately

20 minutes later an identical van parked on Southwest Drive and New Jersey Avenue and began to do the same procedures on that section of lawn. Both groups of workers removed the pipes from the roof racks and laid then in the cordoned off square. They took out shovels and stuck them in the ground. The men then sat on the curb, took out thermos', drank coffee and smoked cigarettes.

Some time later, several other vans arrived on Northwest Drive, Northeast Drive, Southwest Drive and Southeast Drive and all did same work to what looked like dig through the ground to replace pipes. In all there were 12 work vans doing construction in the streets that circled the Capital Building in Washington DC.

A distance away from Capitol Hill at the Department of Homeland Security on Nebraska Street, the Deputy Director of DC security, Chad Hoskins, is summoned to the ground monitoring room. The room has real-time images of every section of Washington DC flashing continuously on monitors that cover the entire walls of this large square office space.

"Chad, we have some suspicious activity around the Capital Building." Delwan Thomas pointed to a frozen frame on the north wall of the room. The 12 work trucks were shown circling the capital building. From the monitor view the position of the trucks resembled the numbers on a clock.

"We checked with DDOT and no repair work was scheduled for that area," Delwan added.

"That doesn't mean anything, Dee. One hand doesn't know what the other is doing over there. It's run like the Army. Dig a hole then fill it up," Hoskins said, staring at the images. "Take me into real time." The pictures showed the workmen at each truck sitting on the grass or eating lunch or digging up the lawn.

"Tell ya what, keep monitoring that area and keep me posted," Hoskins said.

An hour later, Thomas typed an instant message to Hoskins stating that the men by one of the trucks seemed to be working on the pipes in an unusual way. Hoskins rushed back to the monitoring room.

"Blow that up for me," Hoskins snapped at Thomas. "Looks like some kind of handle he's wrenching on to that pipe."

"They're all doing the same thing," Thomas added. The monitors focused onto the other work sites.

"I think we have to get on this. I'm going to call in some teams to check this out closer." Hoskins said.

At Capitol Hill the workers at each truck site concentrated on tooling one of the pipes. They attached a handle, then a sight and then a trigger mechanism. The pipes became RPGs and workers were firing teams. A worker at each site went into the back of the van and brought out a rocket for the RPG. With coordinated timing, they all began to set up in position between trees and aimed the RPGs in the direction of the Capitol Building.

As the firing teams readied their weapons they were unaware that on the streets behind them two armored vehicles screeched to a stop at each location and squads of Homeland Security officers in full SWAT gear ran toward the RPG teams.

Now clearly with loaded weapons pointed at the Capital Building, the Homeland officers didn't hesitate and began firing. The RPG teams turned toward the charging officers and pulled out automatic weapons from underneath their bright red and orange safety vests and they returned fire. Several of the men carrying the RPGs shot their rocket at the armored vehicles and they exploded on contact. A fierce gun battle was on and although outnumbered, the RPG teams had the advantage of the tree cover. They held their own, but very quickly more reinforcements came for the Homeland officers. This second wave were regular US military and the RPG teams were impossibly outnumbered. Of the 24 men that made up the RPG teams, 15 lay dead and the rest surrendered to the overwhelming force.

Just as President Matthews was putting the finishing touches to his speech, a dozen secret service agents entered the room. They were under orders to evacuate the president. Matthews opened his mouth to ask what the hell was going on when he glanced at Peter McKenzie. Peter motioned for him to calm down and leave. Within minutes, The President was on a helicopter headed to a safe bunker.

In the chopper, the President demanded more detail. "Peter, give it to me."

"We successfully stopped a cell of California rebels from attacking Capitol Hill. It appears that Mr. Rivera, the Veteran's Administration shooter was not alone." McKenzie said.

Mathews was in shock at the news. *An attack? What the hell was wrong with these people?* And then a thought occurred to him. He asked McKenzie, "When?"

"Tonight," said McKenzie.

Hearing that, Matthew's face suddenly turned red. *They were trying to kill me. They were attacking my presidency*, Matthews told himself.

"And we think Capitol Hill wasn't their only target. We have reason to believe they were planning on attacking the White House, the FBI headquarters, Supreme Court Building, and maybe more. We're still uncovering facts as we speak."

For the briefest of moments, James Matthews wondered if any of this was actually true. He remembered the words Peter had told him just a few hours before, "plausible deniability." However, after giving it some thought, he realized that it didn't matter. To him, it was real. And that was good enough. He knew this brazen plot was the gift.

"Has anyone spoken to Mr. Rivera?" President Matthews asked.

The McKenzie shook his head. "We found him in his cell this morning. Apparently, he hung himself." The Director paused to let that sink in, before continuing: "But he left a note bragging about what the rebels were going to do tonight. Basically, confirming what we had uncovered. Good thing we found the note in time. I hope that piece of shit rots in hell."

Once news of the rebel plot went viral, the federal buildings were all put on lock down and armed soldiers could be seen on every street in D.C. Public opinion quickly began to shift back to Matthews. This was his moment and he knew it. His speech in front of Congress was rescheduled by just three days.

President James Matthews began to rewrite his talk to the nation immediately after the aborted attack. At the same time, his team drafted a new executive order that would give him extra powers needed to provide him with a fighting chance against the rebels. The attack gave him renewed confidence sense of purpose. It wasn't the first time that he felt he was on the righteous side of history.

When the morning of his address arrived, Matthews' trip from the secure bunker to the floor of Capitol Hill was smooth. Washington D.C. was entirely locked down now after more and more of the conspiracy was being uncovered by the day. No cars or pedestrians were allowed on the streets after six p.m. When the president arrived in the hall, he was surprised that Congress was only slightly more than half full. He was told by his aids that all the Democrats and the delegations from New York and California were boycotting. But those in attendance cheered loudly for Matthews.

They need me, President Matthews thought. *Sheep need their shepherd, or they will get lost or killed by a wolf.* This was generally Matthews personal philosophy when it came to dealing with Congress but he could see it more clearly than ever in the eyes of the Republicans he saw in front of him. This was the sign that what he was about to do was the right thing.

"My fellow Americans," he began. He tried to look strong but vulnerable. "Tonight, we find our great American experiment on a cliff. If we are not careful, the winds of change can destroy what we have spent almost the last two hundred fifty years building. As your president, I will not let that happen. Not under my watch. Not now. Not ever."

The senators and congressmen and women give him a standing ovation for almost an entire minute. When the applause died down, the president continued: "Just a few days ago, the FBI uncovered a plot by a group of radical extremist rebels from the state of California who attempted to take down our institutions and our way of life. Luckily, because of the hard work of our law enforcement, we were able to stop them before they were able to follow through with their plans. But next time, we may not be so lucky. We no longer have the luxury of debating and compromising. That time has now passed. We need to fight back. But to do so, we must do something that others and myself naturally find extremely distasteful." It was at this moment that Mathews laid out his plan. He was issuing an executive order that made it illegal for the press to mention what was going on in California or New York. He also made it against the law to openly support the rebellion in person or over social media. In addition, he was suspending the writ of habeas corpus, allowing the indefinite detention of disloyal persons without trial. President Matthews finished this part of his speech by telling the nation, "However distasteful these may be, I feel that they are the only way we can keep ourselves from going over that cliff. I promise every single American and to the mighty Lord Himself that as soon as order has been restored to our great country, these freedoms will be returned two-fold."

President Matthews took a deep breath before getting to the part that he and Peter had spent the most time on. "It is with great reservation that I am ordering the United States military to suppress the rebellion. To the rebels in California and New York, this is your last chance to disperse and put down your weapons. If you do not, there will be no mercy. I assure you that I will use all the resources of the United States government to bring peace and unity back again to our great nation."

While the president was making his speech, a selected group of the U.S. army—made up predominantly of men and women the Midwest and the South—were streaming over the New York border. Unlike California, the Big Apple had not created any kind of defense force. Most in the state still believed that there was a chance for a peaceful resolution. That was why the army encountered very little resistance on its way to New York City. As the first troops entered Manhattan, some New Yorkers took pot shots at the troops with their legal—and sometimes illegal—handguns. But when the soldiers fired back at them with overwhelming force, usually killing them and everyone around them, the lesson had been learned. From that moment on, people stayed in their apartments. Many tried to write about what they saw or post their pictures on their social media accounts but because of Matthews executive order, no one outside of the NYC was able to read it. In other words, no one knew what was going on.

But Manhattan was not the army's primary objective. Instead, it was to capture Chris Haynes, the governor of the state of New York, and bring him to trial for treason. Because they had been following him for weeks, they knew exactly where he was. He and his family were asleep in the governor's mansion. The soldiers had no trouble taking out the governor's security team who were not prepared for such a brazen assault.

The governor was dreaming about all the money he was going to make as a consultant in his retirement when he heard a loud bang and crash. He sat up out of bed and looked at his wife, who was just opening her eyes, but before he could ask her what the noise was, men in fatigues rushed in, armed with assault rifles drawn.

"Put your hands in the air," a soldier demanded.

The governor's wife immediately put her hands in the air, but Haynes did not. Instead, with his back leaning on the headboard, he asked the soldiers, "Who are you? What is this about?" When the governor did not get an answer right away, he snapped out of the bed. He stiffened his body and began to move toward the lead intruder. He was shaking with anger and his fists were clenched at his sides. He looked as if he was going to attack the intruders. He yelled, "You have no right to be…" He did not get to finish his sentence. The soldiers opened fire on him. The governor's wife screamed as his flesh and bone splattered everywhere from the high caliber weapons. She took the brunt of it as she became covered in blood and body debris. His blood dripped off her face while she wailed. The governor's body landed on top of her, she jerked in fright and she collapsed on the bed in shock.

CHAPTER 15

He Has…sent Hither Swarms of Officers to Harass Our People

Gordon Newton called a meeting of the CMS cabinet immediately after Matthews' address. He invited governor Herrmann and his staff to the meeting. As soon as Herrmann and his people arrived at CMS headquarters, they were led to the largest conference room in the building. Newton and his staff were already waiting inside. The ambiance of the room reflected the substantial financial resources that the CMS had at its disposal. The enormous conference table was naturally sourced redwood, the chairs were ergonomic, audio and video control stations sat on top of the table in three different locations and pull-down screens were evident on each wall. Even the extra side chairs that lined the walls were plush and comfortable. It was acoustically perfect for picking up a speaker from any part of the room and with no matter how many people occupied the space. It was sound-proofed and could lock-down to be impenetrable if needed.

After introductory salutations all around the room, the senior people took seats around the long conference table. Thirty people sat around the table; with the adjunct staff seated in the side chairs that lined the walls, bringing the total to fifty people there.

CHAPTER 15

The addition of the governor and his staff didn't change the mood of the CMS personnel. Many of Newton's people typed away on tablets while they waited for the opening remarks of the meeting. Similarly, Herrmann's staffers did the same. Then Newton called the meeting to order.

"First, I would like to take a moment and ask all of us to honor the fallen Californians who made the ultimate sacrifice for our country." Newton bowed his head. As he stood in silence, everyone in the room paid their respects in the same way.

After that long pause, he resumed. "It is quite clear that we face armed conflict with the United States. Not once has he or his secretary of state reached out to myself or Governor Herrmann to negotiate an understanding of the needs of our people. But, negotiation is not his style in foreign relations. I am not telling anyone here anything new to say that he lives under the delusion that the United States is invincible and can swagger throughout the world and do as it, or more accurately, as he pleases. You all are also aware that his presidency is attempting to build a monarchy for him. Both Governor Herrmann and I have had long personal discussions about the role California will play into Matthews' plans if we proceed with secession. Yes, secession can benefit Matthews and his agenda to take complete and long-lasting control of the United States. We secede, and Matthews makes a strong case to the American people that he is needed to continue leading to quell the rebellion. Even if our secession is successful, Matthews will make the argument that strong leadership must be maintained to prevent other states from breaking off and the eventual dissolution of the United States as we know it today. Much like Franklin Delano Roosevelt was needed in World War II, Matthews may be able to get his terms continued. Our intelligence has reported that his aides have already secretly drafted legislation to propose that the term limit of the presidency be abolished and a new system established. Essentially, this creates the presidency into a life term. I bring this up here today to remind us what we are dealing with here and to affirm our resolve in the necessary steps we must take ahead." He looked around the room to measure the reaction of everyone.

"But, the time for rhetoric is over. We are in an action mode. The California Movement for Secession in partnership with the governor's office has put all the pieces together to secede from the union. Economic, social programs, military, security, education, health, and welfare." Newton paused and looked at Herrmann. "Well, that's all I have to say at this point as an overview of where we are at. I am now going to turn over the floor to the interim President of California, Rich Herrmann, Rich."

The room exploded in applause as Herrmann stood. "Thank you, thank you. And, thank you Vice-President Newton." Herrmann paused as applause erupted at the announcement that Gordon Newton would be his vice-president. Newton stood and acknowledged the applause, then sat again. "Gordon has agreed to come on board in this administration as my vice-present and I couldn't be happier that he will be in this position. We will shape this administrative team as a true partnership with collaboration and delegation of duties very differently than how U.S. presidents have used their vice-president. But, we are not gathered today for accolades or celebrations. We have much to do. This is a War Room. For the rest of this meeting I am asking for full reports from our secretaries of the interior, defense, state, and attorney general."

Herrmann paused, noted the recognition of everyone in the room at the language and titles being introduced for the first time. There was not a single look of surprise. He was naming his administration right then and they were all receptive. This was the evolution of a new country unfolding in front of these closest aides.

"I would like to turn to Tom Huang, the Secretary of State and my former Chief of Staff. Tom…"

Huang stood with a large bound document clutched tightly in his hands that he was going to use as a reference for his report. Huang spoke for forty-five minutes about California's position in the world, the work needed to be done to establish this new nation, possibly making a cooperative relationship with the US, and other big-picture issues of foreign relations. After Huang finished, he introduced and relinquished the floor to the other newly appointed officials of the administration. Each stood with the same lack of fanfare as Huang did. All their reports were factual and, although supportive of the secession, all pointed out the weaknesses that California would experience once the separation was complete. Still, they all concurred that everything was in place, or as much as it could be at this stage, to separate from the union.

The reports lasted four hours, in which they packed in about as much data into these sharp minds as possible. The meeting was also audio recorded so if anything was missed those with security clearance could have access to the replay. A full transcript was promised to be typed up as soon as possible and Newton suggested that this be used like an encyclopedia for staff to use for decision making in the months ahead. The Attorney General report called for a constitutional convention to be convened as soon as humanly possible to draft the first constitution of the country of California. She also called for the current state laws to remain intact until a new constitution was in place. Federal laws will obviously not be applicable to the citizens of California and no federal taxes would be sent to the US.

At the end of the four hours one of the junior staff persons seated along the wall near the back of the room raised his hand and asked, "What's the news on Tricia?"

Newton's eyes softened as he stood to address the question. The room fell silent and no one attended to their tablets, notepads, or cell phones. All eyes were on Newton as he stood pensive for a moment. He looked at some papers spread out on the conference table in front of him. He then glanced at Jaleel Henry. Henry gave the slightest of nods as if to signal his approval to answer candidly. Then Henry punched a text into his phone. Newton thought for a moment longer. A moment that seemed peculiar to most everyone in the room. The silence and the body language between Newton and Henry had everyone thinking the worst about Tricia and her recovery from the attack.

Just as the moment became the most uncomfortable, Newton spoke, "Well, why don't we let Tricia tell you herself?" Jaleel Henry stood and opened the conference room doors. By opening both doors, everyone expected or assumed that Tricia would be making a dramatic entrance in a wheelchair or other assistance. Tears already welled in many of the faces of the staff. Much to the surprise of all there, Tricia walked confidently into the room. There were whispers and a few gasps along with the some 'huhs' and 'what's?' from those that could muster a word out of their shock. Everyone stood spontaneously. Tricia walked over to the conference table and stood next to Gordon Newton and Rich Herrmann. Herrmann appeared as surprised as anyone in the room.

Tricia smiled. "The rumors of my demise have been greatly exaggerated," she said, waving a fist triumphantly in the air.

The room let out a collected guffaw and a round of deafening applause. Then, Tricia motioned for them all to sit back down. "I was grazed in the attack in San Francisco," she continued, "but my wounds were relatively minor. Oh, it hurt, don't get me wrong…" Which was met with more chuckles and soft comments.

"I was released from the hospital within two hours. I was struck by a bullet in my side and another just grazed my right calf. The wound to the side entered into my love handle area…nice way to get an emergency liposuction…" She got her biggest laughs from that quip. She paused as she collected herself as well. "The shot must have been deflected before it reached me because the surgeons said it landed lazily and rested mainly in fat layers and just a bit of muscle. The second shot grazed my calf and I was wounded a bit more seriously than a road rash from a bike fall. I'm fine. Excellent in fact." She smiled and gave a look that conveyed her affection for all there.

Her look turned more serious and vulnerable as she continued, "It was Jaleel's idea to maximize Matthew's aggression against us and use the shooting as a rallying cry to our people." Tricia paused to allow her colleagues to react. There were nods and affirmative statements given with support and relief. "I'm ready to do what is needed to push forward." Strong, controlled applause erupted. Tricia took a seat.

Gordon Newton stood. "Only a small circle of us new about Tricia's condition and now we were ready to let all of you on this strategy. We may have other plans for keeping Tricia's health under wraps to the general public for a while longer, so her vitality is top secret among all of you here today. This is not to be shared with a soul other than those in this room. No loved ones, other colleagues here at headquarters, water cooler chat, nothing. Tricia herself has agreed not to return home and her family has even been kept out of the loop. This is how strategic her condition is to remain."

Newton stopped, looked around the room as if looking into the eyes of each and every one there. He seemed satisfied with the looks he collected back. "We also have another issue to discuss. The fires." He looked down at the papers spread out in front of him on the table, picked up three pages and studied them. "I've been a Californian all my life and I have never seen this many fires, with this much destructive force spreading at one time here. This just doesn't seem like a natural occurrence."

#

Each of the five agents were heavily camouflaged in colors that blended into the terrain of the area. They each carried a locked case that was a four-foot long by 2.5-foot wide rectangle and under normal circumstances you would've presumed they were carrying pool cues or bottles of fine wine. But these were far from normal circumstances.

Their location was not random. One roamed just outside the historic and picturesque town of Ojai,

CHAPTER 15   183

California. The second walked through the brush north of Ventura, California, a solidly middle to upper-middle-class area and the county seat. The third sat against a tree in the foothills of the Santa Monica Mountains on the outskirts of wealthy Bel-Air. The mansions of old Los Angeles families where a stone's throw from that spot. The fourth stood in brown, dry waist high tallgrass near San Fernando, California, a little nugget entirely surrounded by the city of LA. The fifth parked on a street on the outskirts of Santa Clarita, California, a solidly middle-class area and the fourth largest city in LA County and then walked into a wooded sub-division.

The five waited unnoticed and undisturbed in their assigned location. At precisely 1:46 pm on a hot California day their phones rang and each received a one-word message, "Go."

Calm and precise, they rested their case on the ground or opened it and tossed it in the brush. Each took out a long plastic cylinder. Inside the cylinders were thermite and a contact spark ignition. Without any urgency, each held the cylinder by the ends, swung it vigorously six times as ordered no more and no less, then on the sixth swing upward they flung it forward as high into the air as possible. After it went airborne, each of them ran as quickly as they could away from the contact site.

The thermite cylinders did what they were designed to do. Once the cylinder hit the ground, the contact activated the spank igniter and just enough flash was created to ignite the thermite. Thermite is so volatile that a small spark will set it off into an explosion, which then created an intense high-temperature fire that streamed along the ground like lava from a volcano. With planning that took into account the driest summer in California history, the top temperature of the day, and a developing Santa Anna wind that would fuel the spread of the fires, the perfect firestorms were created. The thermite was quickly consumed by the intense flames leaving no trace of its contribution to the fire. The plastic cylinders and the magnesium spark ignitors were consumed as well and their presence was obliterated. The excessive dryness of the foliage in the area kindled the spread of the fire. The hungry flames of the fire became an insatiable hellion that consumed acre after acre in minutes. Any combustible material in the path of the fires in each area disappeared into the raging flames. The path of the destruction was dictated by the fierce Santa Anna wind that was predicted to pick up that very afternoon. As if right on cue, the gentle eight mile-per-hour breeze shifted into an unforgiving forty mile-per-hour bellows for the fires.

Emergency crews and homeowners, even those who had experienced California wildfires in the past, had never seen anything like what was ravaging their countryside so fiercely and so quickly. Of all times for a fire to break out when the drought and the winds were in perfect harmony to create this inferno.

In the oval office, President Matthews just finished barking into the desk phone, "Go," and with a theatrical poke of his index finger he hit the button to end the group call. He looked up from his desk at the group of close advisors in his inner circle for moments like these.

"I'll keep hitting that hella La La Land where they hurt and hurt and hurt. Goddamnit, they will fall into place or pay, pay, pay." He yelled with a combination of anger and exhilaration like a bully in a play lot.

Matthews walked over to one of the chairs that surrounded the two sofas in the direct center of the Oval Office. "They can build up a military, stockpile their resources, but they can't fight mother nature. We'll use their biggest Achilles heel against them. Their own goddamn climate. I'll burn the whole Goddamn state down, then nobody will want it." Matthews' tirade wisely went uninterrupted by his staff. "Five cylinders of chemicals and a good meteorologist. What, about $300 bucks and I can bring down the rebellion?"

The Attorney General Adam Reed, was the first of the staff to speak up, "Sir, there are a lot of your supporters whose homes may be in the paths of those fires."

"Then they should kick those rebels out of their state, don't you think? If they want to save their homes. What the hell?" Matthews responded. "This whole plan is a huge success. I've got scientists working on causing some earthquakes. Between burning the place down or letting it float off into the Pacific, I really don't give a shit. Let's just take care of this problem."

No one else in the Oval Office spoke about the fires. Then the president brought up, "Do you think I can get Congress to pass a declaration of war now that we've been fired upon by the Californians?"

Peter McKenzie, the president's chief administrative officer, responded, "Mr. President, you probably will have a better ear with Congress right now, but I still doubt that they will pass a resolution for a declaration of war on fellow Americans. There will have to be something larger happen to put that many Americans in harm's way. I think the best course of action is to keep operating in the manner we have been. As you are saying here now, we've struck a huge blow with these fires and we haven't needed the Congress yet."

Reed agreed "Congress will tie up for years our ability to respond to California. What's been working for us are quick and decisive responses. You have the power to respond with any resources at our disposal. We don't need Congress."

#

At the safe house the Murakami family worried about Tricia's condition. The family couldn't be kept from social media and news feeds so they believed like the rest of the country that Tricia was barely hanging on to her life. Rowan was informed by the family's security detail, but none of the family was allowed to visit her in the hospital where they were led to believe she was recovering from the attack. They were not told what hospital. They were not allowed to call. They were forbidden from any contact. No flowers, no cards, no texts.

The security personnel kept saying in their daily reports that Tricia was improving every day and that she was going to pull out of this just fine. The Murakami's had little faith in these statements as they contradicted the voluminous reports on the Internet. Tricia was a martyr for the rebellion. News feeds and blogs had already declared her dead. Her body was being hidden so federal agents couldn't kidnap it so she would be immortalized more than she already was becoming. The Murakami family's emotions were absolutely fried from the uncertainty. The social media reports overwhelmed them and they were all on the verge of becoming resigned to the fate of their mom and wife.

The family saw images of a ravaged body riddled with bullet holes and flesh torn open from wounds. Other images showed her on a hospital bed with tubes and IVs injected in her body everywhere. The mythology of Tricia grew viral, just what the CMS planned. But the Murakami's lived in anguish that their mother or wife was dying and they were helpless.

Ezekiel took his mother's condition the hardest because it was his message to Savanah's father, Agent X that informed the federal agents of the rally in San Francisco. Ezekiel felt so proud of his junior agent deductive powers and couldn't wait to brag to Agent X about his mother's next rally. His eager vanity put his mother's life in danger and he knew he was directly responsible.

Ever since the attack Ezekiel had not heard from Savanah or her dad. He was learning the lesson of who your true friends are, in the cruelest way possible.

CHAPTER 16

For Quartering Large Bodies of Armed Troops Among Us

Ezekiel had told Savanah and her dad one other thing: the location of their safe house. He wasn't sure of the exact address, but he had given enough of the landmarks around the house to give away its location. At the time, he had hopes of being rescued by the FBI and being brought to Savanah where the two of them could live happily-ever-after. Now, he wasn't sure that it was a smart thing to have done.

It was the first explosion that woke Ezekiel from his sleep. Looking around his darkened room, he first assumed it was just a part of his dream. But then he heard the helicopters and men's shouts. Before Ezekiel could move, the door to his room opened and his little sister, Grace, ran in. "I'm scared," she told him.

Ezekiel nodded. "Me too." But he had to do something. He looked at his sister and said in as calm of a voice as he could muster, "We have to hide." He grabbed her hand, and they ran to the closet. *Too obvious*, he thought to himself. *In every movie, the kid always tries to hide in the closet. That would be the first place they would look*. He then surveyed the rest of the room for another place they could hide. *Under the bed? Just as obvious.*

As he frantically thought about what to do, they heard gunshots. Not just one or two but what sounded like dozens. Maybe hundreds. Ezekiel wasn't sure but they sounded like they were coming from different kinds of guns. Then more explosions and screams. Their house had turned into a war zone.

"Who are you?" they heard their father's voice asking from somewhere in the house. Ezekiel had to strain his ears, but he heard the answer: "FBI. Now get down on the ground." The answer sent chills down his spine. The FBI had tried to kill their mom. Or maybe had already done so and they just hadn't told him. And now, they SOBs were coming after the rest of the family.

"We have to hide," Ezekiel repeated to his sister more urgently. But when he looked around, there was just no good place to hide. "Can you fit inside the dresser?" But the look on Grace's face was enough to let him to know how stupid the question was. They heard the footsteps coming up the stairs.

"I'll hide in the closet," Ezekiel told Grace. "And you hide under the bed."

Ezekiel made up in his mind that when the FBI came into the room, he would give himself up to them right away in the hopes that they wouldn't bother to look for his sister. He knew it was probably a stupid idea, but he couldn't think of anything else.

Ezekiel helped make sure his sister was out of sight. And instead of going to the closet, he remained standing in the middle of the room. "Ezekiel, what are you doing?" his sister asked from under the bed. But Ezekiel shushed her. At that moment, the door burst open and a group of FBI agents in full SWAT attire and wielding automatic weapons entered. "Where is Grace Murakami?" they shouted.

When Ezekiel didn't answer right away, the FBI agents began to search the room. They lifted the bed and grabbed Grace and dragged her out, kicking and screaming. Ezekiel opened his mouth to say something, but he lost the ability to speak the moment he recognized one of the faces under the mask: Agent X.

After the FBI grabbed Grace, they left. A minute later, the house became completely silent again. It was obvious that they had come for only for Grace. Ezekiel assumed his sister would be used as bait to get at the people with mom, the California rebels.

Rowan found Ezekiel standing in the same spot that the FBI had left him. The moment Ezekiel saw his dad, he ran to him. It had been many years since father and son touched each other, let alone hugged—so long in fact that neither could remember how long it had been. "It'll be okay," he told his son. "They're gone."

Rowan looked around, "Where's your sister?"

"I'm sorry," Ezekiel began. "It's all my fault. I'm so sorry. It's all my fault that they took her."

"It's not your—" Rowan began, but Ezekiel cut him off.

"I told them where we were," he blurted out, as he looked back down at the ground.

"No," Rowan said, not wanting to believe it.

Ezekiel continued to look down as he admitted, "I told them that mom would be at Giants stadium too. It's all my fault she's dead. I'm sorry."

Rowan let go of his son and took a step away. Tears began to well up in his eyes as he tried to understand why his son would betray his family. "Why?"

Ezekiel looked at his father. It wasn't the anger, but the look of hate that came radiating out of his eyes that surprised him most. Rowan grabbed his son by the arm and shook him. "Tell me why!"

"Savanah," Ezekiel murmured.

Rowan frowned. It wasn't the answer he was expecting. His anger faded temporarily. "Who's Savanah?"

"My girl…" Ezekiel started, but then stopped, correcting himself. "This girl from school."

Rowan did not believe in hitting his children. In fact, he had never spanked any of his kids… But without thinking about what he was doing, he knocked his son to the ground. Rowan lifted his hand again when the room filled with a dozen CRM soldiers with Noah leading the charge. Noah went to his father and grabbed his arm before he could hit Ezekiel again.

"I want in," Rowan told Noah and General Brown, the Chief of Staff for the CRM, as soon as he walked in the room. He had been feeling guilty about not supporting the cause. He was wondering if he had done more, would they still be in this situation? "They almost killed my wife, and now kidnapped my daughter."

General Brown shifted uncomfortably on his feet for the briefest of moments. Rowan didn't notice, but Noah did. He didn't say anything at the moment to his father but made a mental note to ask him about it later when his dad wasn't around.

Brown nodded. "We know your background and we could really use your knowledge of rockets once we have taken over some of the bases." This wasn't what Rowan wanted to hear. He wanted to shoot someone now. Preferably the people responsible for taking his daughter. He was about to protest when Brown continued: "You're far too valuable to be playing cops and robbers with the soldiers."

Rowan took a seat on Grace's chair. General Brown was right. Not about being too valuable. He was just being nice. Rowan had never shot a gun in his entire life. Let alone kill something. A memory of him as a teenager popped into his head. The time he got into a terrible car accident instead of hitting the squirrel that darted in front of his car. His father, whom he never got along with, told him he was an idiot for not running it over. Ever since, he had cringed whenever someone used the word *idiot*.

"Do you know where they are taking her?" Rowan asked Brown.

"We don't think she'll be able to get out of California. We've sealed the borders and we're checking everyone that's coming and going."

"And Tricia, how is she?"

Brown smiled. "She is doing much better."

"When can I see her?"

"Soon."

It was not the answer Rowan was hoping to hear. He'd being hearing he would see her "soon" for weeks. But without a way to get in contact her, he was at the CRM's whim. He hoped it would be sooner than later.

Gen. Brown stood. "Mr. Murakami, if you don't mind. I'd like to find your daughter now."

Rowan stood and shook his hand. "Thank you."

A moment later, General Brown was walking back to the car. Noah quickly caught up. "Sir," he began. "What are you not telling us?" Noah began to tear up. "Is my sister already…"

General Brown turned and looked at Noah. "No."

Brown's firm response relived Noah. Like everyone in his family, he was feeling guilty. He was wondering if he could have done more, or if this whole secession thing was a mistake.

Brown put his hand on Noah's shoulder. "We'll find your sister, I promise."

As if on cue, one of general's assistants ran up to him. "We think we've found her." Brown and Noah's eyes met. This was Noah's chance.

In thirty minutes, Noah and his team were on two military helicopters racing toward the location that CRM believed that Grace was being held captive. Noah checked his gun for the tenth time. He wanted to be sure that he was ready to kill the people who had taken Grace. He began to ball his hands into a fist, as he imagined all the things he would do to his sister's kidnappers.

"She'll be okay," Justyice shouted over the noise of the helicopter.

Noah glanced at her. Despite the initial attraction, Noah had made it a point not to speak to her directly or be alone with her. With everything going on, he didn't have time for a relationship, let alone with someone under his direct command.

Justyice continued, "We'll get her."

Noah nodded.

As they rose above the San Gabriel mountains outside of Pasadena, they saw the area below completely engulfed in flames. Both Noah and Justyice had the same thought—although neither of them knew it—they had the feeling that they were going straight into hell.

Noah unconsciously began to pray. "Even though I walk through the valley of the shadow of death, I fear no evil, for You are with me; Your rod and Your staff, they comfort me."

His words could not be heard over the helicopter but Justyice grabbed his hand and joined in. They looked into each other's eyes for a long moment. If Noah wasn't sure before, he knew it then: She felt the same about him that he did for her. Noah thought if this were some cheesy romantic movie, the two would kiss at that moment. But the helicopter banked to the right and they had to let go of each other to keep themselves from falling over. When the helicopter righted itself, the moment was gone. They both said, "Amen" at the same time and Noah began checking his weapon again.

No one on the helicopter was aware of what was going on down on the ground at that moment. At that very second, all the television broadcasts in California were being interrupted by the federal government, who also had the live footage put up on all social media platforms. The first image that appeared on screens was that of a nondescript room that could have been anywhere. When the camera panned down, the audience got their first glimpse of Grace, who was sitting in a chair. There were no handcuffs or restraints, but it was obvious to anyone watching that she was not there on her own volition. No one outside of the new California government or military and her immediate family and friends had any idea who she was. But it quickly became clear her significance.

"Hi," Grace read from the prompter that was obviously just off-screen. Her voice broke as she tried to continue. She looked at someone who appeared to be just off camera. Her eyes widened with fear. Finally, she took a deep breath before continuing. "My name is Grace Murakami; I am the daughter of Tricia and Rowan Murakami. I am currently in the custody of the FBI. To my friends and family, I would like to reassure them that I am being treated well." Upon those words, she pushed her hair away from her left eye giving the audience a glimpse of a growing bruise on her forehead. "The FBI has asked me to plead with those American citizens of California who are actively working against their country to turn themselves in. They are most interested in communicating with my mother, Tricia Murakami. They would like her to turn herself into the FBI immediately." Grace continued like this for five more minutes. As expected, she mentioned the names of the California governor, high ranking officials in the California army and government. She also asked for the release of all the INS, FBI and CIA officers being detained in the state. Most ominously, she mentioned that anyone in California who helped the rebellion would be captured and executed as traitors.

Tricia was watching this broadcast from where she had been sequestered. Tears had welled up in her eyes as she studied her daughter's face. She has never felt more helpless in her entire life. She wanted to reach into the television and grab her daughter to protect her from this whole mess.

Jaleel and Tom Huang, the California governor's chief of staff, arrived in her room before the end of the broadcast. Tom saw the look in her eyes. He knew anything he said would fall short. So instead of saying some idiotic platitude, he took her in his arms and hugged her. He whispered in her ears, "We'll get her back." Tom wasn't sure how exactly they were going to do that, but he had never wanted his words to be truer than at that moment. Tricia buried her head in Tom's chest. She hadn't realized she had made this decision before she said it, but as soon as the words left her mouth, she knew she meant them. "I'm turning myself in."

Rowan was pacing around the room. He was waiting to hear if Noah was successful when one of his security detail came into the room and turned on the television. He, with the rest of California, watched Grace's message. But instead of tearing up, he became even angrier. He wished he could have been with Noah on the raid to rescue his daughter.

When the broadcast was over, Rowan stood there a long time and thought about how he would get revenge on the people that took Grace. He wanted to do something. Anything. He wondered what he could do to help California. Then it came to him. An atomic bomb. Assuming the state had enough uranium, he figured he'd be able to build one that they could drop on all the FBI that took his daughter. He came out of his stupor and went straight to his laptop.

He began researching how to build the bomb. He even began to compile a list of materials that he was going need. To his surprise, it was a lot easier than he had first thought. He knew the difficulty wasn't building the bomb but weaponizing its delivery was going to be the harder part for most people—but not him. He had spent an entire career shooting things into space.

Without even knowing it, Rowan had spent an hour on the idea. He was so consumed by his "project" the time had passed in a blink of an eye. That's why when someone knocked on the door, he didn't hear it. And when the door opened, he didn't turn to look to see who it was. In fact, he didn't know anyone had come in until he heard a voice. "Rowan," a familiar woman's voice said.

Rowan jumped in his seat, startled. He turned and saw his wife standing only a few feet away from him. His first instinct was to run to her, but his feet wouldn't move. *This can't be my wife*, he said to himself. He knew she looked like his wife, but his wife was either dead or seriously injured. This woman in front of him seemed perfectly fine. Tricia wanted to run to him too. But the confused look on his face and the memory of the governor's chief of staff kept her planted to where she was.

"Tricia?" Rowan asked, his voice full of uncertainty.

Tricia smiled. She wondered if her husband could smell Tom's cologne on her. "Who else would it be?" Tricia asked jokingly. When Rowan didn't answer, Tricia continued, "Did you see…?" But she didn't have to finish the sentence; she could see in Rowan's eyes that he had seen Grace on TV too. "I'm sorry. This is all my fault. If I hadn't gotten myself involved, they would never have come after her."

Rowan's mind was racing. Her voice sounded like Tricia's but the look in her eye wasn't hers. There was something missing there. The strength that he had fallen in love with so many years ago with was somehow gone. This was confirmed when Tricia said, "I'm going to turn myself in."

Noah had not said a single word to anyone since he and Justyice had prayed. He kept glancing at her out of the corner of his eyes. But every time he caught himself doing it, he told himself to focus. He had a mission to do. He had to save his sister.

The helicopter pilot spoke into his ears: "We are less than a minute out, lieutenant."

Noah looked around at the others and put up one finger. Justyice, his best friend, Mark Perez, and the rest of his team nodded and then triple checked their weapons. They wanted to get Noah's sister back almost as bad as Noah did. For that, Noah was grateful. It was cliché, but they had become more than a team. They had become family.

Noah looked out the open door. They were in Santa Clarita, about an hour north of Downtown LA. He assumed it would be a subdivision but was surprised to see a strip mall. He knew he shouldn't have been surprised though, because strip malls and this part of Northern Los Angeles County were synonymous.

As the helicopters descended, the pilot interrupted his thoughts: "Lieutenant, command is requesting to speak to you."

Noah was annoyed. He couldn't think of a worse time to talk. Before Noah could say anything, the pilot continued; "It's from General Brown. They say it's really important. It's about your mother."

Noah looked helpless. It was too late to turn around at this late stage, but he couldn't ignore the message from his commanding officer. Mark Perez was listening. He shouted, "I got this, bro. Join us when you can. We'll save the main bad guy for you, bro."

Noah nodded as Mark jumped onto the ground, leading his team. They charged toward the strip mall with their guns drawn. Noah was amazed at how far they've come over the last few weeks. They went from a ragtag group of civilians to highly-trained soldiers. He noticed another helicopter was landing on the roof of the building and those soldiers were getting out a well. Noah stayed aboard. "Patch General Brown through," he told the pilot.

A moment later, he heard the general in his ear. "Lieutenant, your mom is going to turn herself in. We need you to talk her ou—" but Noah didn't hear the rest of it because at that very moment the strip mall exploded into an enormous fireball.

CHAPTER 17

To Bear Arms Against Their Country

The shooting at AT&T Park, Tricia Murakami's assassination attempt, Grace Murakami's kidnapping, and the destruction of the strip mall in Santa Clarita was too much. California reached the boiling point with Matthews and the USA.

The media exploded with the announcement by Governor Herrmann that all federal employees who would not pledge alliance to the new California government had thirty days to leave California or have their property seized and be 'deported.' Further, his executive order entered into law that all federal agents must leave California immediately. He firmly stated that if a federal agent is found to be inside the California border, they will be apprehended and arrested. Herrmann specifically ordered that all California law enforcement agencies and the California Republic Military (CRM) can use deadly force if federal agents offer resistance.

The details of the executive order went on to include all U.S. military personnel stationed within the California border. He did write in a provision that American soldiers can defect to the country of California; they would then be immediately relieved of duty and placed on furlough until passing an evaluation of their allegiance and fitness for duty.

Secession was in full operation now.

Herrmann's order began a California full sweep of both federal employees and FBI and CIA agents. The roundup of federal employees in departments such as the IRS, federal buildings, agencies, etc., was efficient. Addresses and other personal information were readily available to the California government. Email notifications went out personally to every federal employee reiterating the governor's orders.

Rounding up covert federal agents was another matter. With a long history of subterfuge and secrecy, the federal agents were well hidden into the fabric of California. But the CRM had an aggressive plan. The CRM now had the numbers and the resources to blanket California with an exhaustive search. They also had the mobility. Major General Curtis Brown crafted a bold plan: he would deploy the majority of CRM troops assisted with law enforcement throughout the state.

He had the ability to defer these resources because he hedged that President Matthews was nowhere ready to invade California, so a concentrated military was not essential right now. But, in the unlikely situation that an all-out attack was mounted by the U.S., the logistics for the CRM were worked out so intricately that they could be grouped back together very, very quickly.

Although California is a large state, it wasn't as if the troops were deployed over oceans. Thus, the CRM did a bold maneuver to execute Herrmann's orders. They organized an actual sweep of the state. They would canvas every mile of the state.

Another provision of the governor's executive order was to place all law enforcement such as state police, state marshals, homeland security, all other security services, and national guard under the command of the CRM, thus making Major General Curtis Brown in charge of all these forces. As a result of the governor's order, General Brown drew up the logistics to coordinate all the forces now under his command to act as a large expeditionary force to blanket the entire state and flush out any federal agents operating within California. His plan combined the old fashion police work of canvassing areas door-to-door with military might and a sprinkle of high-tech investigation.

Brown's plan, although made purposively very visible inside California, wasn't announced or broadcast across the United States. The logistics of the plan were designed to strike hard and fast as if swatting away pests. In fact, the operation was called, Operation Fly Swatter.

The air operation of Operation Fly Swatter was extremely efficient. Once California took over the U.S. military bases scattered throughout the state, General Brown and the CRM had an abundance of low flying planes, helicopters, and even satellite images they could use to hunt remote areas, forests, parks and other open areas. Even in urban areas, newly acquired technology from the military bases put spy planes in the air that could pick up conversations through buildings with science fiction-like detail. Large numbers of federal agents and sympathizers were identified by the code-cracking knowledge of defected espionage agents.

It was amazing—and frightening at the same time—how all at once the many pieces of such large operation could move seamlessly when there was no federal red-tape to hinder action.

In Sacramento, logically a hotbed of suspected federal agents, an un-manned MQ-1 Predator Reaper surveillance plane picked up a conversation between an estimated dozen FBI agents in a safe house a mile from the California capital building. The Predator operators transmitted the location of the agents to CRM ground forces in Sacramento. A SWAT force of thirty soldiers was scrambled within fifteen minutes and on its way to the FBI safe house. They rode in two matte black troop transports. Another ten minutes and they were in front of the brown bricked three-story apartment complex. Less than a half-hour and the SWAT force was mobilized and ready to encounter a nest of FBI agents. Operation Fly Swatter worked as a fine-tuned machine.

The troops jumped from the transports and took positions near one of the vehicles and waited for orders. Six of the troops stayed in the other armored transport and drove it to the rear of the apartment building to guard against an escape. In the front of the building, a CRM captain reached through the window of the vehicle and grabbed a microphone. A loud announcement barked at the building: "FBI, you are surrounded. You are ordered to exit this building peacefully." He paused, then resumed slowly, "We will hold fast for three minutes. Three minutes only." He repeated, "Three minutes only."

The captain turned to his troops. "They will test us, be ready," he ordered.

A minute passed and then a window on the second floor broke. Although hardly visible, a hand with a pistol appeared through the broken glass, then immediately the automatic pistol began firing.

"Return fire!" The captain shouted.

The CRM troops, who were anxiously waiting for action, riddled the building with their firepower. Three of the CRM troops fired grenades from their rifles through the windows on each of the floors. Explosions erupted from the inside and smoke billowed from the apartment building.

"Hold fire!" The captain ordered and the troops quieted their weapons. The CRM troops waited for any movement coming from the building. The smoke that was so vigorously escaping from every window slowed and then stopped. The captain then gave the order, "Break that door down. Let's get in there."

Four soldiers ran to the front door of the apartment building, lugging a large iron cylinder doorbuster. Without stopping, they reached the front door in full stride and threw the doorbuster through it. The wood door splintered into large chunks and swung open so hard it rebounded back into the charging soldiers who quickly dismissed it and ran forward.

The remainder of the SWAT force charged into the building. Their energy slowed once they were inside the building. On each floor, dead FBI agents lay near the front windows of the building. Their bodies contorted into various positions, some with guns drawn and others face down on the floor as if they were on their way to the windows to support their comrades. Seventeen FBI agents lay dead—much more than the Predator's audio surveillance had estimated. Operation Fly Swatter was swift, deadly and doable.

The remote canvass of the state was just as swift and often deadly. Predators, drones, and helicopters scoured rural and forested areas. The reconnaissance aircraft could fly between one hundred and two hundred and fifty miles per hour while taking images of the ground that could detail a small branch lying in a forest thicket.

One drone flying over farmland in eastern California near the border focused in on a mobile home that looked suspicious. Most mobile homes near farmland are for itinerant farm help. The condition of those temporary housing units is rugged, to say the least. They typically have been in farm families for generations and the occupants are often not the tidy home types. This mobile home looked quite new and still had the tractor cab hooked up to transport the mobile home.

The drone flew closer to the mobile home and its long-range listening capability was activated. It flew around the area, snapped still pictures, took a video, and sent conversations back to the drone controllers in CRM headquarters. Twice, men exited the mobile home for various reasons and although not suspicious looking, they were also not itinerant farmers. Similarly, the recorded conversations didn't pick up anything subversive to California, but the men and women inside weren't talking sugar beets either. The agents inside the trailer discussed weapons, being ready for orders, working out, sports and 'Getting this over and going home.' There was no strategic conversations or discussion of any assignments.

As the drone was casually doing its job, suddenly the front doors of the mobile home swung open and three people all dressed in black stopped a few feet from the front door. One, a woman, opened up a tripod and attached a sniper rifle. Another lengthened a spotter's telescope, sat on the ground and looked up to the sky. The third held an assault rifle and appeared to be searching the area in every direction. With rehearsed precision, the sniper loaded the rifle, aimed, squeezed off one round and in seconds the drone exploded in the air with a flash, sending metal fragments in every direction. Several large chunks of debris fell straight toward the ground and the spotter jogged over and scooped them up. Without any urgency, they all returned to the mobile home.

In two hours, four Apache helicopters landed in such a position to surround the mobile home in every direction. Keeping their rotors running, the doors on each copter slid open to reveal a heavy machine gun and troops with weapons at the ready. A voice made an announcement so loud it boomed over the sound of the rotating blades: "Occupants of this trailer, we need you to exit out of the trailer immediately for a security check. I repeat, all occupants of this mobile home trailer are ordered to vacate immediately and present yourselves for identification checks and security inspection."

There was no response and no movement from the mobile home. The announcement was made again, exactly as it was stated the first time, but again there was no response forthcoming. Minutes passed. All four of the helicopters changed their position so that their cockpits were facing the mobile home. With very visible shifting and noise from the copters' armaments, the rocket launchers and heavy machine guns of these attack helicopters moved into firing position. They aimed directly at the mobile home from all sides.

Ten very long minutes had passed. Still no movement from inside the mobile home. The loudspeaker blared again: "You have three minutes to exit the trailer or it will be fired upon with deadly force." The speaker paused for a few seconds before warning: "The countdown starts now."

Thirty seconds passed and a white bed sheet on a broomstick pushed through an open window. The loudspeaker ordered: "Everyone out, unarmed, hands on your heads. We know exactly how many are in there, so no surprises."

Fourteen FBI agents marched out of the front doors in single file with their hands over their heads. By that time, all the troops jumped from the helicopters. The copter mounted machine guns and rocket launchers remained trained on the mobile home. Twenty-one troops from the two Apache's that landed now formed a semi-circle and guarded the FBI agents as they exited the front doors. The twenty troops from the two rear helicopters formed a straight line and guarded the back of the mobile home.

In the front of the house, the CRM troops patted-down the agents and gave the all clear to their commander. Captain Pete Kellman spoke. He was the voice heard on the loudspeaker. "Is there someone in charge here?" he demanded.

A tall agent in a dark blue running suit stepped forward. "That's me," he responded.

Kellman motioned for his troops to enter the mobile home. "We want any computers, cell phones, paper records, anything of value saved. Don't destroy anything and be careful of any explosives or tricks."

Kellman turned to the lead agent. "If there is anything that puts my troops in danger, you all lose your lives right here." He looked him dead in the eyes. "Is that clear?"

The agent snapped back, "Very."

"Speak up now, because none of my people are at ease," he demanded.

"They won't have any problems in there," the agent assured him.

Kellman called for the troops at the back of the mobile home to come into the front and help with the prisoners. He ordered the FBI agents to be cuffed and led into the helicopters. A soldier shouted at Kellman from the front door. "There's a shit ton of stuff in here, Capt'n."

Kellman thought fast. "Ok, leave it." He turned to his troops. "Anyone know how to drive that rig?"

Four or five soldiers lazily put their hands up. "Draw straws and two of you in the cab. We'll ask the pilots how many of ya'll can fit in with us and the prisoners and the rest get a luxury ride in the tour bus there." He turned and walked toward the group of pilots who were by now gathered together, then he yelled, "OK, let's wrap this up."

On the technology front, General Brown, through the outstanding relationships that Governor Herrmann had with Silicon Valley, had the best minds in technology at his disposal for Operation Fly Swatter. Like Brown, the technology CEO's put all available resources on Operation Fly Swatter immediately. They tracked down federal agents through computer records, social media, employment and personal information such as shopping habits, communications, travel records and other intricate algorithms using the most advanced cyberstalking never used before to capture identities. Email records, tweets, text messages were scanned. The tech companies were in hog heaven with such freedom to cross privacy boundaries.

The tech giants also worked together in an unprecedented way making the speed of this investigation lightening quick. In less than five days, the technology sector handed General Brown the whereabouts of thousands of known and suspected federal agents afoot in California. Brown dispatched teams of four troops to apprehend single individuals and teams of upwards of thirty troops to go after federals living in pairs or larger groups. Every apprehension was done with a large show of force and with urgency. Within this window of opportunity, General Brown had tremendous resources to sweep California clean of federal operators and he used this gift with gusto. Every raid or round-up was conducted with a powerful show of force. This was to quell resistance and to assure that if resistance was offered, it would be met with overwhelming force and stopped dead.

The mass exodus and the federal lives lost to Operation Fly Swatter riveted the United States' attention through constant media feeds. From the onset of the operation, California didn't initiate national announcements of its intent, but obviously, the scope of this operation hit the national media quickly. It also was immediately received by President Matthews who was furious at California's actions. Matthew's grand plan to bring California to its knees through covert action was a dismal failure; in fact, California was stronger than ever with increased security and resolve. Over ten thousand federal agents from the FBI and CIA were in CRM custody. Nine hundred federal agents were killed in Operation Fly Swatter. Four hundred federals escaped over the California border.

On the military side, in the thirty-two military bases in California, 190,160 military personnel were stationed in California. No other state had as many U.S. military stationed inside their borders as California. As a part of Operation Fly Swatter and, in execution of Herrmann's orders, each military base was confronted by armed CRM forces and ordered to take one of three immediate actions: 1–Leave California under the supervision of the CRM. 2–Apply for reenlistment into the CRM. 3–Be detained in an internment camp until such time as they could be transported out of the state.

The numbers were staggering. 123,604 military applied for reenlistment into the CRM. That was 65% of all soldiers stationed in California bases. 41,234 left California immediately, which left 25,322 that were detained in an internment camp. Matthews was losing a huge portion of his military in one sweeping operation.

The logistics of these numbers were stunning given the speed in which this all took place. Although it was chaos to process such large numbers of people, it wasn't unprecedented. Armies took large numbers of prisoners before, but they didn't have to accomplish such a daunting task with such urgency. General Brown had unwavering resolve in completing Operation Fly Swatter in record time even with the chaos that all this processing entailed. Those who chose to leave California did so in every type of transport imaginable: trains, planes, and automobiles were certainly employed, but also unarmed troop transports, for-hire vehicles, boats, and buses were all engaged. For a short period of time the movement eastward out of California mimicked the legends of the California gold rush of the 1800's. All that was fine with General Brown. In his mind, if he would wait for this all to be a tidy, orderly process, the operation would take years and not weeks. Brown could not only live with the pandemonium this all caused, he thrived on it. He had a deep disdain for bureaucracy and the roadblocks it always placed in front of military strategists. He was a doer and a worshiper of General George Patton. Just get the job done and let someone else pick up the pieces. Brown was in ecstasy with the freedom he was given to make things happen. For those twenty-five thousand being detained in California, Brown's orders were to corral them in one place and then we'll figure out how to feed and shelter them.

Interestingly, the usual loud civil rights voices in California were quiet with all this cleansing of the federal presence. Whether it was pent-up anger for President Matthews or the realization that this was civil war or some other phenomena, but no one was objecting to Operation Fly Swatter. The only supportive action the human rights activists showed toward the federals was assistance with transportation out of the state and a large outpouring of aid to those in the internment camp set up at Tule Lake, Northern California, which is located near the California-Oregon border.

In Washington, Matthews aids questioned his strategy. "Mr. President, how long are we going to let this tension in California build before we ramp up our efforts? We've suffered 900 US citizens killed at the hands of these rebels and thousands more suffering from their deportation orders," Stanton asked.

"Jad, you know as well as I that we'll be ready soon for the invasion. In the meantime, all this aggression by California is making my poll numbers rise. When we go in, the timing will be a perfect storm. The country will be solidly behind me." Matthews said. "I mean solidly behind me. I think we'll see numbers like 70 or 80 percent for taking California down." Matthews gloated at the possibilities.

"I'm really getting concerned about world opinion," Stanton said.

"Relax, I've been reassured by Ellis that the rest of the world is frozen. What are they going to do? Side with California? Then they risk our wrath," He paused. "Side with us, Ok, great to be a cheerleader on the sidelines. The world knows we can handle this militarily. But, we won't forget what side they were on. Let me tell you, we're not letting anyone come on US soil to join in this fight. Do that and you'll see those poll numbers drop like a lead balloon."

\#

Noah raced by the security detail outside the safe house in Los Angeles. He didn't have to go through many rooms to find his mom and dad huddled together in front of a large computer screen in what looked like a study. Even with a quick look, Noah could see that they were studying a map of California with a yellowish grid superimposed over it. Two smaller pop-ups on either side of the map had lists scrolling. He saw Grace's name and her physical statistics heading one list.

"Mom, dad!" Noah exclaimed. Tricia and Rowan both snapped up off their chairs. They rushed toward Noah and all hugged with tears in their eyes. "I was on a mission for Grace and…"

Tricia placed two fingers on his mouth. "We know dear, we know."

"Fuck this…fuck Mathews…how could he…" Tears were now streaming from his face.

"Dear, dear…we know about the strip mall. God bless the people there…" Tricia's tone was firm but comforting.

Noah's rage boiled over. He smacked a wall with his fist. "We had the perfect chance, the perfect chance. They're savages, a little girl…" He wailed. "She wasn't a soldier, she was an innocent. This is not the country we can be in. Where's the morals?"

"Noah, listen. People died in that mall explosion, but Grace wasn't one of them. Listen to me, we think she is still alive. We know she is alive. We'll have another chance. Listen to me." Tricia grabbed his shoulder, squeezed him and then her hand moved to his neck and she put his head on her chest like she did hundreds of times when he was a boy.

"She's alive?" Noah said through tears that began to subside. "She's OK?"

Rowan walked over to the two of them and put a hand on Noah's back. "She's alive, that's all we know. The blast left enough evidence around to identify any bodies caught up in it. There were no young persons or females. We're sure of that," he stated with great confidence that had a calming effect on Noah.

"We were just looking over intel on the latest estimates of where they might have her. We have some good data here." Rowan added.

"Oh my God, thanks. That's great news!" Noah became flooded with another concern. "Do you know if they ID'd any of the other dead in that blast?" he asked.

A new sadness overwhelmed Tricia and Rowan. "Oh, that's right, you and your platoon were on the way to that mall right before the explosion. We heard immediately that you were OK and were so relieved. And also, we were still thinking the worst about Grace. We didn't hear anything else about who might have been hurt. We just didn't ask. I'm sorry," Rowan offered.

"How can I find anything out? I tried calling a couple of my troops, but I haven't gotten through to them and then I got reassigned and consumed in the whole Operation Fly Swatter. Which took me near here, so I stopped in here before anything else to see how you both were doing. Phone communication seems to be down. Between Fly Swatter and thinking about you both, I haven't had a second to do a thorough search for my team. It's been a whirlwind." Noah took a breath.

Tricia resumed her nurturing. "Here, sit. Let me get you something. In the meantime, plug into the main computer here. It's a direct connection to headquarters. See what you can find out about your people," Tricia said.

Noah did just that. He settled into the desk chair and went into a CRM communication web site. After he put his ID and password in, a window popped up that stated there was an emergency security hold placed on all CRM communications as a result of the president of the United States actions in retaliation for Operation Fly Swatter. *No wonder why I couldn't get ahold of anyone,* Noah thought. He scrolled down further on the web page and the CRM posted excerpts from Matthews' statement on Operation Fly Swatter. A window with bullet points of the action that President Matthews was ordering appeared.

Matthews ordered:

- A cyber-attack on California in retaliation for the use of electronic data gathering to target federal agents.
- Wherever possible a communication embargo on California. Any phone, radio, shortwave, longwave, microwave, television, cable or any communication links that are controlled by the federal government will be shut-off from use by California.
- Rail traffic controlled by and emanating from the United States will no longer enter into California.
- Blockades will be set up just outside the California borders on all interstate highways entering into California.

As usual, President Matthews dictator-like leadership spoke too soon and he bullied action that couldn't be executed. Within two hours of Matthews' statement, the Internet was buzzing with the news that Washington D.C.

went dark. Washington's entire electrical grid was shut down. Leaked reports from inside Washington indicated that the federal government's tech experts with the aid of the military tech experts were scrambling to figure out how to undo the hack put on the electrical grid. Try as they might, the federal experts kept seeing on their screens an image of the Guy Fawkes mask with an L.A. Dodger baseball cap. The meme laughed out the cry, "Wanna Play Ball?"

Rail traffic continued to roll down the tracks, no disruption in any of the communication systems was experienced, blocking the highways would take the bloated federal agencies months, if not years. Again, President Matthews strong arm tactics failed.

Though his urgency to reach his platoon was stalled by the temporary security block the CRM imposed, Noah had to sit back in the chair and chuckled. He thought, *I bet ol' Gen. Brown is pissing in his pants at how castrated the Feds are. If he was running that show, every one of those things would have been finished and permanent.*

At that moment Tricia came into the study. "What's so funny?" She smiled.

"Oh, just the Matthews show. Or should I say…shit." Noah smirked.

"Shit show is more like it. You saw how the Silicon guys did a little slap down on the latest Matthews tantrum?" she asked.

"Great stuff. I bet you they're having a ball up north. Excuse the pun, given the Dodger's cap on Guy," Noah added. "Google probably ordered pizzas for everyone after that maneuver!"

They laughed together. Tricia poured Noah a Hanson's Ginger Ale, his favorite drink and set down a tray with tortillas bloated with crunchy peanut butter, another favorite. He began to gobble up a tortilla, wash it down with the soda but as he cleared his throat of the chewy snack, he became worried again. "What do you think this might mean for Grace?"

Tricia thought for a moment, "Let's hope she's an extremely minor concern for Matthews with his failures mounting."

"Amen," Noah said with the solemnity of the word.

Rowan came into the study and brought a tray for Tricia and him. The three ate together for the first time in a very long time. With nothing they could do on the computers because of the security block, they talked for a few hours about the state of the rebellion and their roles for the future.

As the conversation began to wind down, Noah stretched and declared, "I'd love to take a nap. I'm exhausted. Can ya show me a bedroom I can borrow?"

Just as he stood, there was a loud knock at the door of the safe house. They all rushed to the front door as it was obviously friendly company that got through the security detail out front. As Rowan opened the door, he saw Grace standing there flanked by three CRM soldiers in fatigues.

"Oh God, Oh God!" Rowan shouted for joy.

Noah and Tricia joined in the chorus of elated shouts and they hugged and kissed Grace over and over.

After the long, loving greeting, they invited Grace and her bodyguards into the front room. "Are you hungry anyone?" Tricia asked.

Grace spoke up, "I'm stuffed, these three here have been treating me like a princess all the way here. Burgers, shakes, whatever I wanted."

Noah looked at the soldiers, "Where did you find her?"

Latrice Peterson, a slim African-American female corporal responded, "We were guarding a group of federals being brought to Tule Lake and we saw this teenager. She seemed out of place and controlled by the military people she was with. We took a closer look and it dawned on us who she was. The Feds tried to keep hold of her, but we basically wrestled her away from them and brought her to field headquarters. Since we couldn't communicate with you all, we just brought her here. Course, we made a couple of stops like she said. She deserved some treats after what she been through."

Peterson's smile lit up the entire room.

"Ten thousand thanks, all of you. What can we do for you?" Tricia asked.

"Kill Matthews!" the male Latino soldier chirped.

They all laughed.

"That's the plan." Noah chuckled.

"Tule Lake?" Rowan pondered. "Noah, Grace, that's the camp where your great-grandparents were held in World War II." Tears welled in his eyes. "Grace, you were retracing family and cultural history. You were right there where the injustices done to the Japanese American families took place decades ago. And, today, we experience injustice again. But, unlike our ancestors, we have the ability to fight against the wrongs." Rowan stood. He looked off into the distance, his head held high and he took several deep breaths. "I know what I must do now. I've been too complacent in the movement. No longer. Tricia, I'm sorry for my past lack of courage and my caution about this rebellion. But all of you, that will change right now. I owe this to all of you and to all my people that came before me."

CHAPTER 18

He Has Kept Among Us Standing Armies

Tricia Murakami did not like deceiving the people of California. But she also understood that she could not come out and just tell the truth anymore. The California Movement of Secession (CMS) had put out a story that she had been on death's door after the attack in San Francisco. Thousands of people from all over the state—and from around the world—sent their prayers for her speedy recovery. It was another one of those galvanizing moments in the movement that Tricia seemed to have a knack for always being a part. Hearing that people had prayed for her health made her feel guilty and she had insisted that the CMS get her time on the air to at least thank everyone.

Tricia and Jaleel worked on a speech for over a week. Tricia wanted to speak from the heart, but Jaleel needed to make sure she didn't say anything that gave any hint of what really happened. In the end, they managed to craft a talk that was both from the heart but didn't give any state secrets away.

A few days later, she was standing in front of a camera in the CMS studio. To make the idea that she had been seriously injured more believable, they had put her arm in a sling and a bandage around the top of her head. Tricia thought it was over the top but didn't put up a stink about it. When the light above the camera turned red, she began: "To my fellow Californians, as you can see, the rumors of my demise have been greatly exaggerated." She did not think that line was funny a second time, but Jaleel had insisted she start her speech that way. And later, it became one of the most memorable moments from it. She went on to thank everyone for their thoughts and prayers. She used the opportunity to warn the people of California that this was just the beginning… that there would be more hardships and that people were going to die. To prove her point, she began to read the names of all the CRM soldiers, police officers, California National Guard, and other law enforcement officials that had died up to that moment during Operation Fly Swatter. She spent extra time talking about the raid in Santa Clarita and the lives that were lost. During this part, she saw that Grace—who was standing off to the side—had begun to weep openly. She had not been aware that soldiers had lost their lives in the effort to find and save her.

Seeing her daughter's reaction, Tricia invited Grace to join her in front of the camera. "By the grace of God," Tricia told the camera with tears filling her eyes. "My daughter was returned to me. People always ask me why I'm doing what I'm doing. I say it is for her and my other two children." She paused and then continued, "I want them to live in a country where all people are created equal, where each person has the right to life, liberty, and justice for all."

Grace smiled shyly at the camera as she raised her fist in the air. Unbeknownst to her, at least at that moment, her image quickly became a meme of not just the California revolution but any protest all over the world for the next hundred plus years.

President Matthews watched the speech from the Oval Office. Seeing Tricia's face made him angrier than the words that were coming out of her mouth. But, to be fair, the fact that Tricia and Grace were alive and well was just the icing on the proverbial cake. He felt so impotent when it came to fighting this growing problem in California. Because the kind of force he knew he needed to use to end the rebellion—a full-scale invasion with armored tanks and a bombing campaign the likes that haven't been seen since World War II—was just not politically and militarily feasible at the time. As it was, the polls showed that almost half the nation as a whole—especially in the West and the South—supported California's right to leave the union. Results below Matthews' dream of 70 percent ratings. And in some parts of the country, the percentages were even higher. Critically, his generals insisted that the military wasn't ready to fight fellow Americans, but they would be ready soon.

If the President was honest with himself, he didn't want just to invade. He wanted to use the full nuclear arsenal on the godless state and wipe out every single Californian off the face of the planet. But even in his anger, he knew how necessary the resources of California were to the nation. The people would be collateral damage. But it didn't mean he couldn't fantasize about giving the order to flatten it. He was in the middle of one of these thoughts when Peter McKenzie interrupted him: "Mr. President, the California president is on the line."

President Matthews sat up. He had been waiting for this call all morning. "President? He isn't the president,

I am." McKenzie wasn't sure what to say, so he stayed silent. After a moment, Matthews told him to, "Send him through." Seconds later, he heard the unmistakable California accent that he had come to despise.

"Mr. President, I'm happy that you're not too busy to make yourself available to chat this time," the California President, Rich Herrmann, began. It was petty, Rich knew that, but he couldn't help getting a dig in about the time the president had ditched him to go golfing when he had come to D.C. to visit.

The President seethed. He thought if he ever gave the order to nuke California, he'd start by targeting the governor's mansion. "Cut the shit," Matthews said through clenched teeth. "I want my people back."

The California President was prepared. He figured this was why the Matthews had called him. "Okay," Rich began. "But you have to do something for me." Rich went on to detail an exchange. California would return all federal officials in custody in exchange for any Californians who had been detained and wanted to return to their home state and there would be a truce placed on all hostilities between the U.S. and California while the two nations, and Herrmann used that language, negotiated a peaceful coexistence.

"No deal," President Matthews said. "We don't negotiate with terrorists."

#

Tricia was taken home right after her talk. Her next assignment was a secret diplomatic mission to China. The Chinese government had made overtures that they were willing to help with the secession efforts but would not do or say anything more until they had a face-to-face meeting in Beijing with a California delegation. Tricia, among a few others, needed to be at the meeting.

Rowan hugged Tricia the moment she walked through the front door. He told her how proud he was of her and hearing that from her husband made her feel good. But the reason she needed to get home was not to see Rowan but instead to talk to Ezekiel. The moment she heard about China, she thought of her middle child. She knew Ezekiel felt terrible about what he had done and maybe this was the way for him to redeem himself.

Ezekiel had been under house arrest since he confessed to helping the FBI. Because the remainder of the Murakami's also lived there, it meant he barely left his room during the day. In addition, Rowan, Grace, and Noah were shunning him. They had not said a single word to him or even acknowledged his existence. Tricia wanted to talk to him but never knew what to say that could make it all better. Instead, she made sure he still ate and tried her best to look in on him when she could.

This didn't mean that Tricia forgave him for what he did. She was still angry and blamed him for a lot of what happened. But he was still her son and she loved him. Most importantly, she was willing to give him a second chance.

She knocked on his closed door. When he opened it, she not only saw the tears in his eyes but the surprise that someone from his family actually wanted to talk to him. "How would you like to come to China with me for a secret diplomatic mission?"

"China? Mission?" a shocked Ezekiel asked.

Tricia nodded. "We will have to sneak out of California and take a flight from somewhere in the United States."

Ezekiel frowned. "Why can't we just fly from here?"

It was a valid question. But for the last week and a half, US military planes had begun to follow any commercial airline leaving the state. The worry was that if they somehow found out that Tricia or other senior leadership was on the plane, they would definitely try to bring it down.

"We'll have to act like refugees fleeing California because everything is being scrutinized inside and out," Tricia paused. "And the hope is that it'll be an easier sell if I have a child with me than if I'm alone or traveling with another adult."

Tricia looked at Ezekiel. She knew her son well enough to read his face. He was excited. Ecstatic. This was not only his chance to prove himself to everyone, but it would be fun.

"When?" he asked.

"Pack your bags," Tricia said with a smile.

Soon, after some goodbyes, Tricia and Ezekiel were headed toward the California border via the I-15 North in a ten-year-old Honda complete with enough dents to make it nondescript. The CMS took no chances. They changed both Tricia and Ezekiel's hair colors to blonde and gave them haircuts, they put fake glasses on them and even gave Tricia a prominent mole on her face. They also packed the car with hastily filled boxes and suitcases full of various junk—to make sure they gave the impression of people fleeing. One of the CRM's most bad-ass Seal trained soldiers would be in the car with them and pose as Tricia's sister. She went by the name, Karen Kane. Others from the

CMS leadership were taking different routes not chancing that the US CIA would be monitoring international flights, waterways and major travel routes into their close neighbor.

By the time they got to the Nevada state border and after waiting in a long line of cars, Tricia and Ezekiel had their stories down. They were originally from Melbourne, Florida, but had moved to Los Angeles in the past year. Tricia was just getting out of a bad marriage and wanted to be as far away from her ex as possible. But Tricia didn't agree with what was going on in the State and knew they needed to leave sooner than later. They had even memorized their fake social security numbers, birthdays, and the same Florida address just in case they were questioned separately.

"Passports and registration" an armed soldier ordered when Tricia pulled up.

Tricia was ready and handed over the forged documents. Karen added hers. He looked them over and then at Tricia and Ezekiel. Just as Tricia thought they were in the clear, the soldier looked at Tricia again. Tricia was convinced that the soldier recognized her. Her first instinct was to gun the car and make a run for it. But before she could do anything, the soldier ordered her to pull over to the side.

Tricia drove over to where the soldier was pointing. She glanced at Ezekiel out of the corner of her eyes and could see that he was fidgeting nervously. "Act normal," she whispered to him. It was advice said as much for her as him. She didn't need to tell Karen. She was already cool as a cucumber.

This time, a group of heavily armed soldiers approached the car. They rechecked the passports and car registration. The soldier in charge shouted, "Exit the car with your hands in the air."

Tricia hesitated, but Karen popped out of the car as if she received an order from a superior. Had Tricia made a mistake bringing Ezekiel along with her? She wondered what would happen to him if they were caught. She had no doubts that she would be executed as a traitor but hoped that Ezekiel would be excused from such punishment because of his age and the fact that he had helped the FBI in the past. She smiled at the irony that his betrayal of his family and the movement might have saved his life. Tricia was even crafting an alternative story in her mind that made Ezckiel more of a hero to the U.S.

With their hands in the air, Tricia and Ezekiel climbed out of the car. They ordered the three of them to put their hands on the roof of the car and spread their legs. The soldiers began to pat them down to check for weapons. Tricia was angry at herself. Who the hell did she think she was? Somehow, she had forgotten that she was just a kindergarten teacher and not some international spy. Tricia opened her mouth to confess who she really was but found that she couldn't find her voice. Karen read her body language and scowled. Tricia dismissed Karen's look and as she was about to try again, the soldier in charge said, "Don't worry, this is just a routine and random check."

Tricia quickly closed her mouth.

The soldier's posture and tone became much friendlier when they confirmed there was nothing suspicious in the car. "We got word that Tricia Murakami was trying to leave California."

Tricia swallowed hard. The soldier didn't seem to notice. "Where are you three headed?" he asked.

"Back home. Florida," Tricia answered casually.

"Melbourne," Ezekiel added helpfully.

"Well, have a nice trip."

The rest of the trip to China went smoothly. They drove to McCarran International Airport in Las Vegas. A little less than thirteen hours later they were landing in Beijing. Tricia did not let out a sigh of relief until she had passed through customs. Only then, did Tricia and Ezekiel remove the silly costumes and smile at their good luck.

Some of the other travelers recognized Tricia, but for the most part, she was just part of the throng of foreigners making their way through the airport. The Chinese government had been expecting her and quickly escorted her out of the terminal. As she and Ezekiel climbed into a black SUV, she saw Jaleel and Tom Huang, already sitting in the back.

Tricia felt like a schoolgirl because the moment she met Tom's eyes, her heart skipped a beat. She didn't think that was possible anymore. It had been decades since she had that feeling. Thankfully, Tricia told herself, Ezekiel hadn't noticed. But, of course, Jaleel had. He smiled knowingly at Tricia, who quickly turned red.

This was a critical diplomatic mission that could hold the entire fate of California's secession movement in their hands and everyone knew it. Having China's resources behind California might just stand down President Matthews and avoid further bloodshed. They didn't have time to rest or sightsee, so they headed straight for the meeting—not bothering to even check into a hotel. Before she knew it, Tricia was at a nondescript government building. An entire military guard was there to escort them inside.

Seeing the soldiers with assault rifles was a wake-up call for Tricia. She had known the importance of this meeting, but it had not completely sunk in. Not for the first time, she wondered if this was what the founding fathers had felt like when they met in Philadelphia. She also wondered what the hell she was doing there. Who was she to negotiate such an important deal? Was she there just for window dressing? Was she some kind of diplomatic pawn in the chess game of international negotiations? She convinced herself that she would keep silent and let the others do the talking, but she also knew that was something that was hard for her to do.

Despite the fact that they were on foreign soil, it didn't mean that they were safe and Tricia knew it. She refused to let Ezekiel out of her sight. This meant that he would be at the meeting.

Jaleel and Tom didn't love the idea, but Tricia was not willing to budge. So, Tricia told Ezekiel to listen, not to talk, and to take notes for her. Ezekiel nodded excitedly, pleased to be part of something so important.

When Tricia entered the meeting room, she was surprised to be greeted by the President of the of the People's Republic of China, Wang Wei, himself. After introductions, they got down to business.

"We have been watching what has been going on in California and believe we can help you with your efforts," the Chinese President began through a translator. He went on to describe a two-part plan. The first involved providing the funding needed to fight a major ground war and also covertly sending military hardware to California.

Wei hated the American president. The two have had an escalating war of words through the press and in social media. As America became more isolationist under President Trump's administration, China filled the vacuum—not just in Pacific but all over the world. But as China rose, America's distrust and outright hatred of China grew exponentially. China's feelings toward the US were the same. Placating California was just an opportunity, a step toward controlling the entire continent, not a love affair. President Matthews had run on the anti-Chinese platform all the way to the White House. Wei had always known that it was just a matter of time before the two superpowers—one on the way up and one on the way down—would have to fight.

The second part of the plan, which was the reason the Chinese wanted to meet in person, involved a coordinated effort to wage war against the United States. Wei was frank with the California delegation. "There is no way your side could win a war against the rest of the United States."

Before the Californians could argue, Wei continued: "That's why as soon as you are ready, with the help of the North Koreans, we will attack all the United States bases located here in Asia. The U.S. will be forced to split its resources between multiple fronts."

"Giving us a chance to actually win," Tricia said.

Wei nodded.

"What if they use their nuclear bombs on you?" Tom Huang asked.

"They won't," Wei assured them. "How do I know? What did you Americans call it during the Cold War? Mutually assured destruction? They know that if they use it against us, we can use it against them. I question President Matthews on a lot of matters, but he is not an idiot. Some of his predecessors may have been, but it is clear, his agenda is world domination."

CHAPTER 19

He Called Together Legislative Bodies

Governor Herrmann anticipated President Matthews to respond in the manner he did. The phone exchange between the two was like a game of verbal chess. Herrmann was politically savvy and putting an offer on the table in an effort to avoid further conflict was a chess move in his favor. Californians and the world could trust that he was not a warmonger. The same could not sadly be said about his nemesis.

Different from his predecessors that started the USA on this narcissistic agenda, Matthews was shrewd. He knew exactly what buttons he was pressing and it worked on the national and international stage without fail. Russia became a country club ally. He made backroom deals and alliances with the Russian president, Alexi Vasiliev. Vasiliev, like Matthews, rose to power in Russia through strong-armed business deals that reportedly made him a billionaire. He was a small, stocky man, yet not fat, but muscular like a Russian weight-lifter, a sport he participated in as a youth. Vasiliev never appeared in public with a smile or even a slight grin, he projected stern confidence through a serious look with lowered eyebrows and a piercing stare.

Since the Trump election, Russia had integrated more and more into the political fabric of the U.S.

Ironically, after the initial uproar over the interference in that election, the silent majority in the U.S. has accepted Russia's participation in U.S. politics. That had been the result of Matthews and his party's effective manipulation of social media. Russia was effectively portrayed as the equivalent of an off-shore marketing machine that aided U.S. elections. It also didn't hurt that Russia went through a horrible five years of poor crops and even though the US was not Russia's primary source of crop imports, it imported all-time highs in American farm produce. Russia had become welcome customers to U.S. farming and farm equipment industries.

Matthews and his administration worked the Middle East in the same way as he had Russia. The Middle East also became country club allies to the U.S. The cozy relationship here was, of course, built upon oil exports, but Matthews tapped into his building product empire background and sold billions of dollars' worth of infrastructure materials, engineering, architecture and other Western-style creature comforts to the Middle Eastern kingdoms and this finally balanced trade between the U.S. and the Middle East. Matthews also opened door after door for the Middle East tycoons to buy U.S. real estate without restriction. Matthews used federal mandates to override state and local restrictions on foreign ownership in the U.S., even dismantling such strict laws in places like Hawaii that restricted land ownership and building by non-state residents. Matthews bargained with the sheiks with card-shark bluffing tactics, walking away from the trade table on several occasions to get guarantees to buy American products at the level that oil had reigned over Western societies for decades. Matthews favorite quote was, "You obviously can't run cars without gas, but Henry Ford made his vendors rich along with him." The U.S. public didn't balk at Matthews' deals as unemployment was at an unprecedented low and wages at record highs. Of course, the rich continued to get richer, and the poor continued to get poorer. Matthews had the support of the U.S. in the palm of his hand.

China, Japan, and the Koreas were all different matters. China stood toe-to-toe with the U.S. as the dominant economic power and it didn't trust or play ball in the same way as the U.S.-Russia-Middle East country club allies. The China-U.S. relationship was irreparably poisoned during the Trump administration when President Trump placed punishing tariffs on Chinese imports. With no regard for international diplomacy, Trump's naïve policies of running the U.S. like a commodity infuriated the Chinese. In fact, Trump's successors did nothing to repair the damage done so China's disdain for the U.S. was as deep as ever. China welcomed dominion over the U.S. by any means possible. China saw the U.S. as a threat to its long-term survival and the country club alliance as heightening that fear. China always looked at geopolitics with a thousand-year vision as opposed to the fast-food attention span of the U.S.

Japan guarded its independence as its biggest strength and refused to be part of the country club alliance with the U.S. as well as staying clear of being a threat to the giant China interests.

The Koreas, now at the best relations North and South had experienced in a millennium and with a closer tie with China than ever before, entered into any economic trade agreements in a strong position. With products made

CHAPTER 19 231

in the south of Korea, the united Koreans conducted business with the concentration on quality products that built their own demand, restrained from price gouging and taking huge profits out of their trade with the world, thus building a strong foundation of economic stability and service to their people. The Koreas didn't need the country club alliance.

When the California delegation reported back to Herrmann with China's support, Herrmann immediately leveraged China with Japan and the Koreas to make formal political and trade agreements with the new nation. Japan and the Koreas listened but weren't as open as China was to working directly with California.

Finally, Herrmann contacted his friend, Governor Raffi Zimmerman of New York to make an alliance with him. Zimmerman was lieutenant governor under Chris Haynes and took over after his murder at the hands of the U.S. aggression in New York City. "Raffi, we're getting our ducks in a row here. Before I pull the final trigger, excuse the pun, I want to make sure New York will support us in some way, really, any way possible." Herrmann bluntly put it to his friend.

Zimmerman laughed, "Rickie," He paused collecting himself. "Too bad we don't share a border because we would unite with California in a heartbeat. We're so fed up with Matthews and his cronies and after Chris's murder, we're ready to explode."

"This has to end Raffi and we are proud here in California to take the first step," Herrmann stated.

"Rich, you have our support. We will at least stay out of any conflict and do our best not to contribute to Matthews' cause. How much we can be visible in this may have to be on a minute-to-minute basis as the events unfold."

"Raffi, thank you, I appreciate this and it's just downright the moral thing to do for your people. The same charge I take as governor. I would make the same decision. Our people come first. Exactly what Matthews doesn't get about leadership," Herrmann assured.

"Agreed," Zimmerman stated emphatically. "Rich, you're doing it right. You've built an infrastructure before making your intentions known. Chris made the critical mistake of reacting when he had no clout. He, and we, paid the price for that." Zimmerman took a deep breath, "Had we been more prepared like you, we could stand with you. As it is, we are totally under Matthews' thumb."

With the strong alliances building, Herrmann felt secure enough to move the rebellion forward. It was now time to make the definitive announcement: California will secede from the United States of America. Herrmann did just that. His statement did not go into all the injustices that his state and other states had been suffering because of Matthews' and his party's leadership. His statement was simple and blunt: "Given decades of injustice, indignity, and inequality, with the power given me to care for the people within this geographic boundary, I declare the formation of a new nation that will now and forever be known as, California."

Social media throughout the world buzzed with what was called the "I" declaration: Injustice-Indignity-Inequality.

Herrmann called for a nationwide (California) census and a special election to officially establish the presidency, the regional elected officials, the form that the government should take, the rule of law, in essence, the foundation of the new nation.

President Matthews insisted on calling an emergency joint session of Congress to again ask for a declaration of war against California. He was granted his appearance before this joint session forty-eight hours after he demanded it. This sent a message loud and clear on the possibilities of the declaration being passed.

As predicted, Congress sent the request for the declaration of war down to sub-committees and the formal declaration stalled until the sub-committees could report on the feasibility and cause.

Matthews' response was to order all borders into California permanently closed and all trade stopped. Within two hours of that announcement, Washington D.C. went dark for twelve hours again. The citizens of Washington D.C. and Maryland were furious with Matthews.

At the Murakami safe house, Noah, Rowan, and Grace watched the events of the nation closely on the Internet. Noah hadn't returned to his unit yet, part of him being home was to add an extra layer of security for the family after the Grace and Tricia incidents. They were in the same, high-security safe house that had been serving them well. Tricia and Ezekiel were still in route home from China.

"Matthews is sealing our borders," Rowan commented while they were all watching a news feed on the computer screen. "Mom and Zeke will need an access point to get back home. I think they are coming back the same way they left. I might be wrong, but I think they are coming through Nevada again," Noah added.

"Noah, if you have communications back up with your commanders, can you make a couple of calls and see what are the plans for CRM to free up a border for their reentry? Or, some itinerary for them?" Rowan asked.

Noah immediately grabbed his android phone and sent a few texts and emails. He received an immediate response. There were no current plans to try to reopen any of the blocked borders. Noah conveyed that to Rowan and Grace.

"Well, it doesn't mean that they won't be able to get through, it's just that the main routes will be all blocked. It's going to add days to their trip back," Rowan speculated.

"And, danger. Any unconventional travel is going to be scrutinized. Let me see if I can get any information from anyone on how they expect to get mom and Zeke home," Noah said.

It only took a few minutes and Noah obtained a sketchy run-down. "Yep, they are coming through Nevada. Seems like that plan went so well that nobody wants to risk altering it."

"Do you know when they are expected to land in Nevada?" Rowan asked.

"Friday."

"I have an idea," Rowan said. "This isn't my place to suggest such things, but…I know the old Route 66 very, very well. It was mythical when we were in college and we would cruise it and drink for the hell of it."

"Dad, you partier you…" Grace winked and smiled.

Rowan shot back a devilish smile of his own and continued his thought, "Noah, can you put together a squad, ahhh…get permission to do so, of course. I just Google Earthed the bridge at the Colorado River that crosses over into Nevada. It's now I-40, but it replaced old Route 66. The guard station there is a pole gate, pretty thick, there's now a steel building on the Arizona side and looks like about a dozen troops on duty. Two machine gun positions set up on either side of the highway and that's about it. What I'm thinking is, why don't we open up that roadway just at the right time for Tricia, Zeke and the rest of the China delegation to zip right through?"

"I love the idea!" Noah said.

"Can I go?" Grace asked, her inflection acknowledging that she knew the answer.

Noah and Rowan just looked at her with raised eyebrows and a blank stare.

"Dad, speaking of which, you keep saying, 'we'?" Noah observed.

"I want to go with. I know the area like the back of my hand and I'm dying to contribute here," Rowan insisted.

"I'm sure we have plenty of personnel that know the area as good as you, dad." Noah had a bit of a dismissive tone mixed with his understanding. "I would enter that debate vigorously and I'm going to insist." Rowan added sternly.

"We'll see, but I have to tell you, that will be well above my pay grade to make that call," Noah said.

"Let me get going on moving this idea up the chain of command. I promise I will make an appeal to get you to be with us in some capacity," Noah added.

Noah took a laptop and went into another room. Rowan and Grace took a break from their constant monitoring of the news to play a video game. Their immediate giggles were undoubtedly a release of tension more than a result of the entertainment value of the game.

After two hours of fun, they both closed their eyes and drifted into a nap on the leather sofa in the study.

Rowan and Grace were awakened by Noah bursting into the room. "The brass loves the idea," he said. "I'm in charge to put together a team to open up the bridge checkpoint. By the way, *they loved* the collateral benefit that this is historic Route 66. The message this sends back to the U.S. will be big-time. Another, B.T.W., our intel shows that this happens to be the one of the least guarded and built up blockades in the whole border. Nice going, Dad!"

"Speaking of going, well…?" Rowan couldn't resist.

"I'm afraid that's a no go. No big explanation, just a big fat NO." Noah walked over to his dad and put both his hands on his shoulders.

"When do you leave?" Rowan asked.

"Immediately, I have to assemble the two squads I'm taking and then we are getting to that area to do an assessment and final tactical planning on site."

Rowan turned his son's gesture into a hug and then rushed out of the room. Noah followed a bit and could see his dad talking to one of the guards in the living room.

Noah began packing. There was a glee about him, glowing that he was getting back into the action. He stuffed his gear into his backpack in minutes and came out from his room into the living room. Two guards sitting in comfortable chairs with legs crossed smiled at him and called for confirmation of Noah's clearance to leave the safe house.

Rowan walked into the kitchen in his version of fatigues: tan cargo pants, a dark green polo shirt, white socks and trail running shoes. He also had a Patagonia backpack.

Noah looked at him. "Ahh, going someplace?"

"You made a couple of calls; I made a couple of calls and BOO YA! I'm on the mission as an advisor!" Rowan effused.

"How…who…whaa…"

"Your stiff colonel gave me a bit of blowback, but I leveled the trump card, excuse that ugly pun," he said. "After using my exhaustive knowledge of the area as my primary argument and the time saving of using me instead of searching through the CRM database to get a soldier as expert as I…all of which he just poo poo'd, then I laid down the, 'That's my wife coming over that bridge. If anything happens, I think I'm owed to be there this time.' Did I say, BOO YA?"

Noah smiled, but his eyes broadcast, *'Now I have to worry about you the whole time.'*

The guard on the phone gave a thumbs-up. Noah ordered, "Saddle up, here we go. And, to coin your favorite phrase, 'By the way,' you're under my command now, none of that daddy-son shit. You do what I say, when I say it, and where I say it. NO exceptions!"

Rowan mocked him with a clumsy click of his heels, his right foot missing his left, and a passable salute.

"Dad, I mean it. And, from this moment, you're Rowan to me."

They hugged Grace, fist bumped the inside guards and walked toward the front door. As they opened the door, Grace yelled, "I'm proud of you, Dad!" Rowan turned, smiled and blew her a kiss. Not enough, Grace ran over to her dad and grabbed him around his waist and gave give a tight squeeze.

Noah and Rowan's black Jeep four-door drove through a barbed wire gate that opened as the car approached. The car drove past the main driveway of a CRM armory and into its adjoining yard. A group of soldiers that equaled two squads waited at ease for Noah to face them.

"I'm Noah Murakami; you're C.O. on this mission. This is Rowan, he is a civilian advisor. He knows the terrain in the area and can be of value." Noah purposely didn't offer his dad's last name. He also didn't look at Rowan. "Given the urgency of this assignment, we'll travel together in an enclosed troop transport. On route, I'll give you the overview of where we are going and what we are doing. But, for now, I want you to know that our work will involve deadly force against U.S. troops. When I was with the other side's military, they never gave me the opportunity I am about to give you," Noah paused and looked over the team. "If anyone of you wants to bow out, do it now."

No one flinched.

"I recognize some faces here but, I'm going to take a roll call to get to know you others a bit."

His second-in-command handed Noah a clipboard. As he got to the fourth name on the list he was stunned, Ja…"

A slim, pretty soldier stepped out from her position purposely hiding behind a group of other soldiers. Justyice, gave a coy smile. Noah cleared his throat, choked down his elation to see her and resumed all commanding officer again, "Justyice, didn't see you hiding over there. Good to have you on this operation. After roll call, maybe you can brief me on how you got out of the mall explosion?"

The other soldiers all turned to look at Justyice as if she was a hero for being in that mess. She was a hero.

"Be honored to, sir," Justyice's responded. Her smile morphed into military attention. Noah finished the roll call. "Ok, glad to have you all. Give me an hour and I'll have a requisition list for all the gear you will each need. Let's assemble here at sixteen hundred and then we leave. Dismissed." Noah turned to his second-in-command, "Get me a desk to work at, STAT."

"Justyice, a word." The corporal seemed to snap forward and be right up on Noah. As everyone peeled off with duties to get ready for the unknown mission, Noah and Justyice stood alone in the yard. "What the hell?" Noah exclaimed. Justyice grinned from ear-to-ear. "I repeat corporal, what the hell? And, you can take that as an order." Noah matched her grin for grin.

"I tried reaching you, but with the communication blackout and not hearing anything, I hate to say it, I stopped trying. Ya know, fallen buddy syndrome. Thought you all didn't make it out of that mall." Noah explained.

"We never made it INTO the mall," Justyice responded calmly.

"Huh? We dropped you right on it."

"I'm embarrassed and yet glad to say, your expertly trained troops kinda fucked up and it ended up saying our lives." She paused, swallowed then continued, "Jacobs, forgot the doorbuster and something else integral to the rescue, so we stayed together, turned around and then the blast hit. There were a couple of scrapes and scratches, torn clothes, but the whole squad made it out alive. Thank God, your sister wasn't being held there."

"What about Mark?" Noah asked.

Justyice's eyes told the whole story. "He didn't make it."

Noah's eyes began to fill with tears, but he found hard to keep them from coming out.

"How come you didn't contact me?" Noah asked.

"I tried as well and the blackout was on. Then I just put myself in your shoes. You were dealing with your mom's assassination attempt; you didn't know if Grace was alive or dead, I even got wind of your brother's antics. I heard you were taken off assignment roster and were at home attending to your family, so I backed off."

Noah, cognizant of being in the open yard, put his index finger on her heart. "I needed you then."

Tears welled in Justyice's eyes. The silence that fell over them created an intimacy that was more powerful than the physical contact they longed for at that moment.

"Now I know…" Justyice choked. She assumed a full 'stand at attention', saluted and as much as a subordinate could and a strong woman willed, she took control of the moment and brought it back to the grim task ahead. "Sir, will that be all? I know you have some marshaling to do and I need to get prepared."

"Yes, corporal, but one last thing: what are you doing here now?"

"Sir, knucklehead, sir. I heard you were putting together a team and I wanted to be close to you," She held her salute, "Sir, knucklehead, sir!" She crisply snapped the salute from her forehead. That huge grin returned unrestrained.

"Well done, corporal, well done. At ease. Sixteen hundred hours." Noah returned the salute.

The hour came and the thirty troops under Noah's command assembled precisely as ordered in the yard of the armory. They were all fully equipped, as was the large enclosed troop transport. Two drivers', an equipment private, an engineer, a videographer and a medic were counted in the thirty total troops under Noah.

CHAPTER 19

By eighteen hundred hours, the truck pulled into a small cave in a bluff one-quarter mile away from the bridge. Rowan directed the drivers to an old hangout spot that still appeared to be secluded from any human contact. This would be their staging area and Rowan earned his keep right from the beginning. It was a perfect spot. A walk from the bridge, out of sight of the checkpoint guards, and a short, quick-step march to the target.

After Rowan gave a tour of the old hangout, the troops settled into their quarters in the cave. Noah ordered, Justyice, Rowan, his second-in-command, Lt. Trae Phillips and the engineer to come with him to patrol the blockade and to graph out the plan to dismantle it. The darkness was perfect for that assignment.

Friday would come quickly, and Noah had the China delegation's flight plan. He also received confirmation that nothing had changed in their travel.

McCarran airport was approximately 45-minutes' drive from the Old Trails Bridge. Noah's goal was to have the blockade dismantled an hour before the delegation's caravan would pass through. The eager engineer was high on using explosives to accomplish the mission quickly and efficiently, but Noah wasn't sufficiently knowledgeable or trusting of explosives to not blow that whole section of the bridge down, thus making it impassable. The ideal effect of the mission was to take out the blockade at this historic spot as a message to the USA. That it killed two birds with one stone and got mom and Zeke to safety efficiently was a side-effect of the larger goal.

Rowan again proved his worth by pointing out, in the dark no less, a maintenance stairwell that led up to the roadway of the bridge just on the other side of the metal hut that appeared to be the blockade guards' headquarters. The patrol spied the staircase, saw where it ended on the side of the shed and noted a hatch that blended into the concrete walkway. If your business weren't bridge repair, you wouldn't notice the hatch concealing the metal ladder. Noah and his advisors were going to bank on that assumption and that would be their entry point to surprise the guards. They would overtake the guards and the engineer would have his fireworks opportunity by blowing the thick gate tube to oblivion. The engineer had only one problem with the plan and that was he couldn't control the demolition of a solid piece of iron the size of the gate. It was huge and appeared to be solid cast iron. He could put his explosives at the base of the riser mechanism; it would be immensely weaker than the solid iron. All of that flash and shrapnel would accomplish would be to plop the iron gate onto the roadway and with its size, no vehicle could transgress the road anyway. They didn't bring along a bulldozer to push the gate out of the way. Up close, the gate was an enormous, solid tube of iron. The engineer could try and put his charges on the length of the metal tube to attempt to blow it into tiny pieces, but he didn't have the firepower to safely blow it up in such a way that it didn't become the world's largest shrapnel generator ever and take out everyone in a quarter mile radius. Finally, he calculated that no matter what plan they would follow, the number of explosives needed to dismantle that gate would have significant collateral damage to the bridge. Orders were to keep the bridge open and accessible. That was the desired effect of the undertaking.

Rowan, yet again, came up with the logical plan on the fly. They had to try and have the gate opened by the guards, and then take them out. They could blow it or dismantle it later. Both objectives would be met if the gate opened and the delegation drove right through it. Rowan even came up with the means to get the gate open.

Friday 9:00 am Pacific
Rowan walked into the small, dirt town of Needles, CA and found the first old car lot he could spot. He looked over the inventory and eyed the worst old junker of a car he could see. He took his time, negotiated a price, took it for a test drive to make sure it can make it the two miles to the bridge. The car no one else would want was a 2001 dark blue Suzuki Swift. Its interior was completely stripped, save the driver's seat. He stopped at the local grocery store and snatched as many cardboard boxes as he could and packed them in an orderly fashion. He drove toward the bridge.

Friday 9:47 am Pacific
Noah and his troops were fully loaded and in the stairwell positioned in single file up and down the maintenance ladder. Noah was on the first step and cracked the manhole-like cover to keep watch toward the gate.

At 9:55 am the Suzuki was chugging toward the gate. At 9:58 am, Rowan reached the gate and was stopped by the border guards. All Noah could see were the duty guards on both sides of the car looking and talking to his dad.

"Hello, patriots!" Rowan greeted the guards through the open window. He did his best at an uneducated, homeless guy's accent.

"Sir, we have to see some ID and know what the purpose of your crossing is?" A fierce looking soldier in a black beret demanded.

"Hell, sure you do. I can tell ya the purpose right off. I'm getting outta that un-American, un-Godly, unpatriotic, un…"

"OK, sir, we get it. You're not alone. Papers? ID?"

Rowan showed them the bill of sale hot off the press. Rowan wisely used an alias. All the guards looked at the piles of cardboard boxes, snickered and they seemed to forget to take a look at his driver's license. The massive steel pole of a gate opened slowly. Even though the guards waved Rowan on when the gate was a bit over halfway up, he waited. He waved his hand and pointed skyward to the guards with an expression on his face as if he was frightened that the iron hulk would crash down on him. The guards laughed and waved back dismissively. The guards turned to get back to their posts as the gate completed its rise.

The gate wasn't completely up when Noah and his assault team stealthily popped out from the stairwell. They divided into two squads and in a crouching run, one squad rushed to the gate area and the other went to the steel building. The gate reached the top of its arc and locked into the up position with a loud clank and jerk before it caught its lock. The weight of the iron pole shook the steel support. Rowan inched his car forward, following the plan to a T as Noah had outlined it. He made it obvious that he was looking up at the enormous pole as if he didn't trust its secure position.

He played the fool just enough to keep the guards from re-thinking letting him pass so easily and three of the guards walked back toward the Suzuki.

The plan called for that gate to remain in the up position while Noah and his troops took out the guards. The plan was working perfectly. In seconds, Noah and the lead squad were yards away from the guards. The guard's eyes were on Rowan and his junker or the gate. Then the assault rifle bursts from Noah's squad announced the raid. At the same time, the other squad broke through the unlocked door of the metal building and a tremendous explosion of rifle fire blasted into the interior of the building. Nothing would survive such an attack into a confined space, particularly with the element of surprise.

The U.S. guard closest to the gate reacted immediately to the attack. He drew his sidearm, a 9mm Glock, in one motion like a cowboy and without hesitation shot a single round into the driver's window of the Suzuki. The glass spiderwebbed and one clean hole appeared about three-quarters of the way up the window. The guard was hit in the chest three times by the fire from the assault squad and his body crumbled to the highway blacktop. The other guards were already leveled and lay dead on the highway. The teams hurried and dragged the bodies into the steel structure. The videographer filmed the entire operation.

According to the plan, Rowan was to drive the Suzuki off to the side of the road into the emergency lane as soon as the guards were taken out, but the car just sat there. Noah walked out of the steel house and that's when he saw the window and the car sitting under the gate just like when the raid began. He ran at full speed toward the Suzuki. He yanked open the door with such force it seemed like it would rip off the hinges. He screamed, "Dad, Dad, Oh My God! Dad!"

Rowan was slumped over onto the space where the passenger seat would have been. His head was resting and several of the empty boxes. The 9mm bullet took off his ear and left a hole the size of a large jar lid where his temple was. Blood was still streaming down his neck and onto his shirt.

Noah reached over and grabbed the steering wheel, threw the car into drive and inched the car into the emergency lane as planned. Several of the CRM soldiers ran over to assist. They stopped the car and began to carry Rowan out. Several hands landed on Noah's back as he leaned into the car to lift his dad's body. The hands spoke volumes of the support and love of their comrade and his dad.

As the attention of the soldiers was on Rowan's body, a motorcade of vehicles sped by the blockade. The speed of the cars showed no recognition of what just took place. The cars roared through the blockade and beeped their horns in thanks at clearing the path. The videographer kept his camera rolling.

CHAPTER 20

In Every Stage of These Oppressions

Noah was still alongside the bridge when he called his commanding officer who went up the chain of command and within 30 minutes Noah was talking with his mom through tears. "Mom, I have horrible news. I'm just going to blurt it out. Dad is dead."

Tricia's words burst out, "What? How? Where was the security?" With Ezekiel sitting next to her sleeping she controlled her emotions as to not wake him.

Choking on his words, Noah detailed the entire operation for his mom including his dad's insistence on being a part of the plans, "I think he finally committed himself to the cause, mom. We have to take his death like any soldier in this fight."

There was a long pause on the phone and then Tricia whispered her son, "Noah, stay put. We have to tell the kids right away before they hear it from social media."

A short time later Noah's cell phone rang and Grace was patched in to a video call from the safe house. Tricia and Ezekiel took the call from the car's monitor and Noah, still by the bridge, joined in from his cell phone. Tricia made the announcement, "Children, a short time ago your older brother told me that your dad was killed fighting…"

Immediately Ezekiel screamed in anger and slammed his body into the car door. He was no longer visible on the screen but his rage was heard in the background, "Damn, damn…I knew this stupid shit was going to kill us all. God damn you both!" Pounding and other noise was heard over the call. Grace remained frozen and she sobbed uncontrollably.

"Grace, I know this is exceptionally hard. Then Tricia raised the volume on the car's monitor so Ezekiel would hear even through his rage. "Both of you, I know this doesn't make it any easier, but your dad died a hero and on an important job."

"I HATE all this!" Ezekiel screamed in the background at the top of his lungs.

"Ezekiel and Grace, Noah and I will stay on the phone with you both for as long as you want. Grace, after we all hang up there will be friends there to help you cope with this." Tricia paused, "Do you have anything you want to say?" The younger kids didn't speak and they all stayed on the video together and cried. After a long time crying together, Noah spoke, "I'll be home in a few hours, somehow, some way, and I'll be there with you both."

Rowan's death was the saddest thing that had ever happened to Tricia. Even days later, every fiber of her didn't want to believe her husband was dead. She wanted to fall apart, but she knew she owed it to Rowan and the kids not to. She needed to be strong. Not just for them, but for everyone in the new country. Because she knew too many of them had already made the same sacrifice that she and her family had.

Grace was taking it the hardest out of all the kids. Before hearing about her father's death, she had in her own childish way, thought of the California secession as sort of a game or at most a movie, and she was the star. But now she saw it for what it was—real life. And in real life, bad things happened—including people dying. It took her father's passing to realize that she didn't have the stomach for it. All she wanted was for things to return to the way they were before. Her father alive. Her family whole and intact.

Tricia had gone to the border to accompany her husband's body back to Los Angeles. When news spread about what had happened, people from all over the state began to line the route. Every man, woman, and child was dressed in black. The men and women stood silently, and the younger children waved. Police officers and CRM soldiers saluted.

The procession drove slowly so the people who had sometimes lined up for hours beforehand could pay their respect to Rowan and their condolences to Tricia. Jaleel forced Tricia to open the window. At first, Tricia felt the need to wave and smile at the crowds, but Jaleel told her that she didn't need to. Instead, Tricia tended to look down at her hands, remembering all the moments that she and her husband had shared.

To the outside world, the procession was remembered in the same way that people recalled Jackie Kennedy going through Washington, D.C. with a rider-less horse after the assassination. People saw strength and courage in Tricia, strength and courage which she herself did not feel. Despite this it became another one of those galvanizing moments that Tricia always seemed to find herself in the center.

Thankfully, for Tricia at least, the funeral was only for family and a few high-ranking CMS officials. Tricia also refused to allow cameras. The procession across the state was one thing, but the funeral was completely different. Only before the funeral, by herself, did she finally allow herself to break down. It came slowly and in waves. At first, seeing his body in the casket all made up by the funeral home, Tricia felt a surge of relief. "He's going to be alright," a tiny voice in the back of Tricia's head said hopefully. And then, just a moment later, a louder voice told her: "He's dead, and it's all your fault." The thought made her legs buckle under her. She would have fallen flat on her face if it hadn't been for Tom—who had slipped himself next to her—and caught her.

Tom was the last person that Tricia wanted to see at the moment. The two looked each other in the eyes before Tricia looked away first. "I'm sorry for your loss," Tom told her as he helped her to a nearby bench. "I came early to see if there was anything I can do."

Tricia blamed herself for everything. If she hadn't gotten involved in the movement, if she had minded her business all the way back at school when she saw the Blue Jackets trying to arrest the father, if she hadn't flirted with Tom, if she hadn't gone to China, maybe Rowan would be alive. It was all her fault, and she knew it. She was without her husband, and her kids were without a father.

"Tricia?" Tom asked.

Tricia looked at Tom again.

"It's not your fault," Tom told her, somehow reading her mind.

Tricia didn't believe it was her fault—she knew it was her fault. And she had to do something quickly before more people in her family died. She had to leave the movement. It was too late to save Rowan, but Tricia thought she could still save her children.

Tom continued to read her thoughts. "You can't quit."

Tricia looked at him. *How is he so in tune with me?* She asked herself.

When Tom saw Tricia's expression, he knew he had gotten it right "I need to show you something," Tom said, taking her by the elbow.

Tricia was too tired to fight. And she hated herself for the sudden jolt of warmness she felt by Tom's touch. She allowed herself to be led up the stairs of the funeral parlor. She opened her mouth to ask him where they were going, but Tom told her, "Hang on, we'll be there in a sec."

A moment later, they arrived at the window on the second floor facing the street. Tricia opened her mouth to ask what she was supposed to be looking at when she saw it. Thousands and thousands of people had come to pay their respect. So many people that they filled every nook and cranny on the street, people were even hanging out their windows, on top of buildings, even some had climbed up light poles.

"They are here to grieve with you." Tom said.

Though California paused to grieve with Tricia, from Washington's end the conflict raged on. President Matthews ordered the Pentagon and his cabinet to orchestrate one of the largest troop movements within the continental United States since the Civil War—the nineteenth century one, not the current one. They had even begun bringing soldiers back from the Middle East, Africa and Asia to bolster their numbers. They immediately started to amass along the entire California border and just off the coast poised to invade. The intricate logistics of military movement were being laid down. It was a classic shock and awe move. In other words, intimidate the enemy with such overwhelming force until they give up before even the first shot fired. It was how America had won almost every conflict since the Vietnam disaster.

Before this, the biggest issue was troop morale and loyalty. But for the past month, all the branches had instituted a test to weed out anyone whose loyalty was in question. This basically meant that any soldier from a handful of states was usually immediately honorably discharged. In the past, losing that many soldiers would have been difficult. But President Matthews made sure that he had enough men and women to fight. First, there was a surge of enlistments in the states who hated California and what they were trying to do. In addition, he passed a law that any person receiving public aid and without full-time employment was automatically enlisted in the United States military.

Of course, many who voted for Matthews hated what amounted to a draft for the poor. Some had even sued the government. The case was currently working its way up through the courts. If it somehow managed to get all the way to the Supreme Court, there was zero chance the justices would rule in favor of the plaintiffs. Matthews was sure of it because he had already given them their orders.

As the U.S. troops were amassing, the first Chinese drone was spotted over the United States Air Force base in Okinawa—the biggest concentration of troops in Asia at the time. The only person who saw it was a Japanese maintenance woman who happened to look up during a smoking break. And she didn't realize what it was or the significance of it at the moment. She assumed it was some toy drone. But even if she had recognized it, there was little that could have been done anyway. Because in the next second, they filled the entire sky. And a moment after that, missiles and bombs began raining down on the base, leveling everything. This same scenario was happening at every U.S. base throughout Asia and the Pacific.

President Matthews was dreaming about his victory parade through the middle of downtown Los Angeles when the ringing of his phone woke him. He opened his eyes and immediately thought he knew why his staff was calling him in the middle of the night. *California has attacked.* He smiled to himself. He had hoped that by amassing a large army right on their border it would provoke California into attacking him first. *I'm a genius*, he thought. Because whatever he decided to do from this moment would now be justified in the eyes of the international community.

He picked up the phone. "Yes? What happened?"

Then he heard the words that changed everything: "Mr. President, China has just attacked. We need to get you to a secure location."

CHAPTER 21

We Mutually Pledge to Each Other Our Lives, Our Fortunes and Our Sacred Honor

China was quick to back up its support for the new nation of California—maybe too quick. "People, this is not good, not good," Governor Herrmann stated as he opened the emergency briefing of his security council. "Our Chinese allies are putting us in a very precarious position. We have solicited their support for our rebellion, and they have begun actions unilaterally against the United States. Not only does this provoke Matthews, it is also a political and publicity win for him. Can you imagine how the majority of the U.S. citizenry will view attacks by the Chinese? Ally of ours or no. It will look like a Chinese invasion not support of our secession. The attack s on the Pacific and Asian bases will have a Pearl Harbor battle cry to it. This is not good for us."

The next day after the drone attacks on the bases in the Pacific and Asia, President Matthews came out of his secure bunker under the east wing of the White House, the Presidential Emergency Operations Center or PEOC. An emergency session of Congress convened and within fifteen minutes, Matthews had his declaration of war against the rebellion in California and its allies. Paranoid of the effects of including China, Congress insisted that the declaration stop short of specifically naming China. They used the technicality that the attacks China initiated were directed by California. California was the enemy. Congress did not want to confront China directly, at least for as long as it could hold out.

China's 'aid' to the rebellion didn't stop with the attacks on the Asian military bases. Beale Air Force Base in Marysville, CA; Edwards Air Force Base in Edwards, CA; LA Air Force Base in El Segundo, CA; Travis Air Force Base in Fairfield, CA; Vandenberg Air Force Base in Lompoc, CA; and McClellan Air Force Base in Sacramento, CA, were all receiving arrivals of jumbo jet cargo planes on a daily basis. The markings on the cargo planes were Chinese. They were loaded with military hardware and troops.

The rebellion was put in yet another vise. It couldn't turn back the aid, yet it was being overwhelmed with equipment and troops that could implode the cause. Herrmann had to act.

"Good morning prime minister Zhou (pronounced 'Joe.'). Thank you for taking my call and offer my greetings to president Wei," Herrmann started his call.

"And good morning to you, Governor, or should I say, President, Herrmann," Responded Li Qiang Zhou ("Lee Qua Joe"), the prime minister of the People's Republic of China. His English was perfect. Li Qiang was a tall, muscular man whose appearance, demeanor and actions defined the meaning of his name: Strong. "I assume you are calling as a thank you for our gifts to your new nation?" Li Qiang's constant serious attitude could undermine his movie star good looks and physical charisma. From afar, Zhou could be taken for a successful salesman or marketing professional.

"Well, Mr. Prime Minister, yes I am calling about your gifts. But, maybe not in the way you might expect," Herrmann's serious approach matched Zhou's.

"Go on," Zhou encouraged.

"Your aid presents logistical problems for us. We've kept your arrival into our country secretive for right now, but we don't know how much longer we can do so. Landing at our military bases was a wise choice and has helped us keep your presence from the general public, but you must have anticipated we both need to coordinate your presence in our country?"

"Go on."

"First, let's just take the feeding and housing of the personnel arriving…"

Zhou interrupted, "Our people don't eat your McDonalds or Kentucky Chicken, Mr. Herrmann. We have brought our own provisions and will replenish as needed. Ours was a carefully planned operation. As for housing, if you inspect our arrival, we have set up portable offices, barracks and supply warehouses. Our intelligence has surveyed the best locations near your airfields to set up our camps. We are there to help, not burden your cause. Is that not the pact your made with President Wei?"

"Yes, but…"

"Mr. Herrmann, the U.S. President is amassing a large force to invade your country. You cannot REACT to such an invasion you have to PROACT. In the next few days, we will be sending over fighter planes and attack helicopters to support your troops. The enemy is at your door, Mr. Herrmann. We do thank you for the fighter escorts you have sent up to ensure our planes have arrived safely and you must know that U.S. interceptors were in the area upon our arrival. The U.S. knows what is happening here. Quite frankly, I think our strong show of support is a good warning for the US President in the face of the conflict that is about to occur." Zhou's tone was condescending.

Herrmann had to take charge. "Mr. Zhou, while we greatly appreciate your gift of aid, I want you to understand that we have our own capable air force. Our air bases were some of the best equipped in the U.S., and we inherited all this equipment..." Herrmann snickered at the mention of inherited, when in reality the CRM appropriated all of the military materials in California. "Do not send over any fighter planes at this time."

"Mr. Herrmann, you have seventy-six F-16 class fighters, twenty-five heavy bombers, three hundred seventy-seven helicopters both attack class and transport, one hundred cargo and troop transport aircraft, sixty surveillance aircraft and two hundred light aircraft at your disposal. If the U.S. would turn its entire effort toward destroying your rebellion, call in all its warplanes from around the world, you will be no match for that power. Further, the U.S. can strike you from all sides as it has bases in every direction from you. We took out the Pacific and Asian strike capability, but that may just be a matter of time before those bases reload. And there is still Hawaii." Zhou paused for effect. "I urge you to accept more air support. It is only a matter of time before the air war will begin."

"Mr. Prime Minister, you make a compelling argument, one in which we have considered greatly, but again, I must insist to hold off any more aid at the moment. Let us coordinate and lead the charge here. And that brings me to the ground troops you so generously have lent us. I must insist that you accept and order your commanders to be under the command of our officers with General Curtis Brown as the supreme commander of all operations. That means he is in charge of your troops as well. That will also include air and sea power."

"We understand, Mr. Herrmann. That is understood. This is your fight, and we are here to help. Let's compromise about the fighter planes. We already have four aircraft carriers headed to the coast of California. Let us keep them on the way. We will cruise close enough to be mustered if needed, but far enough away to not appear to be docking at your ports?"

"I don't immediately see a problem with that plan but let me confer with my military staff and get back to you with a final answer on that. Good?"

"Yes, good. Do that," Zhou's response was terse.

The call ended and both sides feeling they accomplished what they intended. Herrmann turned to his staff seated along the conference table. "I think we have a 'shit show' on our hands here. China knows we're in a push-pull on this. We can't refuse their help, yet we can't let them take over this fight. Any thoughts?"

General Brown immediately spoke: "Let me tour the Chinese installations and assess how ready they are for our command. I'll leave with my staff immediately."

"Good," Herrmann directed. "I'd like to get back to the prime minister and suspend any more 'gifts' until we have that assessment, General?"

"Agreed," Brown snapped.

"Everyone else in agreement?" Herrmann looked around the room at everyone. They all nodded in agreement.

The Chinese Problem wasn't the only 'shit show' as Herrmann put it, in a rare use of vulgarity, that the rebellion confronted at that moment. CRM intelligence reported that assembled in the Central Valley outside of El Dorado, California was an encampment of people that appeared to be militia-like. The number of people at the camp appeared to be growing daily. By the looks of what the intelligence sources could determine, they did not appear to be pro-rebellion. Clearly, they had a stockpile of weapons, and curiously private helicopters periodically landed inside this base, stayed for a few hours and left.

Chet Preston, the head of CRM intelligence, dispatched Zack Harvey, Wes Graham, J.P. Hartman, Mike Koval, and Tom Hauss. They were assigned to infiltrate the camp and find out what they could.

The five agents drove to El Dorado in a used 4x4 Dodge pickup, making sure it looked raggedy and worked in. In the flatbed was an assault rifle for each of them. Their weapons purposely looked as tired and used as the truck. Other provisions filled the truck bed: military grade tactical assault rucksacks for each, two tents and five large duffle bags. None of the equipment was covered so it collected a healthy layer of dust and dirt from the drive. As they approached the camp from a road that was tamped down dirt and grass, they could see a chain-link fence and gate up ahead. They slowed the Dodge to a crawl and approached the gate. When they were yards from the entrance, four guards rushed in front of the gate and stationed themselves to block the truck. They all carried a large rifle that looked like a cross between an AK and a bazooka.

"Halt!" A lanky young man in jeans, a short-sleeved t-shirt and a Kevlar vest walked up to Zack in the driver's seat. "What's up amigos?" he added.

"We hear that there's some action going on here. We'd like to get in on it." Zack said. The young man looked toward the back of the truck where the other guards were already leaning in and looking over their equipment. One guard took the barrel of his gun and pushed around things.

"Yep, we be hav'n a gatheren' here. The militias from around the state are coming together to fight this separation shit," The guard freely offered. "What you boys up to?"

Zack smiled. "Well, that sounds exactly like what we've been looking for." He then turned to his comrades in the truck. "Looks like we stumbled on the dream, men."

Zack turned back to the guard. "How do we sign up?"

"Why don't you get out of the truck, let us nose around and check you all out." He paused and if had a brainstorm, asked, "What unit you all from?"

"We're not affiliated with anybody right now. A couple of us were Sons of the New Zion until that went belly up. We're looking to hook up with kindred spirits.

The guard smiled. "Hmmm…well we gots plenty of those here. Those fuck'd Hollywood people are gett'n us in an evil direction. Come on out and let us have a look." The guard pressed a button on his vest radio and barked, "Front gate here. We got a group of joiners." The crackle of a voice imperceptibly spoke on the other end. Then the guard answered into the microphone, "Yep, check'n em out now. ID'n em and all. Over and out."

Two guards patted down the agents, took their wallets and inspected them thoroughly. While this was happening, two other guards took everything out of the truck bed and took it out of their canvas packs. They laid everything on the ground. It was quite an array of equipment, everything one would need to survive in the wild. The guards didn't flinch at the weapons that were stowed in the back; in fact, they just proved their authenticity as militia types. The guards put everything back as they found it. The agents didn't say a word as that process was taking place. Instead, they sat on a nearby log and rock, smoked and watched the guards do their thing.

After they finished their inspection, the main guard approached the agents who all looked like they were napping during the hour-plus procedure. "All right fellas, go on in, but you have to report to the HQ tent. Just folla the dirt road through the gate and ya can't miss it. Welcome to the real revolution, gents!"

The agents did as told and drove the Dodge through the camp. There were tents and people everywhere. In open areas, there seemed to be small group meetings as if training were going on or some type of instruction. None of the tents were cheap, low-end models and they were uniform in size, color and shape. Dotted along the road were larger, temporary buildings with numbers on the front entrance, except one large one had the sign, 'Mess' over the door.

They parked the Dodge alongside the tent marked 'HQ' and entered. Inside the tent were cubicles surrounding a center open section with café tables, several long tables and a lounge area.

A young man, who appeared to be in his late teens, approached them and asked them to follow him. The teen took them to a corner of the building that was set up like an individual office. Three middle-aged men in green fatigues sat around a fiberboard desk. Behind the desk was an older man, balding, muscular with deep-set penetrating eyes.

"Come on in soldiers," the man behind the desk ordered. "Dwayne out at the front gate tells me that a couple of you had been with the Sons of New Zion?"

Three of the agents nodded.

"Good, then ya can show be your tats?"

The Sons of New Zion all had a tattoo on their inner forearm with a number on it, ala concentration camp prisoners. In this case, the number represented their separation and rebirth from the U.S. government. Their new number replaced their social security number which was deemed a sign of enslavement to the corrupt U.S. federal government. At the beginning of the number sequence was a raised brand with the Sons of New Zion insignia. All the members of that militia had those body markings.

"All right soldiers, raise your shirt sleeves so I can take a look." As the man gave that order the other men in the room took out their side arms, trained them on the agents and cocked them. The agents rolled up their sleeves as ordered but kept their arms to their side. The man got up from behind the desk and walked toward the agents. "Well, let's just take a look and if you are not who you say you are, Jeff, Ted and Tim will just blow your fuck'n heads off. No questions asked, OK?" A sardonic smile filled his face as if he loved this. When face-to-face with the agents, he commanded, "Let me see that tender meat, soldiers."

The agents all lifted their arms to present their forearms and then twisted them to reveal the underside. He grabbed J.P.'s arm first-no tattoo. The barrel of a pistol pushed onto the back of his head. Next, he grabbed Mike's arm-no tattoo. A pistol banged into the back of his head. "Not looking good soldiers…"

The man side-stepped in front of Zack, he looked him in the eyes. "We might just be stopping right here and commence the head blow'n."

He drew his own gun and flicked the safety off with a finger like it was second nature. He grabbed Zack's arm and jerked it forward. A raised brand and a number were prominent in the flesh of his right forearm. The man's eyes widened. Wes and Tom raised their arms voluntarily and proudly displayed their tattoos. The militiaman rubbed Zack's tattoo to check its authenticity. Nothing rubbed off.

"These boys never got a chance to be initiated before the reckoning." Zack cast his eyes on J.P. and Mike. The guns retracted from their skulls. Everyone relaxed.

"That was a damn thing, a damn thing. Sorry soldiers, but we have to be extra careful here. The Sons were good people and good soldiers. That raid was a mess. Damn good people."

The man walked back behind the desk, picked up a cigar butt that seemed like it was a month since a match was taken to it and he smiled. "Welcome soldiers. Where you all from?"

Zack continued to be the spokesman: "We're from Victorville. We all grew up together. Liv'n on the land, survivalists. We hear there is going to be some action, so we thought why not put our skills to work. With the Sons all gone, we were look'n for a belonging." He looked at the other agents, and they all smiled at each other. "What you all have going on here?"

"I'm Ken Karson, commandant of the Unified California Militia. That's Jeff, Ted and Tim, but I already introduced you all before." He chuckled. Jeff, Ted and Tim popped up from their chairs and offered handshakes all around.

"Let me give you the quick rundown. A group of old California fat cats with more money than God got together in the last few months and gave me the mission to bring all the California militias together to overthrow this fucked up, stupid, sinful separation movement. Seems like the LA types and their liberal friends don't speak for all of California when they assume we all want to leave the United States. I don't give a rat's ass why these old California money people are throwing greenbacks at us, I'm sure it's to protect their financial interests. They could give a damn about human rights, federal government and all that shit. They dodge all that anyway. But, anyway, we're very well-funded. We have good soldiers from all over California joining us every day. Mostly we're from the desert region, western Riverside and southwest San Bernardino. But like I said, we have people from everywhere," Karson boasted.

"So, what's the plan?" Zack asked.

"As soon as we can we are going to go to Sacramento and hold a coup. String up that dick, Herrmann." He laughed. "And stop all this shit."

"We're in, right men?" Zack turned to the other agents, they all spoke up in agreement.

"Where can we bunk? We've got our own equipment," Zack asked.

"No need. Ted here will set you up. We have plenty of extra tents. Nice setup. Top of the line, even air-conditioned, toilets, showers. These rich bastards don't know survival from ass wipe'n," Karson snickered.

As the agents turned to exit the office area, Zack turned toward Karson and said, "By the way, just so we can manage our expectations, when is this all supposed to take place?"

"That's the problem, the rich boys wanted it done yesterday. Another thing they know nothing about—warfare. I'm under a lot of pressure to get this done in the next few days before the U.S. goes ahead and invades California, then we can throw out this sham government. U.S. invasion scares the shit outta our benefactors. A ground war on California soil means tremendous collateral damage to businesses and personal property. Their honeypots get eliminated in the process, let alone the retribution from the U.S. and Matthews. That crazy fucker would just as soon level all of California as a punishment and salt the earth. Our people cannot have that."

"So, next few days?" Zack asked.

"We're getting brand new; air-conditioned troop transport vehicles delivered tomorrow. Enough to carry ten thousand plus soldiers to Sacramento. Nothing like starting a coup d' etat in style. Gotta love working with these guys!" Karson roared.

"Seems big!" Zack added.

"Yep, make no little plans, my friend. My only concern is that all these fellas, these soldiers are a rag-tag bunch. No organization as a whole. But, they are as angry as hell and will bite the nose off their own mother. I have to count on that. We'll getter done!" Karson assured him. His expression turned quickly from exuberant to firm.

Once in their own luxury tent, Zack immediately called Chet Preston and let him know the overview of what was to take place, possibly in days. This camp was thrown together so quickly that the outward appearance seemed organized and top-notch, but there was no infrastructure. There was no communications surveillance as Zack and Preston could tell from the CRM security screen of their calls. The coup on Sacramento that Karson and his benefactors were throwing together amounted to a huge mob action. It couldn't even compare to third world takeovers where even the worst of them had the time to be better organized. Regardless, such a march on Sacramento was a diversion and expenditure of resources that the new country could ill afford at such a delicate time. The agents' intel was critical for the CRM to prepare for the assault on Sacramento.

As promised, the next morning, hundreds of new trucks drove into the United California Militia camp. There were over three hundred fifty trucks fitted to transport thirty soldiers each. Some had heavy machine guns above the cab. There were fifty semi-tracker trailers for carrying supplies and twenty SUVs for the leaders.

Zack relayed the information to Preston immediately. Preston reported to General Brown, and Brown put a plan of action into place immediately.

Karson and his leadership greeted the arrival of the trucks like kids at Christmas. Teams of militia looked over the trucks, organized them, made up roll calls of who would be riding in which truck. The activity level was frenetic.

An announcement blared over a loudspeaker for all personnel to report to their tents. A half-hour later the speaker in each tent blasted a further announcement; this time Ken Karson informed all the militia that they would be leaving for Sacramento in two days' time. The remainder of this day was reserved for inspection and organization. Tomorrow, the soldiers were to identify their truck and load their equipment onto that truck. Names were called for a force to be left behind to guard the camp. A practice siren signaled when everyone should load into the trucks. Finally, he led everyone in a prayer for success.

Two days later at 10am the siren went off in the United California Militia Camp. "It's time to saddle up," as Ken Karson bragged.

Although the vehicles in the militia's caravan could have passed for non-military, the presence of over four hundred vehicles beginning a journey on highway US-50 would certainly draw much attention. The thrown together, chaotic organization of the United California Militia didn't think through how telegraphed such a caravan would be. Add on the infiltration of Zack and his team and California was well aware of this force threatening the new country.

The distance from El Dorado to Sacramento was forty-one miles. Reports of a large convoy of trucks tying up traffic on US-50 flooded local 911 dispatchers. As the convoy headed west on US-50 driving at the pace of a funeral procession, it approached Folsom, California in thirty-five minutes. Folsom is twenty-one miles from Sacramento, the half-way point. As the convoy approached the Folsom area, Ken Karson in the lead SUV radioed the other vehicles. "We have a blockade about a quarter mile ahead. Let's slow to a stop and see what this is about."

The vehicles drove further on US-50 until they were yards from a line of CRM tanks lined up across the highway. Behind the tanks was a huge force of CRM troops and equipment. As the stand-off started, more CRM troops and vehicles moved into position to surround the Militia convoy on both sides. Overhead, attack helicopters hovered, then four F-16 fighters did a fly by buzzing the convoy. Evident in the enormous CRM presence was the vast number of Chinese troops that bolstered the ranks of regular CRM military. The combined CRM and Chinese force outnumbered the Militia by five to one.

A voice broadcast over a speaker system directed a warning to the Militia convoy: "You are surrounded and outnumbered. You will not reach your target. Exit your vehicles, drop your weapons. You will be treated humanely."

General Brown was leading the blockade himself. There was no response from Karson. The standoff was on. Minutes ticked off and there was still no movement from the vehicles. Thirty minutes passed in a heartbeat. Then militia were seen rising through the cabs of many of the troop trucks to man the machine guns. The militia soldiers stood by the powerful guns, pulled the lever to load the first rounds and then stood waiting. More minutes ticked off. The CRM force didn't flinch. They didn't make another announcement—they held fast.

The standoff was approaching an hour of constant tension. Karson turned to an assistant in the lead SUV and asked, "Are these things bulletproof?"

The assistant didn't know. Karson called out to anyone in the convoy and asked the same question. No one had an answer, and no one had an idea why Karson would ask such a question. The question made the Militia soldiers inside the stopped vehicles more anxious than they were.

They could see how outnumbered they were. They could hear the roar of the helicopters and the thunder of the fighters. They weren't professional soldiers as much as discontents who met in hidden forested areas and acted as angry, tough, enemies of all bureaucracy. Their fear and lack of confidence in Karson grew by the second. Karson had no way to gauge the fighting spirit of his soldiers, as he always called them. He looked out the side mirror at his soldiers manning the machine guns and ready. He didn't see anyone leaving their trucks. To Karson, his militia was steadfast and resolved.

Karson assessed the situation, then pressed the touchscreen on the dashboard to speak to all the vehicles. "We're not going to just sit here all day. Here's what we are going to do. At my command, get your engines ready to race, gunners concentrate your fire on the northwest quadrant of their force. We are going to blast our way off the highway and around their blockade. Ready…"

It was a terrible decision.

"Fire!"

As soon as the Militia opened fire, General Brown made his own announcement to his forces: "Indiana Jones! Indiana Jones!"

The CRM troops surrounding the Militia swiftly and noticeably began to pull back. The helicopters overhead flew away as well.

Karson barked into his speaker: "Stop, don't move. They don't want to engage. We'll win the day and move forward toward Sacramento. Stop…stand up to them!" Karson watched the retreat, then barked more orders more defiant than before, "Cease fire, save the ammo. We move forward at my command."

Although still within eyesight, but well away from the highway, the CRM force slowed their retreat, as if watching what the Militia would do. Brown ended a call with Herrmann. The highway cleared ahead of the Militia convoy.

A deafening roar dominated the area already quiet from the two forces separating. The four F-16s that did the flyover returned. As they flew over the Militia's convoy each of the fighters released two bombs onto the Militia. In a heartbeat, the rebellion within the rebellion was eliminated.

Herrmann gave his approval to General Brown's plan which he labeled Indiana Jones after the famous scene from the movie when Indy confronts the saber swinging assassin. Indy brandishes his whip as the assassin slashes the air with the deadly saber. A savage fight, saber versus whip, is about to ensue, then Indy drops his whip, unholsters his pistol and shoots the assassin. Brown's decision stopped the opposition literally in its tracks, and the CRM didn't lose a single person.

Chet Preston dialed up Zack Harvey and his team and gave him the details of what happened. Zack, in turn, detailed how they simply stayed back and didn't load onto their assigned truck.

For Rich Herrmann, ten thousand Californians' lives were lost, and it slapped the reality on the momentum of the rebellion that the California secession wasn't a universal mandate.

CHAPTER 22

He has Made Judges Dependent on His Will

As soon as the dust settled, teams of CRM and Chinese soldiers were on the road looking for survivors. Noah had been in multiple war zones and seeing death and body parts strewn all along the road didn't faze him. But when he glanced at Justyice out of the corner of his eyes, he could see that it had deeply affected her. What he didn't know was that before California left the Union, she had been in college, a sorority, planning socials and volunteer work. For the life of him, Noah couldn't figure out why someone like her would even want to be out here.

Noah took his eyes off her when he heard shouting up ahead of them. He noticed a group of Chinese soldiers shouting and pointing their weapons at someone. They had found a survivor. Noah ran to take a look for himself and was surprised to see an injured man on his knees.

"I give up, I give up," the man shouted, as he attempted to get to his feet.

The Chinese soldiers shouted at him in Chinese. But when the man did not comply with what Noah assumed were their orders, they began firing and his body was ripped to shreds before falling with a loud thud. Noah couldn't believe his eyes. He looked at the Chinese soldiers. "Why did you do that?" he asked.

The commander of the Chinese soldiers spoke up. "He enemy." And with that, they continued with their patrol.

Justyice, who had arrived moments before the execution, ran out of formation and off the road. Noah gave the signal to the rest of the team to wait as he followed her. Noah found her dry heaving. "Breathe through your nose," he told her.

When she was no longer retching, he handed her his canteen. She took a few sips. And when she looked up at him to hand it back, he saw that her eyes filled with tears.

"Are we doing the right thing?" Justyice asked. "How do we know we're on the right side anymore?"

It was as though Justyice had been reading Noah's mind, because he had been having that same thought. After a moment, he answered, "I don't know." He knew it wasn't the answer she was looking for, but it was the truthful one. It was easier to know they were on the right side before when they were fighting the US, but now they were killing—executing—fellow Californians, things felt different.

Noah had no idea how to make her feel better. So, he told a joke: "A soldier walked into a bar...Which was lucky because it wouldn't have killed him at any other range."

Justyice didn't laugh. But Noah was happy to see her at least smile. "That was the worst joke I've ever heard," she told him.

"I have more," Noah began. But as soon he opened his mouth to tell another one, Justyice leaned over and kissed him on the lips. It was quick but meaningful. They both sat there in a stunned silence.

#

China's attack on American bases in the Pacific and their presence in North America caught President Matthews entirely off guard. Naturally, he had spoken to other world leaders about California, and they had all assured him that they would remain neutral. He did have his suspicions about his neighbors in North America. He knew of Canada's ambition to bring the West Coast under their control and had gotten intel that Mexico supported California. He had even heard about the secret phone call between Tricia and the Mexican president Hernandez or Gonzalez. Matthews could not remember her name, nor did he care enough to try. He had attempted to reach out to China, but had been rebuffed.

"Mr. President," General Jonathan Tuttle, the chairman of the joint chiefs of staff, began. General Tuttle continued when he saw the President focused on him, "We have come to believe that China is gearing up to invade Oregon, Nevada and Arizona. It's your call."

President Matthews looked at the map on the computer in front of him. The Chinese had also taken over Japan and South Korea. Taken over was not the right word. They had not taken over in the traditional sense of the words. It wasn't Hitler marching through Europe during World War II. China was viewed as a liberator. Japan and South Korea replaced the U.S. blanket of protection with Chinese protection. President Matthews and the United States had become so unpopular in these countries, the American bases were more of an occupying force than a defensive one. So, despite historical differences between these Asian countries, the citizens of Japan and South Korea cheered China's arrival as a protecting military force inside their borders and the expulsion of the U.S. It was an open question however if the Chinese would ever leave.

Everyone was looking at President Matthews. "Congress will be declaring war tomorrow on China. We must hit them back hard, or they'll think we're weak." People waited for Matthews to give further instructions. "Let's bomb Beijing back into the fuckin' stone age."

There was no disagreement around the conference room table. They had all learned that Matthews was not the kind of leader who wanted to debate an issue once he made a decision. Although, secretly everyone had their reservations. It was one thing to attack an outlying base; it was another thing to go for their adversary's capital. Most felt that this was inevitably going to escalate into a full-scale nuclear holocaust. They knew Washington would be China's next target. General Tuttle nodded. "Sir," he began. The other generals hoped that Tuttle would talk Matthews out of this course of action. Obviously, they weren't happy about the bases lost, but they all knew that they had lost those bases—those countries—long before the Chinese had attacked them. Instead, Tuttle told the President: "It would be wise if we moved you to a more secure location."

#

Grace had not left the safe house since her father's funeral. She just wanted things to go back to the way they were before. She wanted to go back to the time when she was in school; her mom was just a normal kindergarten teacher, Noah was a regular soldier, Ezekiel was Ezekiel and her father… was alive.

It was all her fault that her father was dead. At least, that's what Grace told herself every second since it happened. If she hadn't encouraged her mother to join the movement and become its de facto leader, her mother would not have gotten so involved, and her father wouldn't be dead. The guilt was like a tumor. At first, it was small and Grace barely noticed it. But every day, it grew and weighed her down more and more. There were some days lately, the tumor in her stomach grew so large she was barely strong enough to get out of bed.

She tried to bring it up with her mother, but she would only half-listen to her. She always had too many other competing thoughts swirling around in her head. Her big brother, Noah, wasn't about to talk to her about it. But even if he did, he wasn't ever around; he was off fighting. She considered talking to Ezekiel about her feelings, but he was so gung-ho about wanting to fight now that whenever she even hinted at her thoughts, he looked at her like she was the crazy one.

After all the moves and with a new phone every week, she had lost contact with her old friends from school. They wouldn't have understood anyway. The last time she was able to chat with them online, they just wanted to hear about how exciting her life was. She hinted at her true feelings, but they either ignored it or it went over their heads. She figured it was probably a little of both.

This was why Grace had begun to cut herself. It was the only thing that seemed to release the pain—even if just temporarily. At first, the cuts were small and not very deep, but lately, she had begun to cut herself deeper and more often. She knew it wasn't good, but she wondered how something that made the pain go away could be bad.

Ezekiel was at the exact opposite end of the spectrum from Grace. He had never been more engaged in his life. His father's funeral was what he has come to think of as a defining moment. Before that, he didn't know why he was alive. But after his father's death, he knew: it was to fight and die for California. It was his legacy and he was surprised he didn't see it before. From that moment on, he was singularly focused on his goal.

The problem was that he wasn't old enough to be a soldier. Not to mention the fact that he already knew his mom was against him fighting. She had told him that one son in the CRM was enough when he brought up the idea of joining. He had wrongly assumed that with her connections she would get him in right away. Now, it was going to be up to Ezekiel. He had heard from one of the guards that they were signing up new recruits as fast as possible at all California universities and colleges. He would just have to get himself to one.

With so many people coming in and out of their house, Ezekiel found it easy to slip out unnoticed. He made his way down the street and walked all the way to the University of Southern California—the closest school to his safehouse. His plan was pretty simple: show up, act like a college kid, and say he wanted to join. He had even bought a fake ID online that he hoped would be enough to get him through the door. He figured that the CRM needed soldiers and wouldn't do much of a background check. Or at least he hoped that was the case.

Ezekiel got to USC and asked around until he eventually made his way to a table with two CRM soldiers sitting behind a folding table in front of what looked like the campus bookstore. "I'd like to sign up," he told the pretty soldier who looked up at him as he approached.

The soldier looked him up and down. "You're a little young, aren't ya?" she asked.

Ezekiel pulled out his ID and held it out in front of him. Close enough for the soldier to read the birthdate but not close enough for her to really inspect it. "I'm eighteen," Ezekiel said in his most aggrieved voice.

The soldier had looked doubtful until the ID. But now she was smiling. "Great, we can use all the people we can get." She then took out a form and a clipboard. "We need you to fill this out and...."

Ezekiel had come prepared. He pulled out his own application form that he had downloaded from the web and handed it over. The soldier smiled and looked impressed. "A little eager, aren't we?" she asked sarcastically. "You do realize we're about to go war with the United States?"

Ezekiel nodded.

Something about his eagerness bothered the soldier, and she looked Ezekiel over one more time. For a brief second, there was flash of recognition. "Do I know you?"

Ezekiel shook his head. Not trusting that he wouldn't give himself away if he opened his mouth and said anything.

"I've seen your face," the soldier said as she continued to stare. But when she couldn't think of where, she shrugged. "The bus is leaving for Hamilton in ten minutes. If you hurry, you can still make it."

"Thank you," Ezekiel told her and then began running in the direction of the bus.

For what felt like the hundredth time that hour, Tricia couldn't believe what was going on in California. First, it was the number of Chinese troops stationed here and then it was the bombing of all those militia guys. She obviously didn't agree with the militia's politics. But she didn't think that it meant that they should have all been killed. She would have been okay letting them just leave California.

It didn't help that Tricia's real role in the movement was essentially over. She was the symbol of the fight against America and President Matthews. But now that they were on the precipice of a war against the United States, she had become old news. She was now just an emblem of the revolution.

Tricia spent most of her days speaking to the troops as they were being sent to the border or to new recruits. Her job was to motivate them. But she couldn't shake the feeling that her real role was to trick the troops into giving up their lives for the cause. She questioned what she was doing now that Rowan died in the war. The vicious circle would continue: other wives would lose husbands, mothers lose sons, husbands lose wives.

Today, she was in a basketball gym at Hamilton High School near Robertson. There were at least five hundred young men and women in front of her. These were the newest recruits, straight off college campuses. As she was about to give the same speech she had given a thousand times before, she thought she saw Ezekiel standing in the crowd. But when she looked again, he was gone. The shock of thinking she saw Ezekiel in the crowd made her realize she could not do this anymore. Her heart was no longer in it. She made it through the speech, but she was just reciting what had been written for her.

"I can't do this," she told Jaleel in the car on the way home.

Jaleel did not seem surprised. "I was wondering when you were going to say that."

"You're not going to try to talk me out of it?" Tricia asked.

"Do you want me to try?"

Tricia shook her head.

"But headquarters is going to try."

And Tricia knew that they would. She understood that, despite being just a figurehead, she was still very useful. They needed to parade her around in front of the news and the soldiers.

Both Jaleel and Tricia were right. Because that night, Tom was at her door. Tricia had not seen him since the day of Rowan's funeral and he had caught her. He was the last person she wanted to see that moment and at the same time the only one she wanted to see. When she opened her mouth to say something, he kissed her hard on the mouth.

CHAPTER 23

The Civil War

Governor Herrmann, now President Herrmann, was in a frenetic crisis mode. The naturally high energy person was in hyper-drive navigating the two immediate emergencies that unfolded.

The killing of the California militias angered the public, both inside and outside of California. Ten thousand angry, armed soldiers chanting government take-over meant nothing on the Internet news feeds. The CMS held massive rallies and they were beyond outraged when the federal government struck back against their freedom to protest. But, ten-thousand people were killed under Herrmann's direction. Herrmann had his most masterful political dance to do to explain to the world how that was justified. To complicate matters, mix in the role of the Chinese in the incident and it brought a punch to the gut to everyone on the continent and amplified his second immediate emergency: The Chinese problem.

A history scholar, Herrmann poured over historical writings on the American Revolutionary War, the Russian Revolution, Mao's China Revolution, Cuba, South America, the French Revolution, the Irish fight for independence, and everything he could gather. Foreign assistance in all of those conflicts were essential to success. Could California be any different? But in all of those historical examples, foreign assistance was moderated. Some troops helped with the fighting, not huge armies. Some equipment was given, but not a flotilla. And, money flowed to the aid of the cause. Never in history did a foreign power act so unilaterally and so demonstratively. Even when the foreign power's motives were to seize the opportunity to consume the revolutionary country in the aftermath of their rebellion. Make no mistake, most often, that very intent was the prime motivation for so eagerly assisting the revolutionaries. Morality, injustice and altruism in international politics were just slogans covering up self-interest.

Herrmann's study and his own astute political savvy pointed him in the direction of the only course of action possible. He had to send the Chinese presence out of the secession. The trick was he had to put this pit bull back into its cage without it attacking him in the process.

"Mr. Zhou, we have a situation here and I need your help," Herrmann started the call to the Chinese prime minister.

"President Herrmann, we are pledged to help. What do you need? But, don't ask for nuclear capabilities. My hands are tied on that one," Zhou joked in a rare display of humor.

"What I need may be even harder to ask for," Herrmann responded.

"Go on," Zhou's mood shifted back to normal.

"There is no easy way to ask for this, so I am going to come right out with it," Herrmann paused, purposely slowing down the conversation.

Zhou matched Herrmann's silence and waited.

"I need all the Chinese troops and equipment of every kind to leave California immediately."

Zhou didn't say a word. Then, in a deep, baritone he declared, "You cannot defend yourself against Matthews alone."

"Mr. Zhou, we just have to take that chance because I cannot defend California with the Chinese either. My own citizens are compelling me to dismiss the Chinese assistance. I have to listen to the people."

"And how many wars have your people fought against the United States of America?" Zhou said firmly. "In leading a country, a leader makes decisions FOR his people, particularly in matters that they have no experience. I don't know what we can do in response to your request, Mr. President."

"In a democracy, leaders listen and reflect the will of the people without oppression and in respecting human rights. We are building a better democracy in California and my people feel very strongly about the Chinese presence. Furthermore, my people want all the feelings and empowerment that comes with winning this struggle on our own. Doing it without Chinese boots on the ground is critically important."

"Winning is important, Mr. Herrmann. What did one of your sports people once say, 'Winning is the only thing', I believe."

"But you have to win with dignity. And, for your information that was an American football coach from the Neanderthal days of sports. We've grown beyond such brutish principles. In fact, the new country of California wants to be built on a strong moral foundation, not subjugating any persons for self-interest. This is my mandate from the people."

The two men entered another period of silence on the phone. Herrmann could hear papers ruffling and computer keys gently being pressed so as not to make noise.

"Mr. Zhou, you generously gave your pledge of assistance in our struggle here. In our last phone call, you agreed that my military leaders and myself would be in complete charge of the Chinese troops. If you want to frame this withdrawal as a re-deployment of your military, I think that would make it palatable to your leadership and to your citizens."

"But we have a strategy in motion in this conflict. One that has consequences for our position in the world. You may have looked upon our swift engagement into your country as an immediate response to assist a new ally, but I assure you that our actions were carefully thought out," Zhou countered. "I have no idea how this strategy can be reversed."

The phone call became even more tense. Herrmann could feel Zhou resist any back-tracking of the Chinese deployment the more Herrmann tried to convince him of the Chinese pull out from California.

"Mr. Zhou, I fully understand, and this will be the last thing I have to say here. I think you have to look at your deployment of military on California soil as a win for your country. You have shown Matthews that China is all in for California. That alone is a powerful statement. Your clear support of our cause will make Matthews consider all the options before they make their next move. It was an unprecedented and bold contribution. It accomplished what you wanted. In fact, it was what we call a win-win for both of us."

"I know what a win-win is, President Herrmann!" Zhou's words darted out of his mouth as if reprimanding the brand-new president.

The call ended. He had also thought to bring up the Chinese soldier killing the militia survivor—he was glad he didn't.

In the three days that followed their conversation, Prime Minister Zhou sent three messages to President Herrmann. The first, a phone call, was transparent, "My hands are tied. I can't order the military back." Herrmann responded with resolve and just reiterated his statements from the phone conversation. The second communication, an email, was curt, "The troops will stay." Herrmann didn't respond. Finally, the third communication, a phone call, didn't invite discussion. Zhou simply said to Herrmann, "Our military will not move." Then he hung up on Herrmann.

While the dialogue was going on between Zhou and Herrmann, General Brown, commander of all the California military and given charge of the Chinese forces as well, confined the Chinese troops to their base. His orders were pure old school military. He had the Chinese soldiers in training and orientation exercises, base maintenance and drill, drill, drill. The Chinese troops didn't go on any patrols; their officers were not included in any strategy sessions, they weren't even used as sentries or guard duty. They milled about their camp with little to do. Mainland China surely received reports how immobilized their military was in California.

Day five, after the initial phone call between China and California, began with diplomatic silence between the two countries. Without a word from Prime Minister Zhou, the Chinese troops, aircraft and navy began a pull-out from California. The Chinese officers simply informed General Brown that they were being called back to their home country, and Brown stood out of their way. The same flotilla of giant cargo planes that brought them there carried them off again. The Chinese exit took forty-eight hours. As fast as they arrived, they were gone. The chess game ended in a draw.

Californians were elated and relieved. The United States breathed a sigh of relief that China wouldn't be at their doorstep in the looming conflict. Herrmann went on to a media broadcast and thanked China for its strong show of support. At the conclusion of his statements, he emphasized the confidence and strength that California had in its fight for independence.

Herrmann's broadcast had an unusual new wrinkle. With the technology provided by the Silicon Valley companies, Herrmann's address was sent live to every Californian. In a joint development between Apple and Amazon, they created the technology that could transmit voice, video and text-to-voice messages to whatever device an individual is using. The video shows up with backup text on smartphones. On smartwatches the video displays if the watch has that capability, otherwise, just the voice is heard, and a text of the voice is received as a text message. The receiver could not block the live broadcast, it could only turn down or off the volume. On computers, iPads, laptops, the video interrupts whatever is on the screen and the broadcast appears. If any device is turned off, the broadcast is played as the device is turned on.

The new government of California wanted every citizen to be informed of developments as they happened. In the first broadcast, Herrmann explained that this technology was not being used in a 'Big Brother' way, but to ensure every Californian received vital news from one main source. He went on to explain that the new country of California created its own equivalent of the United States' Federal Communications Commission or FCC to set rules for communications in California. California's body would be called the California Communications Committee or CCC. Given that this was a dangerous and tumultuous time in California's history Herrmann explained that immediate, safe and trusted communication to every citizen was essential.

Further, he emphasized that the communication should come from a central source. After the threats to independence lessen, Californians can expect less intrusion by these messages. All interruptions would be kept short and links to more detailed information would be provided. Herrmann emphasized that this system would not replace traditional news sources, attempt to stifle free speech and debate about government announcements, or otherwise curtail the vital role of the media in a free society. He explained it was a tool to directly link your government to you in real time and from the source.

The system was surprisingly well received by Californians as they entered into this tumultuous time. A minority complained out about privacy and protection of individual information, but even they conceded to let this alert system operate and see how it will work. The technology was called: First Alert Communication Technology, or FACT for short.

Matthews' call for a declaration of war against China was heard with deaf ears by Congress. None of the U.S. legislators wanted to engage the China juggernaut, especially after the pullout. The congressional leaders explained away China's involvement as propagated by California. After all, they argued, England didn't declare war on France, Spain, Germany and all the other countries who similarly aided the American revolutionaries.

The Senate and House of Representatives bought that argument and the declaration of war against China was dropped.

Matthews appealed to the unified Koreas and to Japan to return the air and naval bases back to U.S. control, but his pleas were ignored. Japan and Korea staying firm on the new status of the bases was a dramatic and strong statement. The change to Chinese control of these bases allowed Japan and Korea to expand their air and naval forces, something that was suppressed under the control of the United States since the end of World War II. The world was lining up taking sides in the upcoming fight for California independence.

Herrmann still had the PR problem of the deadly force used against the militias. The majority of Californians didn't understand, much less care about the wellbeing of what they viewed as a radical group of anarchists. Secretly, most Californians were happy to see these groups cleansed from their new nation. But to publicly make that stand would be Hitler-like. Many voices across California ranted about the killings. There was a lawsuit filed against the government of California, but it was quickly dismissed when the plaintiffs couldn't prove their relationship to the deceased. The CMS response to the public outcry was to launch a heavy campaign to show that the militias were marching on Sacramento to cause violence and take over the new government at a very vulnerable time. They were classified as an enemy of the state and an assembled hostile army. Public broadcasts and media commercials were frequent. All the statements were blunt, hard-hitting facts about the nature of the ten thousand heavily armed men marching toward the nation's capital. Strategically,

President Herrmann stepped aside from delivering the messages on the topic of the militias and wasn't seen in any of the messages. General Brown was the face of the response. He did a good job. The uproar died down and the action forgotten in the larger campaign for independence.

The second broadcast that Herrmann made over the FACT system was a very positive message. Herrmann announced that the nation of California was officially disbanding the California Movement for Secession-CMS and the California Republic Military-CRM. With California declaring its independence as a nation, the need for these organizations had served their purpose. The CMS personnel were already serving prominent roles in the new government and identifying themselves as employees of the new nation. The California Movement for Secession had no purpose and identity any longer. Secession was here; there was no 'Movement For.' The CRM personnel were in the same position. They were all under the command of General Brown and this was the army of the new nation. From this point forward, they would be known as the California Army, the California Navy and the California Air Force. The future will tell if other branches of military would be needed, such as Marines, Coast Guard or Special Forces.

Herrmann kept this broadcast short. He didn't feel he needed to explain the significance of these changes. Disbanding these organizations marked a significant maturity in the independence of California. This was a big next step in declaring to the world that California was separate. The developmental organizations peel off and become the new nation. This step also announced to the United States, "We're ready...Bring it on."

CHAPTER 23   289

Tricia Murakami, Secretary of State Tom Huang, Jaleel Henry—now President Herrmann's Chief of Staff, General Curtis Brown—now Chairman of the Joint Chiefs of Staff, Vice-President Gordon Newton—the former Chairman of the CMS, were all seated at the conference table where President Herrmann made that address. Everyone at the table was introduced to the public as the broadcast began with both their old positions and their new places in the government. There was little surprise as they all had been functioning in those capacities already. But, the rank and file citizens of California needed to know who the major players were. This was the very purpose of FACT.

After the broadcast, President Herrmann immediately turned to Tricia. "Tricia, you're not being left out of the leadership in this government." Herrmann addressed the noticeable lack of introducing Tricia to California with her new position. "Tricia, you have been the face of the secession and a symbol to the people of California. You've been through a great deal and have given a great deal to get us here. You will have a place in this administration. A place I want you to think about and work with Jaleel to create. Don't let the fact that you are not a life-long politician stand in the way of asking for the position *you* want. I'll let you and Jaleel work that out. But you will not continue as the figurehead for independence. That is the president's leadership role." Herrmann paused and put his hand on Tricia's forearm. "I don't say that with arrogance. It is the traditional and rightful role for a president. I just happen to sit in that seat right now."

Tricia spoke up: "Rich, Mr. President, I completely understand and accept my new role. I never asked to be a figurehead, as you all know, it just evolved, and I freely accepted it for the good of the country. Our new country. You need to be in the spotlight leading the way for us all, not me. I always understood that is the way it will be. I am more than OK."

With that, everyone spontaneously stood and applauded. Tricia kept sitting and burst into a huge smile as tears streamed down her face. She looked at Tom Huang and their eye contact conveyed a virtual hug they shared in the moment. Separated by a conference table and six other people, they never felt closer than at that moment.

In the perfect world, FACT would be pinpointed for only Californian eyes and ears to receive, but its broadcasts could be picked up by other electronic devices. The White House received every announcement made over FACT as it broadcast. Matthews and his top aides sat in the Oval Office and listened to Herrmann's announcement. Matthews' expression while he listened to Herrmann disband CMS and CRM could best be described as 'licking his chops'. The 'Bring it On' swagger of the broadcast was not lost on those in the U.S. government. They had just received their marching orders. Only, it was Herrmann directing them and not Matthews. This movement of California's was declared over. California was not moving anywhere and just said to Matthews, "Come and get us!"

CHAPTER 24

The Enemy at our Gates

President James Matthews III had never been a patient man. It just wasn't in his DNA. While other men waited for things to happen, Matthews had always rolled up his sleeves and got the job done himself. That was one of the reasons he had gotten to where he was in life. If it were up to him, he would have invaded California months ago and killed all the traitors. Or he would have unleashed nuclear arsenal and sunk the godforsaken state into the Pacific Ocean.

Instead, he's amassed the biggest military ground force in the history of the country and stationed it along the California borders. A month ago, showing such force would not have been politically feasible, but the moment the Chinese army had set foot on North American soil, the military brass and Congress quickly accepted the need to have so many boots on the ground and did not put up much of a stink about it.

Matthews was not an idiot. He knew that a ground war would be costly and no matter how much support he thought had, the moment the body bags started to pile up that support would be gone. That's why his plan wasn't just to invade; he was going to send the bombers first. He had given the order to bomb California back into the stone age. His war against California had to be swift and decisive before anyone in the U.S. would be able to protest.

"How far are the planes?" he asked the Joint Chief of Staff, General Tuttle, who was seated next to him in the control room.

"One hour, Mr. President."

President Matthews had chosen the initial targets himself. Instead of going after the military bases—as everyone would expect, Matthews wanted to destroy the heart of California. So, the first wave would go for soft targets like the movie studios, the Golden Gate Bridge, Disneyland, the 405 freeway, Facebook and Google headquarters, sports stadiums, civic centers—even the Hollywood sign was on his list of targets. Once those were destroyed, he would then go after the bases and the rebel soldiers themselves.

Once the heart of California was in flames, only then would the President send in the ground troops on clean-up duty. They would capture the rebel leaders, bring them back to Washington D.C., where they would stand trial, found guilty and sentenced to death. Even though this whole incident has been one giant headache, he was also very thankful for it. This was going to be his Abraham Lincoln moment. He was sure of it. He was going to get to save the Union and finally get his face carved on Mount Rushmore. He had his chief of staff, Stanton, looking into it. If there weren't room for his face, he would get rid of Theodore Roosevelt's—the least important president on that "rock," at least according to him.

"How far are they now?" President Matthews asked.

General Tuttle checked his screen. "Half-hour, sir."

It was about to go down and he felt positively giddy about it. It felt like Christmas when he still believed in Santa. This was the moment he had been waiting for and President Matthews couldn't help himself: he smiled.

CHAPTER 24

There was a continuous live feed of the border where the California army faced off against a much larger US army. Tricia and Tom, like all Californians, couldn't stop watching it. It was like a car accident that was about to happen. Except, they were watching their own accident. They had been waiting for the first shots to be fired for the last day and a half. Both wished it would happen sooner than later, so they could stop waiting for it but also dreaded what would happen after they did.

Seeing the sheer mass of the U.S. army, Tricia didn't think they had a chance. She wasn't sure why she ever thought they did. Maybe it was a mistake kicking out the Chinese army. With them, she thought they might have had a fighting chance. She just hoped they would be willing to return if President Herrmann asked them to.

But most of her thoughts were on Noah. After Rowan's death, she had obsessed over the thought that her oldest son was going to be taken from her too. She had almost asked Tom a thousand times if they could pull Noah off active duty. She knew that Noah would be really angry with her. But at least he would at least be alive. Tricia was thankful that both Grace and Ezekiel weren't old enough to fight. She didn't know what she would do if they were.

Tricia took her eyes off the feed and wiped her eyes. She suddenly wanted to be far away from her new office, which still felt like it wasn't hers. It didn't help that she and Jaleel still hadn't figured out what she would be doing in the new government, which made her feel that she was "playing" government instead of actually doing anything.

Tom looked at her as she got to her feet and started gathering her things.

"I should be with my family," she told him.

Grabbing her hand, Tom looked her in the eyes. "Don't worry. We are going to win this thing and everything will return to normal."

"Normal?" she laughed bitterly. "How can you be so sure?"

"We have to have faith." Just as the words left Tom's mouth, their phones began to vibrate. Both instinctively checked the live, FACT feed, wondering if the first shots had been fired. When they hadn't, they both looked at the message again. Their eyes widened as they read, "Warning, please seek immediate shelter."

"What's going on?" Tricia asked.

"Air raid."

"I've got to get home," Tricia told Tom when he looked up again.

"It's to…" but he didn't finish his sentence because Tricia had already left the office.

"Hurry!" Tricia told her security detail as they drove through the streets. Luckily for them, most of the people had gotten the same warning and were seeking shelter, which meant that no one else was on the road.

When they got to the safe house, Tricia didn't even wait for the car to be put in park. She jumped out and ran through the front door past the security detail. The moment she stepped into the living room, she knew something was terribly wrong. It was in the air, or maybe it was her motherly instincts, but suddenly her feet were glued to the floor and she couldn't move anymore.

"Ezekiel?" she shouted, waited a few seconds, then shouted again. "Ezekiel!" She made herself count to fifty. She figured maybe he just had his noise-canceling headphones on. She looked at the security detail. "Did Ezekiel leave?" she asked. Both the security guards shook their heads. Tricia was thankful. At least he was still in his room.

"Grace?" she shouted next. She was more worried about Ezekiel than Grace because she always had to worry more about her middle child than her youngest. But now she began to think it was unusual that she hadn't come down when she had called her brother's name. "Grace?" she shouted again. And when she didn't get a response, she frowned. *She's probably sleeping*, she thought.

Tricia had to force her feet to climb the stairs one at a time. With each step, her dread grew. What bothered her most was not the unresponsiveness of her children—they were teenagers after all or almost teenagers for Grace—but it was the quietness of the house. It was completely silent. Not a single noise other than her footsteps.

The worst fears went through Tricia's mind: *Maybe they had been kidnapped by the pro-United States forces? It wasn't too crazy. Hadn't the FBI taken Grace earlier? There are no more FBI in California*; she tried to tell herself as she got to Ezekiel's door. But she didn't really believe that. There was no way they could get rid of all of them no matter how hard they tried. *But the security detail is here*; she tried to reassure herself. But didn't they allow Grace to be taken last time?

Tricia's instinct was to just walk into her son's room, but after years of being yelled at by him for just barging in, she knew better. She knocked. There was no answer, but the force of her knock had opened the door slightly. "Ezekiel?" she said as she peeked inside. When she didn't see him, she pushed the door open further. The room was empty. *Where the hell is he?* She asked herself as she ran to Grace's room.

This time, she didn't bother to knock. She entered her daughter's room but found it empty as well. However, she noticed the light in the bathroom was on. Feeling relieved, she hurried to the bathroom door, "Grace, why didn't you answer…?" but the rest of her words died on her lips. Grace laid face up across the bathroom floor. Her left arm was cut open from her wrist to her elbow creating a pool of blood that grew by the second.

CPSIA information can be obtained
at www.ICGtesting.com
Printed in the USA
BVHW030447170123
656259BV00051B/972/J

9 781956 452273